This book was published in cooperation with The Center for
American Places, Santa Fe, New Mexico, and Harrisonburg, Virginia.

First edition, 1999

∞ The paper used in this book meets the minimum requirements of
ANSI/NISO Z39.48-1992 (R1997) (Permanence of Paper).

LIBRARY OF CONGRESS CATALOGING-IN-PUBLICATION DATA

Wild, Peter, 1940–
    The opal desert : explorations of fantasy and reality in the
American Southwest / Peter Wild. — 1st ed.
        p.   cm.
    Includes bibliographical references (p.   ) and index.
    ISBN 0-292-79128-3 (alk. paper)
    ISBN 0-292-79129-1 (pbk. : paper)
    1. Deserts—Southwest, New.   2. Desert ecology—Southwest,
New.   3. Natural history—Southwest, New.   4. Southwest,
New—Description and travel.   I. Title.
    F786.W73   1999
    917.9—dc21   99-6113

THE OPAL
DESERT

Explorations of Fantasy
and Reality in the
American Southwest

PETER WILD

UNIVERSITY OF TEXA
Austin

A better term than "opal" could scarcely be found for describing in a word the color of the desert. . . .

— J. SMEATON CHASE

No other precious stone ever attracted me—diamond, ruby, emerald, sapphire. Any of them can be counterfeited so well that only the highest expert can tell the difference. But no one ever counterfeited a good opal— perhaps it is safe to say no one ever will. Its color and light are not dependent on the faceting but are its intrinsic soul. Keith shared my passion for opals; and when I would come up with a new one he would kneel in his bay window in the sunlight to turn it over and over and tears would often come down his face. Frequently he would say, "I have to have this— take any picture you want."

— CHARLES F. LUMMIS

CONTENTS

ACKNOWLEDGMENTS

One of the pleasures of publishing a book is thanking people who have helped along the way. However, unlike many of the books I've written, this one doesn't have a distinct beginning. Far back in my mind, the project was taking shape even while others were making their way through manuscripts and into print. That is to say that *The Opal Desert* is the result of many years of living in and writing about the desert. Because of this, what was a natural culmination for me frustrates the obligation of thanking the people who, often inadvertently, gave assistance. How do I acknowledge the elderly rancher I stumbled across on a backpacking trip who, perhaps a little lonely himself, took me in and spun desert tales half the night? I remember his kindness but not his name. Then, too, there were dozens, perhaps hundreds, of people who, in hallways and around camp fires, participated in seemingly idle conversations that turned out to be not idle at all. Nonetheless, I clearly name several people especially close over the years with their guidance and good sense: James H. Maguire, Donald A. Barclay, Carl Berkhout, Matthew Rutherford, Lois Olsrud, Germaine L. Moon, Neil Carmony, Peter Steere, and Roger Myers.

George F. Thomson, president of the Center for American Places, gave ready encouragement during the early stages of the project. Later, Shannon Davies, then an editor of the University of Texas Press, likewise helped with an enthusiasm taken up by Sheryl Englund, my present editor at the press.

Several of the following chapters appeared, often in somewhat different form, in the pages of *Puerto del Sol*, and I appreciate the support offered by editors Gail Lavender, Christopher C. Burnham, and Kevin McIlvoy.

I thank my former student and longtime research assistant, Laura Howard, who brought grace to our work, both in libraries and in the field. And, as always, Peggy Flyntz and Me Linda Johnson for their help in assembling the manuscript. Lastly, the long course of this research once again has confirmed what I've always known, that there is a special place in Heaven for librarians.

The Opal Desert

The meaning of the word "desert" has done quite a tumble over the years. When the bewildered mariners in *The Tempest* washed up on the shores of a "desert" island, they meant only that they faced a wild and uninhabited—a deserted—place. No necessary comment was implied about a lack of rainfall. In that time, the Pilgrims applied the term just as readily to the "howling wilderness" before them in the seemingly end-less forest of Massachusetts, as did Alonso, Sebastian, and others in the shipwrecked and soon-to-be-enchanted band stepping ashore on the balmy island of Bermuda, the supposed locale of Shakespeare's romance.

For most of us today, however, the mention of the word immedi-ately flashes a scene of sand dunes and bleak mountains on our mental screens, with perhaps a cluster of palm trees and camels nosing over a bare slope in the distance. Yet the image is not as static or one dimen-sional as it at first seems. As with many concepts in a culture, the pic-ture implies many and sometimes contradictory features beyond our first mental glimpse of it.[1]

The pioneers in the Gold Rush of '49 were troubled by no such com-plexities. In their haste to become rich in California, they all but univer-sally cursed the deserts stretching before their paths as hated barriers to be crossed. And with good reason. Slogging for weeks through the sands, hallucinating from thirst and heat, ambushed by Indians, many of them died out there in that strange, cruel place, whence the naming of Death Valley. For decades those stumbling westward following in their tracks echoed the same bilious opinion. Why had God created such a hellish landscape of useless sandy sweeps and lava cones? For decades flagging travelers damned the noxious wasteland. It was "God's Mistake" and the "Devil's Domain."

Slowly, however, even as the grousing continued, God began to reveal His Divine Wisdom. In the closing decades of the nineteenth century, the U.S. Army bludgeoned the upstart Indians and shunted them off to reservations, while about the same time railroads began crossing the great stretches. Both events took the bitter edge off travel. Some tuberculars, offered little hope by their doctors, found that the desert's dry air brought them brightly back from the verge of death. And trying to scratch a living out there, they found that they could grow oranges, nectarines, and a whole panoply of fruits formerly known only in Sinbad tales. But most of all, gold and silver. In the closing decades of the last century, precious metals started pouring out of the once-despised hills, making some men rich and promising riches to others by the thousands.

It's hard to despise a land that holds out the chance of wealth and well-being at every hand. With that, utilitarianism schooled romance. Why, the desert now seemed even a beautiful place, a place in over-crowded, quickly urbanizing America where the soul might be healed while the lungs were restored and the wallet fattened.

The desert had become the Promised Land.

Somewhat ironically, the more we tamed deserts, the more we looked upon them as desiderata, as repositories of yearnings fulfilled.[2] Here the ironies begin swirling and compounding themselves. Old ideas about exploitation became mixed with new ideas about beauty, spirituality, and notions of regaining our pioneer heritage. Today, backpackers from Los Angeles and Chicago trudge over the lava mountains, hailing their beauty where travelers once died. Great earth-chewing machines level the cactus flats for vast agricultural enterprises, and each year the ticky-tacky of suburbs spreads out ever more relentlessly across the desert. All this while many of the same people benefiting from the region's exploitation (and that means just about all of us) lobby with near religious zeal for the desert's preservation. We shoot rockets over the desert and bury nuclear wastes under its sands. In this water-poor region, we retire in droves to posh communities with well-watered golf courses and myriads of kidney-shaped, aquamarine swimming pools. Then we carve national parks out of the nearby landscape, places officially preserved but overrun by the new, burgeoning population. Today the desert that you see sliding under the wing of your airliner is a heady place of escape for city-pent families and Charles Manson types alike. We build ashrams on it, the better to lead the simple life close to nature, while, nearby, naturalists frantically study its intricate, if fast-fading, ecological web. Equally frantic, but in a far happier mode, real estate developers lay out yet another complex of desert condominiums and begin to count their profits. As the great, desert ranges go through their evening colors and we whisk along at four hundred miles per hour, how those swimming pools flash in the setting sun!

That is, over the last hundred years or so, we have embraced a huge set of contradictions. Our culture has turned the desert, as if it were a limitless, exotic putty, into just about anything people want it to be. In this we keep swinging between the wide poles of fantasy and reality. One of the great urges in humans is to soar beyond the mundane. Eyeing their readers, writers who focus on desert nature want a landscape infused with God, scientific fascinations, romantic mysteries, or some other emotional propellant. The aesthetic issue, however, is not transcendence in whatever guise it appears but the writer's ability to avoid cliché and create a convincing, moving art. The process is the subject of this book.

A few words of comment are in order. On occasion I have used John C. Van Dyke's *The Desert* as a reference point, as a point of comparison for other writers. Not only was its author a rascally and erudite talent, but from his desert book come many of the complex issues that continue to exult, and also frustrate, writers taking their own runs at the subject since 1901. On the other hand, I have not tried to cram in every possible desert writer. Rather, intending this study for scholar and general reader alike, I have kept the focus on a few desert authors who reveal the process at work. The motive here is not to irk aficionados of this particular writer or that but rather to present a large and comprehensible framework providing the context for many other desert writers. Most of the books discussed are nonfiction; the idea being that by very definition novels eliminate themselves from my goal. After all, if reality is to be found anywhere, it should be in nonfiction. That it frequently is not is its own comment on the sometimes delicious waywardness of the human psyche and entirely germane to the point of this book.

Lastly, although desert writers have loved heaping the coals of moral failure on civilization, attitudes toward deserts have changed, as alluded to above, largely due to a whole complex of interrelated phenomena, many of them economic and demographic. Did writers with their talent and enthusiasm for a new land set the trends, thus leading the nation, or did they merely reflect what already was bubbling in the culture? If I had to guess, I'd say likely more of the latter than the former. Yet in any case, a great deal of interaction was going on among the currents and countercurrents; and, especially in those days when the written word was a prime shaper of public opinion, many of such books discussed below were large influences on people's feelings about the arid sweeps. At century's turn, John C. Van Dyke's poetic descriptions of sandstorms whirling up off the deserts in great, Rubenesque billows of gold couldn't help but soften the negative prejudices and excite the positive imagination of his large reading audience. Telling on this score, Van Dyke's book went through edition after edition during his life, and it remains in print today.

None other than Edward Abbey cautions that "you cannot get the desert into a book any more than a fisherman can haul up the sea with his nets" (*Desert Solitaire* xii). Despite the warning, writers have not stopped trying. The resulting number of books about deserts is daunting; together, they would fill a good-sized library. The volumes selected for the bibliography below will provide entrées for readers eager to pursue their individual interests. In the meantime, because I think a grasp of the overall picture is important, let me recommend three books, each excellent in its particular field. Already mentioned in a note, Peggy Larson's *The Deserts of the Southwest* offers a clear and well-illustrated introduction to the natural history underlying artistic responses to deserts. Franklin Walker's *A Literary History of Southern California* is a thorough study of its subject, although unfortunately the book is a bit cluttered for the non-specialist, and in any case it ends about the time of World War I. While W. Storrs Lee gives but moderate attention to literature, otherwise the sine qua non, hands down, to understanding the dynamics in the changes from negative to positive attitudes toward deserts is his *The Great California Deserts*.

1

CABEZA DE VACA

Flaming Entrails,

Burning Trees

In the summer of 1859, famed newspaper editor Horace Greeley jolted in a stagecoach across the continent to report back to his readers on their prospects for settling Out West. When he reached the desert, this visionary of an America of rose-covered farm cottages made no bones about his opinion. "Here," he declared, plowing across mile after mile of choking alkali dust, "famine sits enthroned" (231).

It was not an unusual sentiment, and it pretty well summed up the nation's opinion of those strange lands out there, recently acquired by the Mexican-American War. The growing country wanted water and greenery for potential homes, not a vast expanse of useless sand and rock. So useless that congressmen scowled that they wouldn't appropriate a penny for investing in those hideous places. Except, well, those places lay dead in the path of settlers headed for the lush Pacific coast, and legislators grudgingly allowed that this agonizing land, to be crossed as fast as possible, deserved at least a trickle of money for military outposts to protect travelers against wild Indians and for surveys preparatory to easing travel further by building a railroad to California.

However, humans have a marvelous capacity for holding two contradictory ideas at once. In 1851 Americans picked up a translation by Buckingham Smith, the first rendering into English of a Spaniard's account of crossing the desert some three hundred years earlier. English-speaking readers knew, if vaguely, of the Spaniards' exploration of the Southwest, knew of the riches they had found in Mexico and Peru, and of the riches they had failed to find in the barren deserts. With Alvar Núñez Cabeza de Vaca, however, if the desert described was not a pleasant place, it was nonetheless a mysterious place, a land where the strangest things could happen, a land of gold and precious jewels, and even of miraculous happenings. What made all this odd was that Cabeza de Vaca's account was far different from that of other Spaniards who had stumbled across the lands; and, furthermore, his report was eminently believable. So unique and persuasive was this account that it drove a wedge into the chink of the standard wisdom about the desert, and for this it deserves a brief background on its context created by other conquistadors.

Sailing west to reach the glories of the East, Columbus bungled into a new world lying in between. He thought he'd found his goal, the fabled riches of the Orient. More than that, buoyed on centuries of hubble-bubble about fantastic lands, he believed that the very Earthly Paradise lay but inches away from his fingertips.

Taking fire with the news, his fellow Spaniards swarmed after him across the ocean and started hacking their way into the jungles in search of the dream. It was a dynamic time for Spain, a moment of possibilities. Gathering forces had converged, soon propelling the nation into a world empire. After centuries of battle, the country had finally driven the pagan Arabs back into Africa. Fueled with patriotism and religious zeal and armed with new technologies, Spain's noblemen, brawling among themselves, plunged off into the unknown lands to conquer the kingdoms already existing as bright articles of faith in their heads.

First Hernando Cortez emerged, arms dripping with gold fleeced from Montezuma's staved-in treasury; then Pizarro sent ship after ship back to Spain so loaded with silver that they wallowed up to the gunwales. And so the fever to be first in the next great find reached the point of hysteria. As would happen centuries later in our own Gold Rush to California, the mad scramble for riches was a cruel lottery. Most men returned bedraggled and poorer than when they left, or they rotted in swamps while the dream still burned in their heads. Yet with human beings, extravagant stories of success outshine the dull mass of failures. In such an atmosphere, the discovery of a gold bell in the smoldering ruins of a sacked village or rumors about a swarthy potentate robed in feathers and dripping trinkets, even heard third or fourth hand, were evidence aplenty to spur desire and send yet another expedition charging off pell-mell into trackless places.

To their astonishment, on the other side of the jungles the Spanish found the deserts of what now is the American Southwest. Physically, these barren places slowed the expansion, but in some ways they increased the fervor. The pain-maddened last words quivering from the lips of a tortured Indian telling of entire cities of gold lying still farther to the north dazzled his tormentors. After all, an all-wise God must have put these deserts here for some reason, and if they were of little use for farming or raising cattle, then they must, to justify their existence, hold wealth beyond imagining—so went the logic of the day. So off went Fray Marcos de Niza and after him Coronado, plumes flying, their horses clomping for hundreds of miles into the stony places. They found only mud houses, although in the sunset they glowed *like* gold, surely evidence of the real thing ahead.

One would think that the accounts of such enthusiastic forays would reflect the mental frothings lying behind them. Sometimes they do, but far more often they do not. After all, these were practical explorers, bent on getting their itching fingers on the solid stuff of precious metals, not littérateurs devoted to honing their prose into airy loveliness. Many of them left accounts of their desert travels, but most often these were written out of bureaucratic necessity. Adventurers needed to justify the expenses of their expeditions to the king's hawk-eyed accountants, and when their searches failed, they further needed to offer the king promises of fortune just over the next hill, if he'd only fund yet another try. Writers of such pleas needed to sound sober to their skeptical king. For the most part, then, these are bare-bones accounts written by explorers with other than literary niceties on their minds.

There are notable exceptions. Accompanying Juan Bautista de Anza as chaplain, feisty Father Pedro Font spices his record of the desert journey across Southern California by carping about the drunken dallyings of the soldiers with maidens in native villages. Though he swears that what he says is true, another man of the cloth, Jesuit Juan Nentvig, exercises his imagination in describing the arid lands. There, in that overheated, unknown place where reality easily blurred with fantasy, the good padre assures us a tarantula leapt out of the bushes to bite off the hoof of a galloping horse. His pen getting the best of him, the Jesuit offers poetic soarings about two-headed eagles and tales about inexhaustible troves of gold kept secret by the Indians.

Some of his marvels have practical applications. As this bit of hopeful advice to the wanderer bitten by a rattlesnake:

The most common and efficacious remedy consists of securing the head of the snake between two sticks, keeping the head in such a position that the snake cannot bite. Then the tail is held firmly and stretched out so that the snake cannot coil. The victim of the snakebite then bites the snake. At this point something truly remarkable happens. The patient does not swell, but the snake does, monstrously so, until it bursts. (31)

Fetching as such passages can be, far more typical are the no-nonsense jottings in Pedro Vial's diary for December 1786. Dutifully ending with the number of leagues plodded that day, the entries are unrelieved by magical happenings:

15 *I set out to the north, going right along the Brazos River until I stopped for the night on the same river. 5*
16 *I set out from this place in the same direction, and slept without any mishap by the same river. 5*
17 *I went in the same direction from this place until I arrived at an arroyo with water. 8 (Loomis and Nasatir 273)*

Vial's head may have boiled with phantasms, but drudgery was his daily lot.

Valuable to scholars piecing together the history of the Southwest, the bulk of such material makes tedious, hardly revealing reading for the nonspecialist. Perhaps the most remarkable exception is Alvar Núñez Cabeza de Vaca's *Relación.* The sixteenth-century account of shipwreck, followed by eight years of slavery among the Indians, escape, and a crossing of unknown lands bringing him back to civilization, in itself is the stuff that has schoolboys dreaming.

Yet there's much more here, so much so that to this day the little volume holds scholars bewildered. If at times writers such as Nentvig rattle on about wondrous cures and extravagant gold mines hidden in the hills, such claims, although the priest likely believed them, today have a charming translucency typifying an age when whim-whams often passed as truth. Not so the book of Cabeza de Vaca. This story of conquest gone sour, only to yield an unexpected triumph, is a solid work of journalism, anchored in everyday details, persuasive in its author's earnestness. Seamlessly woven into this is an artful set of parallels, ironies, and foreshadowings, resulting simultaneously both in a convincing historical account and a compelling work of art. Taken by this, when miracles begin to happen—although we may not believe in miracles as earthly phenomena—we can't help but believe, if for the moment, that they *did* happen for this king's nobleman. That is, we hardly feel that Cabeza de Vaca is bamboozling us, and for scholars the issue becomes not one of explaining away the impossible but of trying to figure out how such impossible things seemed to have happened.

All this, or much of it, took place in the desert Southwest. The impact of these things was immediate. Cabeza de Vaca's story was directly responsible for the further and ever more avid probings of the Southwest by the already mentioned Fray Marcos and Coronado, now convinced more than ever of the forbidding desert's potential. And the impact of Cabeza de Vaca surged through the ages, lasting to our day. Before Cabeza de Vaca, the deserts to the north of the Mexican settlements were vague, forbidding unknowns. Now the man who had crossed them brought back news of what lay out there. And it was exciting news. For this wanderer was the first to appoint the desert, not only as a land of earthly wealth, but also as a place stimulating the soul and adorning it with noncorporeal riches. On this latter point, his is a tale that continues to be told and embroidered by the region's spiritual searchers.

To know a thing, we must name it. As would John C. Van Dyke nearly four hundred years later, yet in a different way, Cabeza de Vaca made the desert a place by giving people a desert vocabulary of both words and ideas.

Whatever the wonders revealed before our eyes in this account, Cabeza de Vaca tells his tale in several quite rational and discrete sections. The approach gives bizarre events a believable context, and it is, no doubt, part of the writer's method of building confidence in his readers.

As was customary in such documents of the day, the *Relación* begins with a brief address to His Majesty, King Charles V. Thereafter, the book unfolds chronologically. Cabeza de Vaca covers the voyage from Spain, ending with landfall on the island of Hispaniola, one of the supply centers in the New World. He next recounts the invasion of Florida in 1528 by four hundred men and their disastrous trek inland through unexplored swamps and palmetto tangles. There, the soldiers, many of them mounted, bright with armor and confident of their firearms, are quickly humbled. As they wade helplessly through swamps, Indians pepper them with arrows, and disease further decimates the large force until it's reduced to a handful of desperate men. Piled on top of their misery, they fail to rendezvous with their lifeline, the supply ships supposedly following them along the coast. After that, the expedition in ruins, this becomes the twisting tale of attempts to save themselves by reaching civilization. At the time, geography largely was a matter of wishful thinking. The Spanish outposts in Mexico actually lay over a thousand miles westward, but the soldiers believed they were nearby. In a last hope for survival, the men construct jerry-built barges and sail off westward along the Gulf Coast. When they land for water, Indians greet them with showers of arrows, and storms take a further toll of the overloaded and flimsy craft.

The men weaken to death from weeks of bright sun, dire thirst, and aimless floating. Then a great wave hurls Cabeza de Vaca's barge up on the coast of Texas—on what likely was Galveston Island. The shipwrecks tumble out, naked, cold, and starving, only to be made slaves by the local Indians. More agony follows. Kept half-starved, the Spaniards are forced to dig roots until their fingers bleed at the touch. On top of that, their new masters beat them for the sheer perverse pleasure of it.

At this juncture, an already suspenseful plot turns into a prolonged cliffhanger. Weary of the abuses, Cabeza de Vaca and three others, the last of the known survivors from the Florida invasion force, make their escape. Practically naked and unarmed, they plunge westward into the wilderness. Their plan is still the same, to reach Mexico. This time, however, their prospects of survival are more dismal than those during the sailing fiasco. The land, where even the natives often go hungry, becomes more and more arid and bleak the farther they go, until out in the desert they're reduced to eating powdered straw. Worse, the four strangers in a wild land will run a gauntlet of unknown tribes, with no guarantee that they'll be any less ruthless than their former captors on the Texas coast.

One thing saves the four distressed wanderers. Along the way, they observe medicine men curing—or attempting to cure—ill natives by breathing on their patients, laying on hands, and other traditional remedies. Such seems laughable to the Spaniards, until to their surprise they find by accident that they, too, can do this—yet, throwing in a few Hail Marys and the Lord's Prayer, they succeed to an even greater degree than do the shamans. They have such success that at one point Cabeza de Vaca raises a man from the dead. Astounded at this, the Indians think the strangers walking across their lands are divine creatures, Children of the Sun. As the four travel westward, they are lavished with honors and gifts as Indians by the hundreds crowd around them, eager to touch the hems of their garments. The escape that began as a forlorn hope turns into a triumphant progress.

Finally, the foursome, crossing the Southwest into what is now northern Mexico, meets a party of mounted Spaniards. Ironically, these exploitive men, out on an expedition to capture Indians for the slave trade, look on the admiring throngs surrounding the wanderers as a windfall, but Cabeza de Vaca stays their hand. With this gesture, he completes his eight years in the desert wilderness.

Such is the barest outline of the *Relación*.[1] Simply recounting the main events, however, misses the genius of its execution. If history is the assembling of facts into patterns and literature the working of language into refined effects, Cabeza de Vaca's work is a masterpiece of both. For with his book Cabeza de Vaca has created a deft setup. The surface excitement of the story distracts from a cluster of issues at once dicey and profound. Radical as they are, his messages are very much there, seeping through subliminally as the book progresses. In short, the writer is trying to save his own skin while also trying to reverse Spain's approach toward the conquest of the new lands.

In evidence of Cabeza de Vaca's subtle ways of working, he begins his strategy with disguised innocence on the very first page, with the customary apostrophe to the king. As expected of a loyal subject, Cabeza de Vaca goes through the obligatory hoops, addressing his king as his "Holy, Imperial, Catholic Majesty." Further flattery follows. Of all the princes of the world, men most clamor to serve him, yet, even when, through no fault of their own, men like Cabeza de Vaca fail in their earnest desire, they remain diligent and eager for further service. This hints at the first of several dire problems in a morass from which Cabeza de Vaca hopes to extricate himself with his following pages, for now he is back in Spain, where an autocratic rule has with fiendish vengeance put men to the stake for far lesser shortcomings. Cool in standing before the king, the writer nonetheless is shaking in his boots. This, then, is a man making a bold move. He's trying to save himself, as well as promote an agenda, through a work of art.

As earlier mentioned, despite the chance for extraordinary riches, participants in the Conquest were playing a lottery in which most men lost far more often than they won. Pámfilo de Narváez, leader of the Florida invasion, disappeared in the journey of the barges. Now Cabeza de Vaca, the treasurer and second in command, stands to take the blame for the endeavor's dismal collapse. Not only did the expensive venture fail to find gold or other precious metals, but the king's treasury was drawn down by the loss of hundreds of soldiers and their equipment. Adding to the predicament of Cabeza de Vaca, he must explain why early on he revolted against his leader, Narváez.

Cabeza de Vaca saves these and other ominous issues for later. For the nonce, though he will try to show that his accomplishments were far more splendid, of greater royal service, and even ordained by the Divinity, than any Spanish sacking of a pagan trove for mere earthly gain, he begins humbly, but not without flashing a lure. For now, he doesn't try to dupe the king by hollow protestations about the Florida disaster. Admittedly, the expedition had a "disastrous outcome" (*The Account* 28), although in remaining faithful to his king, perhaps despite his misfortunes he can entertain a man weary of reading bureaucratic documents with his novel tale and in the process suggest ways to help the throne be even more successful in conquering the wild world across the sea. Cabeza de Vaca is going to win over Charles V by the amazement of wrapping him in an artistic web.

Yet whatever his grand aims, an artist is a practical person, calculating step by step, building his elaborate work to persuade by its overall and overwhelming impact. Long before the axiom was touted in creative-writing classes, Cabeza de Vaca knew the first truth of writing: to show rather than tell. Realizing that the king was beset by hosts of sycophants trying to editorialize their way into his favor, Cabeza de Vaca takes a different tack. Knowing he has a good story to tell, he presents events unfolding, with the hope that, thus shown the drama, the king will piece things together and on his own arrive at the right conclusions. This is no better illustrated than by the *Relación*'s treatment of the expedition's leader, Pámfilo de Narváez.

A great self-promoter and one of the sleazy, though inefficient, weasels of a Conquest abounding in unsavory types, Narváez came to the Florida venture with his reputation already soiled. Years before, when the Crown sent him to rein in Cortez, who was having visions of grandeur in the aftermath of his Mexican triumph and threatening to start his own empire, the charismatic Conqueror of the Aztecs had won over Narváez's soldiers by his dazzling talk and slapped leader Narváez into a dungeon. A weaker, less skilled man would have brought up this disgrace, rehashing the sordid business of Narváez with the king. But Cabeza de Vaca realized that he didn't have to. Aware that Charles V well knew this background, a scandal throughout the empire, Cabeza de Vaca avoids wearying his monarch's patience by regurgitating the story. Cabeza de Vaca thus marks himself as an unusual gentleman, a man with noble aims who is above such unpleasant tactics.

Nothing quite so blatant for Cabeza de Vaca. Instead, he begins drawing a subtle picture of malaise, convincing with the real and stepping into the unreal. Working on a man prone to suspicious beliefs, the supplicant tells his king that the times are out of joint in the New World. Weird things are happening over there, and because of this the venture was ill-fated. On the first page of the account proper, 140 men desert upon their arrival in the West Indies (30). Then Cabeza de Vaca notices "bad signs in the weather" (31). They prove worse than imagined. Storms plague the fleet. While Cabeza de Vaca is in Trinidad gathering provisions, a hurricane sweeps the island. But this is no ordinary storm. It is preternatural, with qualities beyond comprehension. In a night of horrors, houses and churches are blown down, and the fearful men wander, desperately locking arms against the blast. Added to that:

While we were going about we heard all night long, especially from the middle of the night onward, a great uproar and noise of voices, and a great sound of little bells and of flutes and tambourines and other instruments that went on until morning, when the storm ceased. Never in these parts had such a fearsome thing been seen. (32)

Just the atmosphere to catch the attention of a king schooled in the mischief of devils in that Inquisitional age.

The next day, Cabeza de Vaca counts the losses: two ships, sixty people, and twenty horses (31–32).

Then Narváez appears on stage. Added to this ill-starred atmosphere, Cabeza de Vaca shows that Narváez is a brash man, doomed to take the whole expedition down with him. Landing on the west coast of Florida, he decides to plunge inland toward a fabled city called Apalachee, while the ships sail on to meet the soldiers again at a harbor rumored to exist farther north. The second in command points out the folly of this, but to no avail. Headstrong Narváez upbraids Cabeza de Vaca for his caution, then leads the soldiers inland, burning and plundering the Indian villages. He's also leading the men into the maws of the jungle, where the alarmed Indians wait, already nocking their arrows (36–37). Little by little, the Spaniards are worn down by the swamps and guerrilla warfare until they reach the coast again. There, out of contact with their ships, they make the desperate decision to escape the hell of green tangles by building boats.

In this situation, despite his waywardness, Narváez starts losing his nerve, and in response Cabeza de Vaca shows that he must assume command. Up to now, it is his good advice that has been ignored, but when the little flotilla of pitiful barges sets off, Cabeza de Vaca lets drop that his craft is in the lead. "My boat was first," says Cabeza de Vaca (49). The king will get the message. The greatest ignominy of all, cowardly Narváez has taken the strongest soldiers to man the oars of his boat, and when things get tough, he rows off, never to be seen again, calling back over his shoulder that now it's each man for himself (53). In contrast, Cabeza de Vaca tries to keep the little bobbing band together. Later, when, despite all his efforts, only four survivors remain, it is Cabeza de Vaca who plots their escape from captivity (74) and Cabeza de Vaca who performs the most dramatic cures (80). However, all this is presented as the facts of events, delivered without boastfulness. Cabeza de Vaca shows himself to be nothing more than an honest man devoted to the service of his monarch.

Still, the failed explorer remains in an extremely dangerous position.

It was bad enough that he was standing before his king trying to patch up why a mighty expedition leaving Spain had been reduced in the New World to four stragglers. On top of that, he had to exonerate himself for resisting the Crown-appointed leader of the venture. So far, Cabeza de Vaca has handled the situation perhaps as well as anyone could, citing plausible explanations and, throughout his account, showing himself a loyal servant acting as best he could in bad circumstances. Yet all this is but a prologue to defuse the most perilous issue of them all—a shocking religious violation. The miraculous cures the wanderers had performed, saving their hides in dire circumstances by winning over the Indians, now have backfired.

It bears emphasis that in the Spain of those days, Church and King were tightly allied. In their efforts to shore up their power and keep the nation under strict control, they were eagle-eyed, quick to punish even hints of unorthodox behavior, either secular or religious. For far lesser acts of getting out of line, men had been dressed in the sanbenito of the Inquisition, a garment painted with flames and devils, hauled away and given over to the real fire and devils that eagerly carried off the souls of condemned heretics. Suspicious leaders' eyebrows must have shot up at Cabeza de Vaca's unorthodox cures, which sounded very much like dabblings in black magic.

Of course, Cabeza de Vaca might have made a pact with his fellow survivors and tried to stifle the issue entirely. Wisely, he did not. Rumors of such things almost inevitably leak out, and circulating hearsay can metastasize into far worse stories than the events of their origin. More than that, almost in a Zen way Cabeza de Vaca handles this issue as he does other negatives in his account. He deftly turns sore disadvantages into favorable outcomes. It is the great risk, and the major accomplishment, of the *Relación.*

An essential part of his major message, the solution is smoothly interwoven with other complex features of his story, for the genius of the book lies in its series of surprising parallels, foreshadowings, and reversals. The little gold bell found by the greedy explorers in Florida, a promising hint of further riches ahead, is echoed many pages later by a Spanish buckle Cabeza de Vaca sees an Indian wearing as an ornament, indicating that civilization is near. Made a slave by the Indians and cruelly treated, toward the end of the story Cabeza de Vaca is appalled by a similar inhumanity on the part of Spaniards bent on enslaving his Indian friends. The farther west they go, the lower the shipwrecked men fall. Starting out in armor, they end up naked. This is the point of the book. The aggressive ways of the Spanish will not work in the

New World. Disaster can be avoided, and in fact even more prosperity and riches can be gained for the king if he will institute kindlier, more Christian, methods of winning over the new lands. The *Relación* is an immense tour de force, an attempt to change the entire consciousness of the empire.

In the long run, given human resistance to change, Cabeza de Vaca failed in his monumental efforts at reform. Nonetheless, his book succeeds in stating its noble case—a success borne out by the very practical fact that the king later appointed the writer to implement more enlightened policies as the governor of a colony in South America.[2]

Meanwhile, Cabeza de Vaca's sleight of hand in at least temporarily wresting triumph from almost sure defeat crowns his literary skill. Further, what turns out to be the crowning glory of Cabeza de Vaca's progress across the continent occurs in the desert, a land, he leads his readers to believe, of riches, miracles, and mystery. In this scenario, one that has lived on to this day, the Southwest is a region both of physical and spiritual wonders.

To effect such an enormous change in attitudes among hardheaded empire builders gleefully swinging their swords as they plundered the land and its Stone Age inhabitants the writer persuades by accretion of detail rather than by loud lectures. He builds subtle notes into his story ending in his triumphal reentry into Spanish civilization. Almost from the start, he begins preparing his readers, showing them that this is a strange place in which the aggressive European ways lose their power and become useless. Storms on the voyage to Florida almost overwhelm the ships, and not only are they inordinately powerful, as we've seen, their mysterious voices and sounds of flutes indicate malevolent forces at work. Although the Indians, like any humans, are capable of kindness, they are plagued by the dark instincts of the unsaved. Worse, evil itself runs rampant among them. For instance, this dramatic hellion:

These Indians . . . said that a man whom they called "Evil Thing" wandered that land. He had a small body and a beard, but they never were able to see his face. When he came to the house where they were, their hair stood on end and they trembled. Then there appeared at the entrance to the house a burning firebrand. Then he entered and took whomever he wanted and stabbed him three times in the side with a very sharp flint, as wide as a hand and two palms long. He would stick his hands in through the wounds and pull out their guts, and cut a piece of gut about a palm in length, which he would throw onto the embers. . . . They told us that he often appeared among them when they were dancing, sometimes dressed as a woman and other times as a man.
(80–81)

That certainly got the attention of the king and his counselors, for here was the very sort of evil that the Inquisition wished to stamp out.

The other side of the coin, Cabeza de Vaca slowly begins to suggest, is that the antidote is Christianity, a proposal that his stern auditors hardly could deny. So Cabeza de Vaca had turned the tables on his potential enemies within the court. For not only was there a need for Christianity, God already was there, despite all their suffering guiding and preserving the four survivors, as if they were the vanguard of the Gospel. At one point, Cabeza de Vaca tells his king that when he was lost and freezing, "It pleased God that I should find a burning tree," whose warmth saved him (77). How else could such desperate Spaniards survive in that savage place unless the hand of the Divine was actively working in their favor?

This is a nearly perfect segue into the miracles. Antipodal to the stuff of black magic, they are ordained by God Himself, are but one in the many miraculous ways He worked in bringing the wanderers through. Why, the cures and the great impression they made on the Indians even allowed the foursome to do a little preaching, sowing the religious seed among these eager heathen, a seed that will flourish if His Majesty seizes the advantage (79). In such a way, the New World, at that point resisting conquest, can be the king's—won, not through expensive armies destroying the land, but through the ministrations of far cheaper men of God (115). Thus, the king has a supreme opportunity to demonstrate his true Christian spirit.

But Cabeza de Vaca also knows that virtue can be quickened by the hope of earthly favors. The farther west he goes the bleaker the land becomes but also the better the prospects for wealth. The desert can be a hideous place, but it also contains fertile lands (106) where "we saw many signs of gold and antimony, iron, copper and other metals" (107). Here, the Indians live in real houses, just as the Spanish do; their intelligence has increased, for they cunningly work fabrics and precious stones (103); and, My Lord—one can almost hear Cabeza de Vaca whispering into the ear of his mesmerized king—farther on there are rumors of pearls and unnamed "best and richest things" (116).

Cabeza de Vaca had checkmated his adversaries.

How sincere was Cabeza de Vaca? In an age saturated with blarney, no doubt he was telling his share, but no doubt also, as with the priest Nentvig, he also likely believed much, if not all, of what he was saying. In any case, there can be little doubt about his innate idealism, as his following efforts to put it into practice as governor of a colony in South America attests. The essential difference lay in Cabeza de Vaca's vision

of the New World, not as a battleground, but as a pacific garden, a fulfillment of the old dream of a paradise on earth, achievable if men only
would employ their better instincts. That, as noted, he failed, and was
shipped back to Seville in chains, is beside the point. Cabeza de Vaca had
provided evidence of the desert as a dawnland for the human consciousness as well as for human purses.

The strength of that vision has lived on and grown, though, as often
happens with well-known books, the *Relación* took on a life of its own,
one often violating its original intent as people turned the story to their
own purposes. The appeal of riches that Cabeza de Vaca held out as a
lure quickly outshone his appeal to idealism. The little book set off "the
chain of events that ultimately prompted the colonization of the Southwest" (Pilkington 69), and the great irony is that the conquest by Europeans showed little of Cabeza de Vaca's gentle and tempering ways.

Swinging to the other extreme, Cabeza de Vaca sparked modern "feel-
good" approaches toward the Southwest. Large in the contemporary literature of the American West is the hero combining physical struggle
with spiritual rebirth, and the wandering, miracle-working Spaniard of
old serves as the prototype. Novel after novel has tumbled off the presses
presenting Cabeza de Vaca as a Saint Paul undergoing a conversion. Setting out on a destructive expedition, Cabeza de Vaca is struck down.
Confused and humbled, he sees a redeeming light, and it suffuses his
whole being with "altruism toward the Indians" (Cheaves, "Prologue"
n.p.). In this tradition stand Abbey, Bowden, Nabhan, and a whole host
of modern writers who ascribe their newfound physical welfare and spiritual salvation to the wonders they find in the desert. Even more than this,
they often either imply or state directly that our society as a whole can
recover its muscle tone and spiritual sheen if it will turn—all the millions of us—to seek renewal in this miraculous land.

This philosophy finds ready listeners in an industrial age, on the
one hand plagued by overcrowding, rattled by rapid social change, and
schooled to think about nature in terms of Disney's *Bambi,* and on the
other so fattened by prosperity it eagerly feeds on pleasant, if vapid, notions. Yet the attitude perhaps becomes never so cloying as in Haniel
Long's modern appropriation of Cabeza de Vaca. Turning wayward, this
son of a missionary rewrites the *Relación* according to what he envisions
its author should have been, according to some modern tastes. In Long's
words:

*My account of Núñez is not the account he sent the King, apart of course from the
actual facts. But I believe it to be the account he wished to send the King. I preserve*

the core of his narrative . . . , and I try to show what, quite plainly, was happening to the spirit of the man. That is, I allow him to speak as though unafraid of his King and his times. I wish him to address us four hundred years later, in this world of ours where human relation is still the difficult problem, and exploitation the cancer. (viii)

Thus, we get a hero who, indeed, sees a "light" (1) and beating his breast over "man's inhumanity to man" (xii), swells with "mystical feeling" (ix) as he staggers about in a state of spiritual "drunkenness" (23). The moral being in Long's revelation that, if all would do likewise, the world would be a much better place.

Thus, also, we learn far more about Long and his comfortable perspective than about the historical Cabeza de Vaca, thirsty, starving, and his feet bleeding as he tries to escape captivity among the brutal Indians and reach civilization. Long has his sweet-souled suppositions, but no evidence, to support his revised version of Cabeza de Vaca. Admittedly, the spiritual impulse is a strong light in the *Relación*, but Cabeza de Vaca's spirituality hardly is as simple and as pure as Long pleases himself to imagine. Rather, Long conveniently glosses over the Spaniard's belief in the superiority of European culture; he ignores the Spaniard's willingness to use Christianity as a tool to subject the natives; his massaging the king to action with repeated promises of riches; and his hoodwinking of the Indians to inflate his reputation as a miracle worker and thus increase his power over the tribes he's passing through.

Long has turned this practical and complex, though enlightened, conqueror into a bag of clichés, a spiritual ninny. And not only does Long rudely violate the man, he violates the landscape, turning a harsh region, as cruel to Cabeza de Vaca as it was to his starving Indian companions, into a wondrous stage for a trite morality play in which love conquers all. This remains, however, an opulently saleable concept. Hence, Cabeza de Vaca, the early desert writer, transformed into our first desert saint by wishful writers coming after him, eventually will become a stock character, a man of honey, locusts, and good feelings, stumbling dazzled through much of our desert literature.

2

WILLIAM L. MANLY

The Classic Account of

Deserta Horribilis

Despite his earnestness, Cabeza de Vaca's airy view of deserts was shared by almost no one else. If gold and associated wealth could be extracted from those bleak and unyielding lands, well and good for the Spaniards and those who came after them. A few priests drove themselves to attempt redemption of the heathenish souls dwelling out there, but for the most part the hot, hellish places drove the self-appointed rescuers back. Deserts were worthless, pernicious jokes played on bewildered men believing in the biblical charge to make the earth fructify.

Today, we may have an air-conditioned romance about deserts, but the older, negative view of them is perfectly understandable, if not eminently sensible. Some desert reptiles have the ability to spend most of their time sleeping underground, avoiding extremes of desert temperatures. Human beings have no such luck. They have to eat regularly, preferably several times each day, and they have to scurry around making things to clothe themselves and put roofs over their heads. All the while, they're burdened with raising offspring that, unlike newborn lizards, cannot fend for themselves. Instead, they take years draining parents' time and resources before they mature and can provide for their own needs. Such tasks are difficult enough almost anywhere on earth and even under the best of conditions. In a nearly waterless expanse where food is scarce and the afternoon heat soars past endurance, life approaches the impossible. That is, humans weren't made to live in deserts.

This would seem to contradict Mesa Verde, Casa Grande, and other ancient ruins where tourists presently wander—whole cities where people not only lived by the thousands but apparently prospered. The key here is the changing climate. Tens of thousands of years ago, the Southwest was a lush place, a place of bears and fat ground sloths, mammoths, and great lakes fringed with palm trees—a paradise for hunters. As the centuries passed, however, the climate became hotter and drier. In response, people retreated to those ecological nooks where water and soil conditions still made agriculture possible. When the water failed even in such refuges, civilization collapsed.

White people would have their nasty words for deserts, yet at the time of European contact with arid-land peoples, it's difficult to believe that even these sinewy dwellers were having a sanguine time with their lot. Along the Colorado, the Southwest's greatest waterway, the Mojave Indians grew fine crops of corn and squash on riverside plots. Reflecting the Mojaves' power and good fortune were their trade routes, radiating from riverside villages for hundreds of miles. In contrast were the Mojaves' cousins living in the desert outback. Far less blessed, they wandered in small family bands from water hole to water hole, snatching up snakes and eating them raw, regaling themselves after good hunting days with rodent stew. No doubt, when their bellies were full, they sang and danced, but during droughts they died of thirst and malnutrition. Sometimes the hardiest survived by taking advantage of a "second harvest," picking out undigested seeds from their feces. Whether or not such people were generally happy cannot be said; it can be said, however, from what we know of them that in dry times they constantly struggled merely to survive (Clifford Walker 1–68).

Sweating in their armor, impatient for riches, the Spanish ground their teeth as they stumbled over these devil-cursed lands. In the accounts they left us, hardly a conquistador has a favorable word for such blazing places. After them, the Mexicans hunkered in isolated settlements where a spring or a live river made crops possible, surrounded by scalp-raising Indians and pitying themselves for their exile from civilization to the south. The first English speakers to cross the deserts of the Southwest likely were experienced frontiersmen, toughened trappers such as James O. Pattie. Pulling themselves from water hole to water hole, they, too, picked up the lament, grousing as they crossed the sandy, Godless wastes, inexplicable obstacles to the rich promises awaiting on the California coast.

Actually, such groups were far better prepared for survival in the desert than the wave coming after them. Of epochal proportions both in size and naiveté, the huge migration would bring the desert into the nation's consciousness and fix it there with a harshness and indelibility whose sharp edges have not yet completely worn smooth after a hundred and fifty years. As to the invading Spaniards, they came with some experience of aridity from the high, dry, and sparsely settled plateau of their native Spain. Then, too, they were soldiers, steeled by hardship and propelled by greed, unencumbered by families or by the softness that comes with general concern for humanity. Besides this, time was on the side of psychological adjustment. Their encounter with the deserts lasted nearly three centuries, time enough to accept the barrenness to the north as fact, a puzzling fact, but one they could choose to avoid by withdrawing after their failures to the settled, more amenable southern climes in the heart of Mexico.

Although they hardly fared any better, and perhaps worse, the Mexicans after them, a blend of Spanish and Indian blood, poverty stricken and not tortured by high expectations from the European side of their ancestry, stoically clung to their green patches, suffering the theft of their cattle, and sometimes their wives and children, by the Apaches. To the hardiest, most savvy, and wilderness-wise group America ever produced, the mountain men—hard-drinking, whoring, innovative, used to dismissing daily threats of brutal death from grizzly bears and merciless Blackfoot with dark, roisterous humor—the desert was but one more trial added to lives already honed to the keen edges of hilarity by constant dangers. If on their way to California, their water ran out and they fell to their knees, forced to crawl, then crawl they did, lured on by dancing visions of sloe-eyed señoritas and sleek beaver pelts awaiting them on the other side of the sands.

In contrast to these hardy types, well chafed and chastened by frontier experiences, imagine a farmer living near a New England village in the late 1840s. He and his family have enough to eat, but it is common fare. They rarely travel more than a few miles from their home; their view of the world is from the Bible and Milton's *Paradise Lost.* Life can be good, though it promises no great excitements or prosperity, no relief from the daily round to the barn, the woodpile, and the potato patch. For such people, God keeps the world in a sensible order, and it is a green world, of woods and streams and familiar neighbors down the country lane. If there is a better life before the one that comes after death, it will be much like this one, only greener. Then the family hears rumors about California, recently acquired by the Mexican-American War. They hear about pastures and soil rich beyond anything they've imagined, about a climate that is spring year-round. And, taking the breath away, about the gold being dug from the earth, at that very moment turning hard-working farmers into princes. After much discussion, they sell their farm and most of their goods. Piling what's left into a wagon, they set off to claim their hope, little knowing what lies between them and their dream.

The dream came tinged with apprehension. After months of jolting across the continent, the travelers would face California's Sierra Nevada mountains. The immigrants probably have heard about the range, that it is the highest in the United States and that fearsome winter storms swirl around its great peaks, choking the passes with snow many feet deep. Not wanting to suffer the horrors of the Donner party, the wise pioneers have left the East early in the spring, timing their trip to reach the passes while they are still clear.

But for that, just enough of a danger to speed their pulses with anticipation, a picnic atmosphere often prevailed in the pioneers' camps. After they crossed the Mississippi River and left the familiar forested country behind, they struck the Great Plains. In the spring, the grasslands stretching over the rounded world's horizon could be lovely, dreamscapes bursting with flowers and providing ample feed on which their draft animals and livestock tagging along fattened. If this was all there was to it, well, then, California was all but in their grasp. At night someone got out a violin, and there was singing and dancing around the camp fires.

And then, and then . . . Topping a ridge months after they had left home, they stood stunned, slapped in the face by a nightmare.

America's classic account of crossing the desert serves as a baseline for changing desert attitudes thereafter. It was written by William L. Manly, a man born on a farm in Vermont. Young, full of fun, naive, and only rudimentally educated at the time of his adventure, Manly sticks to the unfolding details of his journey, giving us a tale so realistic and immediate that step by step we go with him, suffering the thirst and hunger that left the trail behind him dotted with corpses. And yet, though he titles his book *Death Valley in 49*, featuring the crossing as the main crisis of a life otherwise quite normal in its circumstances, Manly tells the story of his life from birth to old age. Thus, we get no mere recitation of horrors, dramatic as that would be standing by itself, but the entire context of a central event that reverberated through Manly's years.

At least that's how it might seem at a first reading of this cliffhanger, and one can imagine that a wily Cabeza de Vaca, calculating as he bites the end of his pen, would have changed the convincing, homespun quality entirely, subtly manipulating readers with planted hints and literary tricks, dazzling readers with miraculous events. In contrast, Manly is a meat-and-potatoes writer. With him we have John Bunyan, not San Juan de la Cruz. And yet the world is full of gripping adventure stories, few of them remembered long after the excitement of the first reading. Bright as Manly's surface events are, they contain their own set of subtleties, their own set of parallels and contrasts when compared to Cabeza de

Vaca's great work. Because of such qualities, Manly becomes the American Everyman of his age, and his book sticks in the mind, continuing to work in the consciousness of our nation.

Whereas on his very first page Cabeza de Vaca begins lubricating his readers, preparing them for an unexpected message, Manly disarms by establishing himself as a humble farmer's son, wearing homemade clothing spun from homegrown flax, laboring honestly, attempting to better his life through dogged toil (1–5). "You will have to depend on yourself in all things," his father lectures him (23), and it will become a theme of the book as the following story reflects how well young Manly learned his lesson. Not that the youth is grim with an overbearing sense of duty. He has fun and adventure in his bones, and after the family's move to Ohio in search of better lands (6), the youth strikes out on his own. He'd rather "catch chipmunks for a living" than endure the drudgery of splitting rails (22), and off he goes into the Wisconsin wilderness with his gun (31), making his living by hunting and trapping and leading an independent, Huck Finn life.

The pattern certainly was not unusual for a boy growing up on the frontier, but the background prepares us for Manly's future heroism. Like Cabeza de Vaca, the writer is cautious to be self-effacing, or at least leads us to believe that he is. When the wheels begin coming off the pioneers' dreams and lost and stranded they start dying in an earthly hell, it is yeomanly Manly, solid of character and used to making do in the wilds, who steps forward, equipped better than anyone else to lead the befuddled wilderness neophytes and their trembling wives and children to safety. In such a way, Cabeza de Vaca also prepared his readers. When need calls, both he and Manly take charge during dire times.

From the beginning, Manly portrays himself as a typical American with solid, middle-class values. He keeps yearning to improve his lot, keeps yearning toward the West. When in the winter of 1848–1849 news arrives of gold discovered in California, he throws up everything and joins the fevered throng (53–54), pockets empty but hiring on as a wagon driver for a pioneer family (56). But he doesn't go all the way. In present-day southwestern Wyoming, he and six other light-hearted youths conclude they've seen enough of oxen's posteriors and decide to paddle down the Green River into the Colorado and on to the Pacific coast (69–72). Logically, floating rather than jolting made a good deal of sense, although geographically the idea was folly. The ill-prepared seven would have been ground up in the maws of the Grand Canyon. Fortunately, friendly Indians dissuade them and point the youths overland to Salt Lake City (87–92). The hilarious, though nearly disastrous, side trip serves a serious purpose in the book, illustrating an ignorance of the Western landscape that will get the travelers in even greater trouble a few weeks hence.

At Salt Lake City, the Mormon center where pioneers regrouped and bought flour, bacon, and other supplies, Manly's desert story proper begins. Here, he bumps into Asabel Bennett and his family, friends from Wisconsin, and is invited to travel with them to California (99–100).

At this point, a word or two needs to be said to counter the beneficent image of white-topped prairie schooners making their stately progress westward. Most pioneers followed the Oregon Trail to South Pass, in western Wyoming. Once over the continental divide, the trail divided. One route went on to Oregon, while the gold seekers turned south to the Great Salt Lake. From there, the course was across northern Nevada and over the steep California sierra toward Sacramento, the center of mining activity. However, the region between Salt Lake City and Sacramento was all but unexplored, travel by wagon across it was relatively new, and as a consequence the route branched into a lacework of trails. Told by the Mormons that the season was too late and that the impatient pioneers might find the northernmost route to Sacramento blocked by snow, they decided on a more southerly branch. So far, so good.

Other factors entered into what would become a fatal mix. Again contrary to the picture of stalwart and selfless pioneers acting out the nation's destiny, wagon trains could bristle with conflicts. Setting off from Missouri into the wilderness, each train drew up a list of rules and elected a leader. Yet group cohesion was voluntary, and as the journey took its toll on men and animals, high spirits were rubbed raw, tempers flared, and disagreements arose over what route to take. Often, spatting members broke off, forming smaller groups, and even if they all stuck together, the captain appointed in happier circumstances in Missouri likely had several nerve-worn successors by the time the travelers saw the Pacific Ocean (Quaife xix–xxi). Also, the geography of the route was particularly cruel. The hardest part, crossing the desert and the mountains, came last, after disease, Indians, long months of travel, and personal disputes had worn down the travelers' bodies and enthusiasm. In such an abraded condition, both men and oxen faced their worst trial, across new landscapes appalling in their demands and totally unfamiliar to the Easterners. They had never seen mountains rearing two miles high. They had little concept of a desert or the significance of one that stretched hundreds of miles wide in their path, demonically waiting their crossing.

Yet cautious with inklings of difficulties ahead, Manly's group wisely hired Jefferson Hunt, a man familiar with the route to the California coast. And so they were off, 107 wagons (447) bearing the hopeful into the barren lands stretching west from Salt Lake City (102–104). In the following weeks and months, they would split and split again into quarreling factions, until in Manly's party all wagons were lost, and a handful of sunken-eyed, near-raving people staggered out of the desert.

The trouble began early on. Eager to reach California and fill their pockets with gold before the thousands pressing behind them, the travelers lost their heads over a map that somewhat mysteriously appeared in the wagon train and began circulating from hand to hand (106). Of primary attraction, the map showed a shortcut from Hunt's route that would shave five hundred miles from the trip (445). At night, men argued the point, sawing their arms around the camp fires. Admittedly, Hunt had experience, but his way was the long one, while there, there on the map was a fine road, with the water holes marked and showing places with good grass that would get them to California with speed and ease (107). The more Hunt was shouted down as a mossback, the more alluring the promise of the map became. Despite Captain Hunt's warnings, wagons began peeling off into the unknown. But now they were leaderless, one group passing another in the race, and, worse, the map was completely wrong. Finally, as they stumbled doggedly on, following faith rather than reason, chaos reigned until, remarks Manly, "we were completely lost"—not having any idea how to extricate themselves from this mess (126).

And Manly's little party of seven wagons (132, 453) was lost not on some flowering prairie, where the grass grew thick for their livestock, water was abundant, and following a stream eventually would lead to a settlement, but in a static upheaval of the earth, a chaos of jumbled rock, sand, and bare mountains, a place almost waterless and with little game to supply their dwindling larders. Manly shows the slow disintegration. They send out scouts to find a way for the wagons through the rocky mazes, and the scouts return dejected. Strange mirages bewitch with promises of lakes that disappear upon the approach of the thirsty (116). When real water is found, it often tastes of salt and poison. Indians are all around them, and against Manly's advice the hungry travelers break into the food caches they find and gorge themselves (124).

Time after time, the hopeful scramble up a slope, expecting to see the lush valleys of California inviting on the other side, only to see yet another Dantean landscape stretching endlessly before them in a "desolation beyond conception" (135). Back in camp:

The four children were crying for water but there was not a drop to give them. . . . The mothers were nearly crazy, for they expected the children to choke with thirst and die in their arms, and they would rather perish themselves than suffer the agony of seeing their little ones gasp and slowly die. They reproached themselves as being the cause of all this trouble. For the love of gold they had left homes where hunger had never come. . . . (127)

Tortured by day, at night they are tortured again by dreams of wading in pools of water and breaking great loaves of bread (128, 465). Finally, in order to eat they are reduced to killing their starving oxen. Not only that. Fuel is so scarce that the pioneers begin burning their wagons to roast the meat. The travelers destroy their very means of escape in order to survive. In a radical pitch of fortune, the issue has changed from how to reach California to how to stay alive.

People begin looking at one another with "a strange look in the eyes," and the single men begin to abandon the slow-moving wagons with their wailing children, slipping off on foot in hopes of saving their own skins (147). One night the dozen or so adults remaining in Manly's party face reality. They are all about to die. As a last resort, they decide to pitch camp by a little spring in what is now Death Valley National Park. They'll try to hang on to life there while Manly and his friend, John Rogers, the two strongest men in the little band, go for help (151–152).

And so the two youths, faithful to their charge, shoulder their guns and slog off through the sand. They begin passing the bodies of others who splintered off and tried it afoot. They hope to be back in ten days (151). They are gone for nearly a month (205).

We have, then, slipped from a travelogue into a story of suspense and rescue under the severest conditions. Having set the tone for the central portion of his book, Manly keeps the suspense going by portraying the daily events of their crisis. The two put bullets in their mouths, trying to raise saliva (157). They become so distraught that when they see little tufts of grass, they rush forward as if they've found gold, clawing up and eating the thin blades for their little moisture (157–158). But nothing works. They are so dehydrated they cannot swallow the little dried oxen meat they have. At night the two weary men lie down, but they are so maddened by thirst they cannot sleep. Wearily, they stumble on in the moonlight (158). All there is to do is keep moving in hopes of saving themselves in time to return and save their friends left behind.

Eventually, they climb a snowy ridge, then stagger like drunken men into the green valley on the other side. It's a grassy sweep, with a stream and fat cattle. They fill themselves from a brook, kill a yearling steer, eat, then stumble on like men in a dream. Soon they reach the rancho of a Mexican couple, are treated with kindness, and directed to a mission. The wanderers can't speak Spanish, but they communicate with signs. Their ragged condition speaks well enough of their plight, and they receive supplies for their return trip (184–185). When they depart with horses and a mule, Manly relates a touching scene. A señora "came out with four oranges and, pointing to her own child and then to the east, put them in the pack, meaning we should carry them to the children" (188). After more trials, Manly and Rogers arrive back in the nearly hopeless camp and lead their friends over the trail to the good Mexican people, who greet them with more hospitality and send them on their way to Los Angeles. It would become an old story of pioneer survival, yet one never so keenly stated as here. Manly does go on to recount the rest of his life, his moderate success in the gold fields of northern California, his further wanderings, and his long life as a farmer in San Jose, though most of this is forgettable when compared to the desert trek, which left Manly with "Every point of that terrible journey . . . indelibly fixed" in his mind (265), left him, despite the passage of decades, shaken and bewildered. As it would, vicariously, the rest of the nation, a humid-land nation rattled by the desert as if it had beheld the Devil Himself in its own back yard and puzzled how best to handle Him. As eminent desert historian E. I. Edwards states the case with finality, Manly's is the "classic" account of that encounter ("Death Valley's Neglected Hero" 63).

For all that, perhaps Manly's main ploy is too successful. At the low point, the pioneers sit dejected in Death Valley, and not with a great deal of zeal, their leader, Mr. Bennett, suggests that Manly go for help. Bennett says, "He knew one man well enough to know that he would come back if he lived" (152). That decided, Manly picks friend Rogers as his companion, and the two pack up and leave on foot. The decision and departure are so sudden that the significance of Bennett's little speech is easily missed, for the events in this narrative of survival are so exciting in themselves that we might read right past both the smaller and larger subtleties behind them. This may be put down to Manly's skill as a straightforward but not an especially sophisticated writer, a person who, more than anything else, wishes to get across the most important story of his life, yet the subtleties, if often undeveloped, nonetheless are there.[1] For instance, Bennett's little speech reflects a very real worry for those who will be waiting behind. A man lucky enough to make it out of the desert might easily decide that by then his friends likely are all dead and, thus rationalizing, prefer pushing on to the alluring gold fields to the north rather than returning to the hellhole he had just left. It's a point that another writer might have easily enlarged upon to create more psychological tension in the narrative.

Or we may be selling Manly short. In "Death Valley's Neglected

Hero," Edwards analyzes the text and compares it to versions of the same events recorded by other pioneers surviving the disaster. His conclusion: Manly may not be an urbane writer, but he is a clever one (64). *Death Valley in 49* is a story of heroism. Throughout his tale, Manly appears to be self-effacing and modest, the model of the humble but capable yeoman, yet he keeps stepping forward when circumstances call for a man of strength and selfless deeds. For instance, points out Edwards, in telling his long story of reaching the coast and returning with aid, the central and most riveting part of the book, Manly acknowledges his companion, John Rogers, only as a rather faceless functionary plodding alongside him. Thus, Manly reduces Rogers, deserving equal credit for the rescue, to a "meaningless appendage" (63).

Edwards makes a tight case. Rogers, indeed, is the "neglected hero" of Death Valley's most famous event. Yet Edwards' conclusion needs to be modified by several factors. Human nature comes into play here. We tend to see ourselves in favorable lights, to remember circumstances in terms of the roles we played in them, especially when our own personal heroism was a large part of the main event. Thinking back over the decades on the most chromatic segment of his life, one that already glowed in the annals of pioneer folklore, Manly naturally enough would see himself as central and sterling. Though for far more complex reasons, Cabeza de Vaca also did something very similar in writing his *Relación.* Furthermore, and consistent with his purpose, Manly's emphasis throughout is on action and description, rather than on development of character, either that of himself or of his companions. In this view, Rogers, deserving as he is, is no more slighted than any other of the travelers, and if Manly leaves an overall impression, it is one of an undistinguished freeman living through an exciting patch of history.

Not that, rough-knuckled writer that he is, Manly is devoid of the literary niceties that make reading an account more than an act of absorbing information. Writers who are blowing smoke often show their hand by their vagueness when it comes to facts. In contrast, step by step Manly gives the convincing particulars. He names the ranch of the kindly Mexicans, the Rancho San Francisquito, where he and Rogers first found succor (271), and, as we've seen, he passes on the touching vignette of the señora giving the returning rescuers oranges for the starving children. True, to follow Manly's route, we might wish for more place names, but their absence cannot be laid at Manly's door. Likely the first English speakers to see much of that desert territory, Manly's company faced a land without names, at least without English names. Yet in recounting the fearsome grandness, backwoodsman Manly gives, as Carl I. Wheat, another Death Valley scholar, puts it, an "almost photographic description of the wild country" (4). When Manly describes a great, snowy mountain lying directly east of the camp in Death Valley (209), there it is on modern maps, now known as Telescope Peak, soaring over eleven thousand feet above the desert floor. So accurate are such descriptions that Wheat was able to map Manly's route. And the above illustrates another virtue of the prose, whether Manly put it there consciously or not. Lawrence Clark Powell observes that Manly keeps us reading by constantly shifting perspective, zooming from grand prospects to minute detail, "modulating from wide-angle views to close-ups" ("William Lewis Manly's . . ." 32).

In another sophisticated switch, the book keeps the colors of the prose changing by alternating between extremes of emotion. Building up the suspense, when the two youths return to the camp in Death Valley, they remember evidence of Indians dogging the wagons through this forsaken place and wonder if the weakened families haven't been slaughtered during their absence. They approach the camp warily. There the wagons sit bleaching in the sun, one hundred yards away, without a sign of life. Closer, and still no sign. Perhaps all their friends are dead, and this is an ambush, and they have suffered weeks of torture only to be tomahawked with the rest.

As Rogers levels his shotgun, at the ready, Manly fires a shot into the air from his repeating rifle. The result: "Still as death and not a move for a moment," tenses Manly, and "then as if by magic a man came out from under a wagon and stood up looking all around. . . . Then he threw up his arms high over his head and shouted, 'The boys have come! The boys have come!'" With that, the others appear and, though bedraggled, rush toward their deliverers (203).

Suspense has turned into rejoicing.

Manly doesn't stop there. He continues to work the camp scene, producing yet another set of emotions. Despite the high spirits at their return, Manly makes clear that he and his friends are by no means home free. Trekking to the coast with Rogers was bad enough. Now, leading these starving, staggering people, all afoot except a few women and children perched atop weakened oxen, will be an even greater, and perhaps impossible, task. Sizing up the situation, Manly says, "We must succeed or perish," although he keeps his grim thoughts over their prospects to himself. He's not too grim, however, to note Mrs. Arcane. To lighten their loads, people strip to essentials, but Mrs. Arcane refuses to abandon her best clothes. She's hauled them halfway across a continent, and now she's not about to leave them for some Indian to find, then strut about wearing his new prizes. Indignant at the prospect, she prepares for the trip by putting on several of her finest dresses, one over the other, and tops off the bizarre travel outfit with her best hat, trimmed with extra ribbons (213).

All goes well, until her ox bolts. The huge animal plunges and dances dangerously, while serene

Mrs. Arcane proved to be a good rider and hard to unseat, clinging desperately to her strap as she was tossed up and down and whirled about at a rate enough to make any one dizzy. Her many fine ribbons flew out behind like the streamers from a masthead, and the many fancy "fixin's" she had donned fluttered in the air in gayest mockery. (216)

The scene, caught by Manly's eye, becomes a pleasure for the reader's.

With such a gay picture, we get the tension-breaking humor of comic relief in the midst of trials as Manly humanizes his companions.

Yet the bright portrait of the whirling lady streaming ribbons belies the seriousness of the situation. A few pages later, though out of Death Valley and while Manly has hope they'll make it through, the pioneers sag at the prospect of more desert ahead. "They seemed to think they stood at death's door," says Manly, "and would about as soon enter as to take up a farther march over the black, desolate mountains and dry plains before them, which they considered only a dreary vestibule to the dark door after all" (222). Once again, Manly has swung back into the conflict of his main theme.

What, then, are the two leaders to do? They come up with a ploy:

We said to them, "We are not going to leave you two ladies out here to die, for there is not a sign of a grave to put you in." And it was a pretty tough place to think of making one. We told them of the beautiful flowery hillsides over the other side and begged them to go over there to die, as it would be so much better and easier to perform the last sad rites there instead of here on the top of the dismal mountain. It seemed like quite a grim joke, but it produced a reaction that turned the tide of thoughts and brought more courage. (223)

Thus Manly has combined humor with psychology, using the just-over-the-next-hill approach that, despite its cliché, often works with flagging spirits. With words Manly has manipulated the people of his party as well as his readers.

He's effective in exploring further intricacies. He is quick, almost in an obligatory way in this book about heroism, to praise his fellows for their bravery and nobility in response to crises. At a time when water has become far more precious than gold, and people are cursing the "yellow phantom" that has lured them into this plight (467), Manly cites men who denied themselves by sharing their canteens with perishing friends (469). But the author's view of mankind is complex. There's also a sardonic, and more convincing, edge to Manly's observations of those around him.

Soon after leaving Salt Lake City, when the fatal debate breaks out over whether to follow the route of experienced Captain Hunt or change course according to the promises of the map, Reverend J. W. Brier energetically helps sway the crowd. Bringing to bear his erudition, he energetically supports the case for the map, discoursing "learnedly and plausibly" on the matter (107). Weeks later, when the map proves false and the wagons have split up, each disheartened group starving, thirsty, and lost in a no-man's-land of rock, Manly passes Brier's camp and witnesses a strange sight. Approaching extremis, surrounded by hostile Indians sending up smoke signals, the reverend is delivering a lecture to his sons on the benefits of education (136). However, perhaps out of concern for pioneers still alive, Manly doesn't fully explore other, darker, and more dramatic sides of behavior emerging when the press of surviving begins to operate on human nature. He reflects on one particularly bad day of struggles, when people with any strength left passed former neighbors unable to go on:

William L. Manly

> *Looking back on the scenes of that day, the way the selfish dispositions of people were made manifest is almost incredible. Every one seemed to think only of saving his own life, and every spark of human sympathy and kindness seemed extinguished. A man would drink the last cup of water even if his neighbor choked. (464–465)*

One gathers from the bleakness of the passage that such occurred far more often than the noble deeds Manly praised. In contrast to events in Cabeza de Vaca's tale, the desolate land has brought out the desolate side of human beings.

Not so with the animals. A former farm boy and a youth who had spent years supporting himself by hunting and trapping, Manly hardly was queasy when it came to eating meat. But as often happens to people who work closely with animals, those along on the journey became creatures with personalities, and to Manly they are companions. Fellow sufferers through this hideous place, they are very much part of his drama.

By comparison with the perfidy of some of the humans about him, the oxen are patient and enduring, a foil to their sometimes grasping and conniving owners, and Manly is pained at their misery:

Months had passed since they had eaten a stomachful of good nutritious food. The animals walked slowly with heads down, nearly tripping themselves up with their long, swinging legs. The skin loosely covered the bones, but all the flesh and muscles had shrunk down to the smallest space. At a dry camp the oxen would lie down and grate their teeth, but they had no cud to chew. It looked almost merciless to shoot one down for food, but there was no alternative. (248)

Again bringing differing emotions into play, Manly uses such creatures for more than objects of pity. Old Crump—Manly sometimes calls him Captain Crump (247) or Old Crump the Christian (266)—makes it, staggering out of the desert alive, the two children on his back delivered to safety. When, in a chance encounter years later, Manly recognizes the ox, fat and happily feeding in a field in the San Joaquin Valley, the rider dismounts and gives his old friend a pat. But sparing us cliché, the writer says wryly, "I doubt not that he too was glad" (389). Offering yet another tonal color on the subject is "a poor little one-eyed mule" (189). Manly has doubts about this new acquisition, purchased on the coast and meant to carry supplies to those waiting in Death Valley, but she's all he can afford to buy. However, she turns out to be persistent and scrappy. Scrambling over ledges, refusing to give up, she becomes the heroine of the rescue, her pluck an inspiration to the weary families walking out to the coast.

Further than the animals, nature itself becomes a character, the central character, for without it Manly would have no story. Slowly, having left the green landscapes behind, the travelers realize that the map they followed is a lie and, worse, that now they are lost in an abominable, trackless, and nearly waterless expanse. Their dreams have been betrayed, and, full of bitterness, they sit down and curse their surroundings:

One fellow said he knew this was the Creator's dumping place where he had left the worthless dregs after making a world, and the devil had scraped these together a little. Another said this must be the very place where Lot's wife was turned into a pillar of salt, and the pillar must have been broken up and spread around the country. . . . Thus the talk went on, and it seemed as if there were not bad words enough in the language to express properly their contempt and bad opinion of such a country as this. (140–141)

These are not people who hate nature; Manly himself says that he is one of its admirers (298). Rather, their bile is due to the radical contrast of the country before them with what they think nature should be. From the well-watered forest and farmlands of the East, they carry in their heads the template of an ideal, a nature of greenery and abundance, beautiful with flowers and trees, with fat cows and soil that produces ample crops for feeding their families (298–299). In contrast, they face a land they had not even dreamed of, a perversion of nature, a "purgatory" (299) of "dreadful sands" and "bitter lakes" (260). The very existence of such a place in a world ruled by a loving God leaves them bewildered.

Yet practical as he could be, for writer Manly this was not simply a world divided into "good" and "bad" nature. There was a Gothic streak in the romantic culture, and when Manly stands on a mountaintop beholding not a tree nor a blade of grass in the views stretching to all the horizons, he is awed at the desolation (135). Negative as the scene is, he feels the thrill of a person trembling with vertigo as he gazes into an abyss, and though he goes away shaken, he is fascinated. After Manly, the idea would grow. Those who came in the following generations often crossed the desert in a few hours by train. Gazing out the windows as they rolled along, they felt that the long desert trek of the threadbare, starving pioneers had little to do with their pleasant journey. Often city people, able to afford the comforts of the industrialized life that bored them, they were not settlers confronting a hard, crushing reality but escapists looking for thrills in a strange land. Unlike the stumbling pioneers, they could afford to indulge, even cultivate, their frisson at the desert's desolation.

Following a rather different route, in their views of deserts such people arrived at a position close to Cabeza de Vaca's: the desert as a place of high emotions, launching spiritual flights akin to religious soarings. Manly could not go that far. As an accomplished hunter and a man who had, while nearly dying, walked across the lands that others, coming later and riding in trains, reverentialized, he was too practical, bore too much of the burden of actual experience. He did return briefly to the desert in the early 1860s, but it was in search of gold (Belden 28).

Both remarkable accounts of daily desert survival, the stories of Manly and Cabeza de Vaca are two classics, each outstanding in its rather different virtues. A nobleman bound up in the intricacies of royal politics, Cabeza de Vaca writes a highly sophisticated work laced with subtle, literary tricks. His ploys are designed with no less an aim than to reshape the entire empire's approach to the New World. In major ways, Manly's book is at loggerheads with that of his Spanish predecessor. Though Manly manipulates language, calculating shifts of tone and scene, proving himself a more-than-capable storyteller, he is no littérateur. To the contrary, he's proud of his humble origins and of his accomplishments as an independent, self-reliant yeoman. That is the very point of his book. Countering the standard wisdom, Cabeza de Vaca shows the desert as a new place, a land of spiritual rebirth, while Manly chromatically confirms the desert's traditional, ghastly image. Where Cabeza de Vaca's purpose is to champion new values over old ones, Manly's is to show that, even when tried to the extreme, traditional values are found true and carry the day.

However, despite this divergence—of the radicalized nobleman and the rough-hewn democrat—it would not be long before the two strands found a strange convergence in the desert, where an idealized type in literature became the spiritually sensitive man wandering through the desert wonderland in the toughened body of the capable frontiersman.

3

J. ROSS BROWNE AND

SAMUEL W. COZZENS

Happy Travelers

through Lost Lands

Born in 1820, William Manly lived into the next century, dying in 1903. Over his eighty-three years, he saw enormous changes come to California as civilization gradually took root and spread over the wild, trackless land of his youth. He saw orange groves with locomotives chugging through them replace the open ranges of the footloose vaqueros, city governments responsible for paving streets, electric lights turning the places where Indians once roamed into a yellowish version of day, women's clubs, churches, and grocery stores signaling the amenities of European culture. A believer in progress, old farmer Manly no doubt nodded and approved of such changes.

We can guess, however, that one thing continued to bewilder him. He had seen, firsthand, "desolation beyond conception" (135), vast prospects in his path where not a tree or shrub or blade of grass grew—and not only had seen such landscapes but had stumbled through them. He had seen his fellow pioneers sit down and die and had felt his own tongue blacken and cleave to the roof of his mouth. At night he had watched the brave oxen slump to the ground. There they had ground their teeth through the hours, out of habit going through the motions of chewing their cud, even though their mouths and bellies were empty.

As with prisoners of war and survivors of shipwrecks, such a hellish experience leaves a mark on a man. Dragging himself for weeks across Death Valley, ever but one step ahead of death, Manly saw the trek as central to his life. In fact, the journey became its main event, the central reference point coloring his outlook over his long years. We can only imagine, then, that the bearded old man shook his head in wonder, as old men do at baffling change, when others traveling over similar landscapes proclaimed them "grand and beautiful," called lifeless stone peaks "perfect models of architectural beauty" (Cozzens 207), and declared the very act of crossing the hideous sweeps that nearly sucked Manly into his grave "a pleasure trip" of "exploration and adventure" (Browne, *Adventures* 11). Surely the world had tilted on its axis and men had turned fools.

Perhaps in a sense they had. It was not simply a case of the rapidly industrializing nation, growing by leaps and bounds as it quickened the cultural pace, leaving old Manly, the hidebound pioneer turned farmer, behind. Nor was it a case of notions about deserts changing overnight, leaving Manly holding his bag of antiquated ideas. Rather, it involved the evolution of parallel and sometimes contradictory attitudes toward nature generally, at work long before Manly was born and securely in place by his adulthood. Such things can be easily linked, but this calls for some background to show that the new desert celebrants were but cousins of different fortunes to such grim travelers as Manly.

As a youth going west, Manly was keen for fresh experiences. But that was not his main goal. His motive, and even more so that of the families in his party, was economic. In a sense, such people were refugees, going west to improve their lot in life. Their concerns, then, were mundane, each day striving to get a better toehold on their futures. This involved few dizzying flights. Finding good pasturage, building a comfortable home, and guiding their children into the future were uppermost in their minds. And when they unexpectedly were confronted by a waterless desert, a gloomy forest, or an impossible mountain pass choked with snow, challenging their way to modest prosperity, that was viewed as an obstacle to their staid, middle-class vision of what their lives might be. For the most part, the pioneers wanted to be burghers.

This did not hold true for the adventurers who came soon after the earliest Western pioneers. Young, often single, eager to be tested, this new breed looked to the West as a romping ground, a land of challenges where they could shed their boredom in exchange for the thrill of adrenaline surging through their veins. Perhaps the most extreme and colorful examples of such types were the bored European royalty, often bearing such lavish names as Prince Maximilian of Wied-Neuwied, and at times traveling with a lavish baggage train (including cases of champagne) matching their titles. They sailed across the sea, not to ditch and grub, as did the peasants in their homelands, but to dash about chasing buffalo or to test their prowess against the monstrous grizzly bear, much fabled for its man-tearing habits. If in the process the avid travelers had a nasty skirmish with the Blackfoot or a bear ripped off someone's arm, all the more the adventure. And all the more to write about and awe their readers when they returned to their manses and castles and put their thrilling exploits between two covers, as did the above prince in his lively *Travels in the Interior of North America*.

Yet even then democracy of sorts held sway in the wilds. After all, you didn't have to have a fancy rifle, servants, and fine wines to have fun out there. Anyone with a will could cavort in the wilderness, as did the mountain men in the Rocky Mountains, happily boozing, whoring, and dodging arrows even while Manly lay, a babe in a crib in Vermont.

The attitudes generated by such a footloose life were far different from Manly's. His is a grim, factual account of earnest events and grinding survival, while adventurers in the new lands tended to exaggerate, letting their fancies run wild, often beyond the exaggerated lives in which they gloried. For instance, this famous tidbit as rough-and-tumble Moses Harris (known among his trapping cronies as Black Harris), taking a breather in St. Louis in the 1830s, astounds a fashionable lady with a tale about a strange land he's seen:

A putrefied forest, marm, as sure as my rifle's got hind-sights, and she shoots center. I was out in the Black Hills, Bill Sublette knows the time — the year it rained fire — and everybody knows when that was. If thar wasn't cold doin's about that time, this child wouldn't say so. The snow was about fifty foot deep, and the bufler lay dead on the ground like bees after a beein'; not whar we was though, for thar was no bufler, and not meat, and me and my band had been livin' on our mocassins. . . .

"Hyar goes for meat," says I, and I jest ups old Ginger at one of them singing birds, and down come the crittur elegant; its darned head spinning away from the body, but never stops singing, and when I takes up the meat, I finds it stone, wagh! (Ruxton 8–9)

That is, to such minds, strange lands generated tall tales, and the stranger the land, the greater the appeal to the storyteller's fancy.

Just when the edges of civilization were foaming around the petrified forests and scientists were telling the public that the stone trees were perfectly explainable in geological terms, and as a result the restless nation was feeling a bit crimped for adventure, travelers began penetrating the Southwest's deserts. And so exotic they were — so completely different from most people's experiences — that the region became a gold mine for the imagination. As well as a rich mine in fact. For wasn't this the land of the Seven Cities of Gold, almost found centuries before by the Spanish conquistadors? So one fantasy fueled the other. In the desert, a man not only could feel the thrill that he might get rich, he could have a jolly good time while doing it. Rendered into books, this was a powerful combination, keeping the reading public agog and writers happy over their royalties. The change, however, was not entirely linear, and neither was it smooth.

As we've seen, the keys to the dream were not only technological developments easing travel but the U.S. Army, holding at bay the tribes that had bedeviled settlement for centuries. With the firing on Fort Sumter in 1861, the dream collapsed. Desperately unprepared for war and short of manpower, the federal government began withdrawing its troops from the desert outposts for service on the eastern battlefronts. That left the Southwest exposed to its old nemesis, the Apache Indians. Seeing most of the soldiers leaving, the nomadic warriors claimed victory in their long guerrilla warfare with settlers and came tumbling exuberantly out of the hills. All but overnight, the bright hopes for the desert went up in the smoke of burning ranch houses, torched wagon trains, and the flaming camps of miners, often decorated with arrow-riddled and obscenely mutilated corpses. As we'll see with our first happy adventurer, in some cases military escorts still were available, and travel was by no means stopped completely. But in places the countryside was all but depopulated as the whites fled, and the few citizens remaining huddled in their adobe houses, many of them fearful of tilling their nearby fields.

Yet, reflected in the second adventurer's story, the dream ballooned at the end of the Civil War. In 1865 the nation was rapidly industrializing, former soldiers were restless and eager to get on with new prospects for their lives, and wave after wave of immigration from Europe was pushing the population once again westward. In this new, more confident turmoil, the Southwest again became important if for no other reason than as a place to be crossed to reach California. The wheels of the nation's economy began spinning as never before, and it needed the fuel of resources. Men had not forgotten the gold and silver lying out there in the desert hills waiting to be claimed, and, as happens with dreams embroidered by distance and time, they hadn't forgotten the freedom, the footloose adventurous life, and the exotic strangeness of the abandoned lands. Once again the military returned and began establishing order. Once again the desert became a place where young men on the make came for excitement, although the region remained just dangerous and unknown enough to whet the edges of their desire.

The turmoil during the Civil War and the reconquest of the desert after the conflict ended form the roseate atmosphere in which, with telling titles, J. Ross Browne wrote *Adventures in the Apache Country* and Samuel Cozzens penned *The Marvelous Country*.

By the time of Browne and Cozzens, the frontier was still wild, still a violent place where bandits and Apaches prowled and often held sway. Yet though a man could still get lost in the desert expanses and lose his scalp, if he were wise he traveled in organized, well-armed parties, and in numbers discouraging attack, and thanks to earlier exploration, they knew where they were going, where the main routes, mountain ranges, and rivers lay. The military provided protection, sketchy though it might be at times, and stations for stagecoaches afforded travelers water and a semblance of safety. Furthermore, the land was believed to be so rich in mineral, timber, and agricultural potential, a veritable treasure trove, that there was little question that the dynamic, expanding nation sooner or later would develop the riches, and then settlement would sweep in and take hold. By the time of Browne and Cozzens, life and death was still a concern, but it was an issue diminishing in importance as excitements grew brighter. Dicey though life could be on the frontier, the question now was not *if* civilization would come to such lands but *when.* Yes, they took care to watch their backs, but, more and more, such travelers were on a lark, and their prose happily seethes with an ebullience foreign to Manly. And we shouldn't neglect to mention a shift in audience, too, as the country became increasingly middle class, educated, and literate, as well as urban and bored. Readers were changing. They wanted not so much the earnest trials and moralizing of John Bunyan but the titillating entertainment of Jules Verne. His *Journey to the Center of the Earth* and *Twenty Thousand Leagues under the Sea* even then were roiling urban imaginations and lining the pockets of the father of modern science fiction.

Springing from this complex background, most immediately fascinating about the books by Browne and Cozzens is that they are at once remarkably similar and remarkably different. Both men wander over common geographical ground, the territory that is now Arizona and New Mexico. Both keep their audience keyed up with awe and suspense, having much to say about fights with Apaches and fabulous treasures, about gruesome scenes hinted at with Victorian allure, only hinting at the obscenities endured by women captured and carried off by heathenish Indians applying the ingenious deviltry of their tortures to naked and screaming female flesh. But ultimately not taking themselves too seriously, they balance daily hardships with comic relief. Thus, working their audience in an increasingly romantic age, the two books take readers through a full panoply of emotions. And together they represent the sometimes conflicting values toward the deserts that in their pages at once beg for exploitation and astound with beauty. The essential difference—one that will become ever more common in desert books— revolves around the question of accuracy. No matter how embellished with literary curlicues, one is in the main a reliable account, the other, largely a fake.

J. Ross Browne was born in a village near Dublin in 1821, as Donald M. Powell says, with itchy feet and "ink in his veins." Due to his liberal politics, his father was jailed, then banished. He sailed to America with his family, where J. Ross began a whimsically peripatetic life. Still a teenager, he signed on a Mississippi riverboat plying between Louisville and New Orleans, then rambled afoot across parts of Texas (ix).

Not yet in his twentieth year, Browne started publishing sketches of his travels, sometimes bearing his own drawings, in *Graham's* and in other popular magazines of the day. The early success fueled his visions of a life of travel and literary ease that had its share of bumps. He set sail as a common hand on a New Bedford whaler but recoiled at his tyrannical captain and jumped ship in Zanzibar. Demonstrating the pluck that would carry him through in touchy circumstances, he explored the island of Madagascar, worked his way back to the United States, and published *Etchings of a Whaling Cruise, with Notes of a Sojourn on the Island of Zanzibar*, a book, significantly, reviewed by Herman Melville (x).

Despite this success, Browne found, as does many a writer, that his pen alone could not support his new wife and growing family. With his eye on his first love, however, he engineered a series of government and journalistic positions that kept him happily moving about and money flowing with his ink. He traveled extensively in Europe and the Near East, turning out books and drawings as he went, then settled permanently in Oakland, California, in a fashionable home called Pagoda House, overlooking San Francisco Bay (xi–xii).

Adventures in the Apache Country came about through a chance meeting on the streets of San Francisco. There, in early December 1863, Browne bumped into his long-lost friend Charles Poston. An old frontier hand, Poston now was superintendent of Indian affairs for the Arizona Territory, bound for a tour of the land of his new responsibilities. Part of Poston's job was to put a lid on the Indian uprisings, largely through distributing gifts, and tagalong Browne thus had a dual advantage as a traveler through that lawless, desert country in 1864 (28). Thanks to Poston and his strong military escort, the tenderfoot in a dangerous land kept his scalp. Due to Poston's official duties and important connections as a government representative, Browne enjoyed an unusually intimate entrée to the territory, one turned into a series of articles for *Harper's* before appearing as a book (Donald M. Powell xii–xiii).

The result was, again in Powell's words, "the earliest Arizona classic of the American period, and one hundred and more years later still one of the best" (xiii). Yet this is a classic in a far different sense than Manly's *Death Valley in 49.* If Browne had been traveling as had Manly, dependent on his own resources, the two books might have been quite similar: two grim tales of desert survival. Whatever his dash, Browne, however, was no frontiersman, and given the upheavals in Arizona at the time, he likely would not have even considered going there alone, and if he had risked the venture, tenderfoot that he was, the chances were good that he would not have come back.

By nature, Browne was a raconteur with a light touch. His eye was quick to pick up on the ironies of life, and his pen rendered them into gentle, sometimes self-mocking humor. He also was a reliable reporter of detail, helped, no doubt, by his own artistic instinct as he sat with revolver on his hip and drawing pad in his lap, scanning the scenery before him. First of all, he was, then, a gentlemanly entertainer. His association with agent Poston had everything to do with the shape and tone of his book, for Poston's presence, and that of the soldiers keeping the threat of attacks at a distance, allowed Browne to see this new land, where other men were then taking arrows and fleeing, in the sanguine light of his previous accounts of travels through more civilized places. For Browne, speaking truthfully of his experiences in the desert, this is "a pleasure trip" of "exploration and adventure" (11). If, journalist that he is, he doesn't ignore, even bemoans, the deaths of settlers and miners by Indians and the rich land's silver potential abandoned as a result, such are not his immediate concerns. Instead, traveling in relative safety, his is a schoolboy's awe at the ragged mountains changing shape before him as the miles unfold and his the enjoyment of traveling through a "glowing, hazy, mystic atmosphere" of adventure (75). Appreciating his privileged mode of travel, Browne continues: "It was all easy, holiday life, with just adventure and danger enough to give it zest." Then he adds, teasing in a playful mood, "I had some notion of giving up civilization altogether myself, and devoting the remainder of my days to hunting Indians in Arizona" (163). The statement would have astounded less fortunate men in Arizona at that time, but it at once shows how a writer's personal circumstances can color his prose and sets the romantic tone of desert literature, growing ever stronger, more colorful, and lyric, as travel in the region becomes ever safer. Not that dangers will disappear from desert writing. Authors will keep them at the fore—whether threats from rattlesnakes, Indians, greedy land developers, or the press of overpopulation in the Southwest—as convenient pricks to their readers' alarm. And, rather than threats *from* the desert, they will evolve into threats *to* the desert. Whatever their nature, in inept hands they become stock villains dragged out on stage to arouse the audience to gasps and hisses.

Poston and his entourage left San Francisco by steamboat and skimmed down the California coast to the Los Angeles area. Given their mission, the itinerary was perfectly logical. With horses and wagons, they crossed the Colorado desert, enjoying the "tolerably good" water at four reliable wells along the way (50). At Yuma, the Army fort on the California-Arizona border, overlooking the Colorado River and commanding a settlement of Indians, they parlayed with the tribe and distributed gifts. Then they took the pioneer route in reverse, eastward along the Gila River to the villages of the Pima Indians, south of present-day Phoenix. From there, the direction generally was south, to the crude and ribald outpost of Tucson, then farther south into Magdalena, Mexico, with side trips to visit military outposts and investigate the rich but Apache-plagued silver mines along the way, before retracing their steps back to San Francisco.

Essentially, this was, in the travelers' minds, a journey from civilization into the fascinating barbarism seething on the nation's underbelly, the raison d'être of the book. In consequence, *Adventures* is a travel book studded with bright anecdotes. Browne passes on the lore of the country, featuring the curiosities of the land and the eccentricities of the frontiersmen that would keep Eastern readers in a state of wonder. The thread of the narrative, then, is accurate, describing geographical points and historical figures, many of them readily identifiable today. When the party passes Picacho Peak, Browne notes its shape and offers his drawing of the prominent rock spire north of Tucson, today looking much as Browne depicts it (128–130). On the Gila River he mentions meeting trader "Pie" Allen, a pioneer who can be easily found in the history books (99). *Adventures in the Apache Country* has the convincing ring of a writer who names people and places and gets them where they should be.

Yet, foremost, Browne is neither a geographer nor a historian but a man obviously enjoying his trip through a new land. And his anecdotes not only reflect this, they keep readers turning pages by playing up and down their emotional scales. The distribution of gifts to the Yuma Indians is a farce of government largesse, and, despite his host's duties, Browne doesn't hesitate to mock the occasion:

Every man received his share with satisfaction, and with gratitude to the Great White Father in Washington. When they shook hands with us for the last time, and we were about to part, the scene was really affecting. I almost shed tears at it myself, unused as

I am to crying about what can't be helped. In squads, and couples, and one by one, they affectionately took their leave, with their hoes and axes, spades and shovels, gimcracks and charms stuck all over them—in their sashes, breeches, clouties, blankets, and pina-fores. One went with a necklace of mattocks around his neck and three Collins axes in his girdle; another with his head thrust into a glittering pile of tin-ware. . . . (63)

Browne similarly passes on the romance and lore creating a roseate aura around the region, much of it earnestly believed but entirely bogus. The Hopi villages in northern Arizona, he tells us, are the home of ex-patriates from Wales. Centuries ago, following political dissension, their ancestors sailed across the Atlantic to become a tribe of blue-eyed, light-skinned Indians. Browne has this, he informs us, on the best of authority, an English missionary, but given the ease with which he's shown how white men are duped in Arizona by wild tales, we know that the writer is passing on the widely believed tale with a wink (28).

With more serious and cutting humor, he describes the frontier out-post of Tucson, "a city of mud-boxes, dingy and dilapidated, cracked and baked into a composite of dust and filth; littered about with bro-ken corrals, sheds, bake-ovens, carcasses of dead animals, and broken pottery. . . ." Bad enough are the Apaches lurking in the surrounding cactus flats. The town itself is a "Sodom and Gomorrah," a nest of mescal-soaked gamblers, petty thieves, and psychopathic killers (131). The frontier town is the flypaper for the outcasts of civilization, its main contribution to decent society. Browne's portrait is biting in its sarcasm and entertaining in its exaggeration as he shows the "Sonoranian buf-foons, dressed in theatrical costumes," strutting about in the midst of violent lunacy (133).

Darkening the emotional colors, he recites the tale of the immigrant Oatman family, ambushed along the trail to California by Apaches. The Indians slaughtered and mutilated the father and mother in front of their two daughters, who in turn were carried off as slaves. Browne shows the two girls, beaten and barefoot, dragged into the Apache encampment to the anticipatory glee of its filthy, drooling inhabitants. Here, they are "placed in the centre of a large circle, and compelled to witness sights so brutal and obscene that they . . . prayed that they might die before they should be subjected to the cruel fate that threatened them" (96). One of the sisters dies from abuse. Ransomed five years later, the second is so shell-shocked by her experiences that, upon her rescue, she can only moan and cry (98).

This is about as far as the propriety of the day allowed Browne to go, but his allusions to the sexual acts inflicted on the girls must have kept

J. Ross Browne &
Samuel W. Cozzens

Victorian imaginations sizzling. The restraint did not apply when he comes upon an Apache crucified by the Maricopas, an enemy tribe. The body was twisted, dried by the desert air, and "the head hung forward, showing a few tufts of long hair still swinging about the face." Making as much as he can of the scene, Browne plays another ghoulish card. Further shocking his readers' perspective, the traveler notes wryly that, if the pagan Maricopas had learned little from their Christian missionaries, they at least learned this, that the crucifixion practiced by whites makes an excellent form of torture, one hitherto unknown to the heathen Indians (104).

Such a ghastly sight as the corpse of the warrior hanging on his crude cross, Browne informs us, is typical of the country (104), but from the overall impression created by the book the reader knows that Browne exaggerates, speaking here with momentary color and for dramatic impact. Far more typical of Browne's pages is the author's enthusiasm for this strange and new country.

With the romantic zest of the desert travelers who will follow him, Browne celebrates both the beauty and dangers of the country, its eccentric characters, its mountains, nowhere else so awesomely spired, and its potential for adventure offered to young men of derring-do and vision. Why, the winter climate alone—another appealing note that will be played louder and louder right down into contemporary times by chambers of commerce—"is finer than that of Italy." His conclusion: "It would scarcely be possible to suggest an improvement" (56). The desert lands, then, are a vast playground, exhilarating for both body and soul.

However, the aesthetic and physical attractions, together with Browne's literary skill in rendering them, aside, one feature is the cornerstone of all this dreaming. To Browne's credit, though in an unusually inflated passage, he frankly admits the human psychology involved by pointing to the essence:

The unclouded sky and glowing tints of the mountains; the unbounded opulence of sunshine, which seemed to sparkle in atmospheric scintillations, inspired us with a perfect overflow of health and spirits; and it was no wonder we built many castles in the air, and revelled in dreamy regions of enchantment in which the glittering silver mines of Arizona played a prominent part. (226)

That is, the beauty of a sunset in itself is fine, artist Browne knew as he sat with his sketchpad. But the colors in the sky are enhanced immeasurably until the eager heart fibrillates if the scene is matched by the colors of gold and silver in the surrounding landscape. Whatever Cabeza de

Vaca's religious fervor, this was the sine qua non of his position on the desert and the very lure that in later years drew William Manly back again into the sandy expanses where he had suffered. Over the following years, imagined fortunes from vast irrigation projects, from alfalfa ranches, and from all manner of get-rich schemes would fuel the impulse based on the earlier silver and gold. It is easy to think of a rich land as a pretty place. So great a friend is greed to beauty.

And phantasms the powerful companion to reality. Browne, as we said, delivered a mostly reliable account graced by literary flourishes. But once the heart of a culture gets worked up, it can become a machine whipping out ever more weltered froth. This both for writers avid for sales and for readers' expectations of what they'll find in books about a far-off region.

Little is known about Samuel Woodworth Cozzens. Born in Marblehead, Massachusetts, in 1834, he studied law and eventually served as a judge in the Arizona Territory, then died in Georgia in 1878 ("Cozzens, Samuel Woodworth").[1]

45

J. Ross Browne & Samuel W. Cozzens

Whatever the details of his life denied us, we do know its most important feature as concerns the desert. In 1876, close on the heels of Browne's *Adventures,* Cozzens published *The Marvelous Country: Three Years in Arizona and New Mexico.* Furthermore, in many ways the book is a mirror image of Browne's work. Cozzens traveled through a similar territory; his progress is episodic, rich with anecdotes about scenes and adventures along the way; and, as with Browne, the echoed timbre of the land is of great beauty and financial promise combined with the condiment of danger. While providing large doses of comic relief contrasting with horrors, both writers celebrate the territory's mineral wealth and scenery; both rail against the Apaches; both recite the romance of the Spanish conquistadors and the glory of the ancient Indian civilizations before them; and both repeat similar tales, for instance, that of the captivity of the Oatman girls by the Apaches. Such correspondences might be expected of travelers wandering across the same frontier at about the same time and eager to vacuum up material for books.

Having read the first volume, however, the reader need not fear boredom when picking up the second. If the contents are similar, the treatment is so different that we feel with Cozzens that we are being transported to an entirely different land, one not of this earth. Hardly a mirror image of Browne's work, Cozzens' is more the glass of an Alice in Wonderland. If Browne is the journalist skeptical about tales of Welsh Indians and bonanzas of gold, Cozzens has no such hesitations. He delivers almost everything as fact, and they are facts in the superlative.

While with hints of sarcasm and disbelief Browne passes on stories he's heard, Cozzens tells them directly, as if he'd been a reporter present at events, busily scribbling down notes. Regarding the captive Oatman sisters, in Cozzens' version the younger not only dies, the author has her singing hymns as she soars off, "ushered into eternity" by her own, sweet voice (95). When it comes to precious metals, the region's mountains are chockablock with the stuff, "filled with silver, gold, and copper," as well as "rich in precious stones" (41).

Such gushy hyperbole about the desert's wealth was not unusual for the day. However, when it comes to Indians, Cozzens spreads his creative wings and takes flight, quite outdoing his run-of-the-mill literary competition. The judge gives a stentorian ring to the common wisdom of the day, asserting that "without doubt" the Indians are descendants of the celebrated Montezuma, whose fabulous Aztec empire astounded Cortez in Mexico over three centuries before (199). More than that, in an astonishing display of talent, Cozzens has Cochise, the famed Apache chieftain, step forth from the book's pages as a loathsome brute and a noble savage all in one! Here is Cozzens' first encounter:

It was a beautiful day in June that I first saw him, naked as he came into the world, with the exception of his breechclout and moccasins. He was a tall, dignified-looking Indian, about forty-seven years of age, with face well daubed with vermilion and ochre. From his nose hung pendent a ring about five inches in circumference, made of heavy brass wire, while three of the same kind dangled from each ear. His body had been thoroughly anointed with some kind of rancid grease, which smelled very offensively. His stiff black hair was pushed back and gathered in a kind of knot on the top of his head, while behind it rested on his shoulders. One or two eagle feathers were fastened to his head in an upright position, and swayed with every breath of wind. As he came near me, he laid his bow and arrow down upon the grass, and extended an exceedingly dirty hand, with finger-nails fully an inch in length, saying, in pretty fair Spanish,—

"Me Cochise, white man's friend. Gim me bacca." (86)

Given the unfortunate lack of information about Cozzens, we'll probably never know if he was aswarm with his own bombast or privately guffawed at the genius of the stroke when he topped off the vignette with the linguistic conundrum.

Either way, Cozzens was just warming to the grandness of his subject. As to scenery, Browne's appreciation of delicately shifting hues seems timid and mundane by comparison. In Cozzens, pinnacles soar so high, challenging the laws of physics, that in reality they would topple from their own giddiness. Chasms yawn so deep that, as the explorer descends, he trembles, feeling the shadows falling on his shoulders, until he is groping through a land of perpetual night. Yet he has a mentor for such Dantean trials, a guide no less than the aforementioned great Apache chief Cochise (98).

In a similar vein, whereas Browne repeats stories of Indian raids heard around campfires, Cozzens is actually there, time after time embroiled in frays and blazing away with six-shooter and carbine. At one point, the writer drops a warrior from his saddle with one shot, at a distance of nearly half a mile (226–267). No matter that Cozzens' Spanish is flavorful but atrocious, that he has pine trees growing on the desert where there were no pines, sacred flames burning in secret Indian shrines where no such flames glowed—and that he gets his geography so scrambled and distorted that we cannot recognize Arizona and New Mexico but think we are reading about another planet.[2] Such lands, then, at times in Browne, but almost always in Cozzens, are indeed lost, in that they never existed, but in the books describing them glowed with an appealing never-never land aura. For all that, Cozzens makes a thrilling read, ironically far more compelling, and in the bizarre way of science fiction, convincing, than Browne's tame and more realistic travelogue.

We should not laugh at our ancestors' gullibility in often accepting such dizzying inflation as fact. Books were their main source of information about the desert, and, as with the mysterious map leading the Manly pioneers astray, often the more appealing the fantasy, the more readily it was believed. And we shouldn't assume that an age of television, easy travel to the Southwest, and an abundance of readily available scientific information about the arid lands has immunized us against being pulled gladly by the nose into even greater desert phantasms than Cozzens spouted. Over the decades, Browne has vied with Cozzens, and although in the fog of the continuing tussle, first one has held the field, only to yield to the other, down to our day the legerdemain of the fabulist has received most heartening applause from the sidelines. And not only that. Sometimes the writer is so swept up by his imagination and the sound of clapping hands that he begins to believe his own, bright whim-whams.

4

CHARLES F. LUMMIS

The Showman with the

Shining Right Hand

Surely there were many in the host of book buyers back East who read a man like Cozzens with flickering smiles of skepticism at his elongated peaks and ingenious exploits with a rifle. Such people knew little about the region, but they were not naive. They realized that successful pen-wielding could involve a good amount of literary high jinks, just as they realized that in attending one of Phineas T. Barnum's extravaganzas they probably would come away the laughing and willing dupes of the circus man's profitable pranks. As would those who paid a nickel to "See the Ass with His Head Where His Tail Should Be and His Tail Where His Head Should Be"—only to find the creature standing backward in his stall. Customers knew that Barnum's mockery lay in wait for them, but still they eagerly bought their tickets and crowded in.

Added to that, there's a huge difference between knowing something intellectually and accepting it emotionally. To use a modern example, while many people today know that nature doesn't work according to the fetching values in the world of Bambi, those values have enormous appeal, and it's tempting to view nature as if it were indeed soft, warm, and fuzzy-wuzzy because we would prefer it to be so. At a certain point, the colors in the picture wax so strong that the facts of the matter become extraneous.

Added to that, in the late nineteenth century fact became the servant of fancy and, in turn, fancy, the handmaiden of fact. After all, there *were* fabulous gold strikes in California, bubbling mudfields and geysers in Yellowstone, things unbelievable out there, except that travelers had seen them and written about them. And if the West was a different place, a place of possibilities stretching the former limits of credibility, the sub-region of the Southwest was its most exotic exemplum. About the time that Cozzens wrote *The Marvelous Country*, Currier & Ives was printing a popular series of lithographs about California. One of them, *On the Coast of California*, showed "tropical flora, grass-roofed homes built on stilts, and a mountain in the background that closely resembles Japan's Mt. Fuji" (Holmer 51).[1] In such an atmosphere, whether people were skeptics or believers hardly was the operative issue. The Southwest was a marvelous place. Whatever was going on in the right-hand part of their brains, they continued to buy the world sold by Currier & Ives and by Cozzens and his colleagues. Then, as now, the media could project un-forgettable images overriding the facts. What began as travel fantasy was becoming cultural fact with a life of its own.

Setting the stage, the roseate aura glowing over the Southwest devel-oped into more than a convenience for the next set of writers, it was their windfall. Cozzens and Browne had poked their noses into the arid lands, had their flings, then moved on to other places and other books. Not so another set of writers coming immediately after them, around the 1880s. By then the desert was fairly safe. Newcomers had little fear of Indian arrows, of dying of thirst, or of losing their way in a trackless land. To the contrary, many of them were urban people traveling on trains and blessed by the comforts of Los Angeles and San Diego—so blessed that at times when they sallied out into the dry outback they had to manufac-ture desert dangers in order to keep their readers' juices flowing.

Not only were they city dwellers, a good number were converts, people with problems who had found solutions in their new home. Weary of the pinched, gray routine of life back East, they saw Southern California as having everything—for starters, an ideal climate, an easy pace, a romantic, Spanish-Catholic heritage, and a booming economy. There, one could bask in the year-round sun, have spiritual flights—and be wealthy to boot! That is, Southern California had the answers to Life's Problems. Buoyed by this, they became boosters in a near religious sense, spreading the message of salvation. If they made the desert dance to sev-eral different tunes, of fearsome place, beautiful place, and place of dan-gerous mystery, so much the better. Part of the exhilaration stemmed from how one thing could be so many others, depending on one's needs. And if what the writers called desert we'd now call grassland or a semiarid plateau, that didn't matter, either. "California is a land where nature her-self knows how to sing" (Lummis, *The Land of Poco Tiempo* 218), and the sandy places could sing, too, share in the glory of one landscape slopping over into a far different one nearby. Romanticism thrives on such hazy enthusiasms and rosy vagaries.

That is, boosting the Southwest turned into a promotional carnival run with zealous conviction, and, as is true of many converts, its barkers became larger-than-life campaigners for an almost holy cause—the redemption of mankind.

How much of this was idealism, how much celebration of ballooning egos, cannot be said, but the phenomenon was entwined with the life of a nation eager for excitements, for thrills pulling people out of their humdrum lives. Every age has its exciting fixations. In 1869, the country's network of telegraph lines sizzled with speculation that John Wesley Powell's expedition of little rowboats had been ground to splinters in the raging maws of the unexplored Grand Canyon. In our grandfather's day, after Charles Lindbergh sailed off into the fog of the Atlantic, the country held its breath for a day and a half until the lone, young pilot touched down near Paris, emerging from his cockpit the very image of heroism. Other excitements of times past yielded to new ones and are forgotten. We forget that in 1913 newspapermen breathlessly watched a naked man smoke a last cigarette, then, shaking hands with the reporters, slip off into the Maine woods. Joseph Knowles reappeared two months later, wearing the skin of a bear he claimed to have stolen from the animal with his bare hands. The nation was dazzled, and in Boston crowds cheered as the wilderness hero, still wearing his shaggy coat, passed by in a motorcade. If such is an ego-feeding performance, it also dovetails with the needs of a society living vicariously on doses of assurance that a special one of their number can soar beyond the mundane.

Though sociologically telling, there almost always is a certain irony in such exploits. In Knowles' case, whether he actually lived on roots and berries for two months, then slew a bear, is beside the point. Only four or five decades earlier, he would have been thought daft, for people then commonly and by necessity were living, not always happily, cheek by jowl with wild nature in cabins dotting the nation's vast wilderness. Now, with the great woods all but gone and many people laboring in factories instead of tracking bears, Knowles' adventure was an affirmation for city dwellers feeding on a lost past of primitive wholeness and dreaming that the free pioneer spirit lived on. So erumpent individuals suckle a culture's sustaining myths (Nash, "Conservation as Anxiety" 85−87).

In a similar vein, in September 1884, Charles F. Lummis, a young reporter, announced an astounding thing. He was going to walk from his home in Chillicothe, Ohio, to Los Angeles, California. Again, but a few years earlier, people would have paid him little mind, for the western spaces then streamed with settlers plodding toward the coast in wagons and afoot. Now, however, railroads spanned the spaces, and a person doing such a thing for the sheer fun of it must be an exception, a sterling and romantic adventurer.

Note, however, that Lummis didn't simply walk to the outskirts of the little farming community and begin hoofing it across America as might a more modest sort. As did some of those both before and after him, he turned his trip into what we'd call today a media event. Lummis had struck a deal. He would send off weekly dispatches, one to his hometown newspaper, the *Chillicothe Leader*, the other to the more prominent *Los Angeles Times*. Furthermore, a plum waited at the end of his plodding. If he completed the arrangement with the *Times*, upon his arrival he would be crowned the paper's city editor (Fiske 16–17).

Lost was the irony that Lummis had the benefit of the U.S. Post Office to forward his weekly installments, that he walked well-traveled roads, and for much of the way followed railroad tracks. For all that, despite the towns marking his route, knocking off 3,507 miles across mostly open land was no mean feat in itself. And although settlements already were taking root, the West was by comparison to Chillicothe still a rather wild place. Ruffians were not unknown on the dirt highways, and south of where Lummis passed through Arizona, the Apaches continued to kick up their heels. Just the stuff of adventure.

Lugging a revolver and a sturdy hunting knife, the young minister's son didn't disappoint his readers. In Colorado he reported that two convicts tried to kill him, told of an encounter with a wildcat, and the exhilaration of watching the stars swirl above him as he stood atop Pike's Peak. The land, as the nation watched, was turning this tenderfoot into a Westerner. Expediency, pluck, and quick wits were the name of the process. Lummis had to talk himself out of dicey situations, and, out in the blazing desert, Lummis' dog went mad, and his master had to shoot him. Fate got pretty rough in toying with this adventurer. Near Winslow, Arizona, he broke an arm. What to do out there in the wilds? "There was but one thing to be done—the arm was to be put in shape right there."

The one-handed man would set his own arm! But how?

Lummis tied one end of his canteen strap to a tree, the other to the wrist of the painful arm:

Beside the tree was a big squarish rock. Upon this I mounted, facing the tree; set my heels upon the very edge, clenched my teeth and eyes and fist, and threw myself back-

ward very hard. The agony, incomparably worse than the first, made me faint; but when I recovered consciousness the arm was straight. . . . (A Tramp across the Continent 226)

Capping such adventures, late on the night of February 1, 1885, with his left arm in a sling, Lummis victoriously tramped into the streets of Los Angeles with Col. Harrison Gray Otis, the *Times* chief editor, striding beside him (Fiske 28). The next morning Lummis sat at his city editor's desk, ready to command the *Times.* What a guy!

The nation loved it. "Somehow," mused one reporter of Lummis' dispatches, "the articles have a strange, indescribable interest and people have got to talking about Lum all over the country" (17). Showman Lummis had turned his trek into a circus, and he would keep the circus going, spinning ever more wildly as the crowds cheered, for the rest of his life.

As he grew more and more into it, Lummis the man became more and more his own act, the actor himself becoming the role he loves to play, until the first is indistinguishable from the second. For during those 143 days between Chillicothe and the City of the Angels, more had happened than a man and his shadow crossing an expanse. Deep in Lummis' New England bones lurked an "extravagant flair for the romantic and dramatic" (Bingham 9), and on this trip when he hit Santa Fe, it emerged to ravage him like a beneficent and lifelong virus.

He'd always been prankish, with a wee bit of the rebel threatening to break out, and also a little fey, a fiend for moonrises over lakes who published his own first collection of poems on thin sheets of birch bark. Charles Fletcher Lummis was born in 1859 in Lynn, Massachusetts, the son of Reverend Henry Lummis, a Methodist preacher and educator.[2] His mother died when he was two. After that, frail and precocious, Charles grew up learning Latin, Greek, and Hebrew from his scholarly father, then followed his father's footsteps and entered Harvard. Of this, Lummis later reflected, "From my cloistered life I had come to the Tree of Forbidden Fruit. I climbed that tree to the top" (Fiske 7). That is, he became a maniac for sports, poker, and daredevil exploits, though his native genius carried him through.

Or almost carried him through. According to rumors, because a college liaison resulted in a child, he took up with a second woman to escape the tangles with the first (14). Whatever happened, he married Dorothea Roads, a young medical student, then flunked out of college. The marriage began on a second strange note, what we'd call a long-distance relationship. Charles went to Ohio to manage his new father-in-law's farm, while Dorothea remained in the Boston area to complete her medical degree. Farmwork couldn't hold him, and neither could editing a small-town newspaper, the *Scioto Gazette*. An ebullient young man who as a boy grew up absorbed by Captain Mayne Reid's *The Scalp Hunters*, a book that out-Cozzens Cozzens, Lummis had Great Ideas swirling in his head— and he was off. The restlessness, visions, and troubles with women would characterize the rest of his life, as would, contrary to the standard wisdom about luftmenschen, the ability to turn his wild energies into solid accomplishments.

"Mr. Southwest" would find, however, that in the process of achieving national, yes, international, acclaim, the gods would put him through the wringer even while they gave him wings. When the twenty-six-year-old, continent-crossing wunderkind stumbled into Santa Fe, New Mexico, a town of adobes and fiestas and far more Hispanic than Anglo, he had an epiphany:

Though my conscience was Puritan, my whole imagination and sympathy and feeling were Latin. That is, essentially Spanish. Apparently they always had been, for now that I had gotten away from the repressive influence of my birthplace I began to see that the generous and bubbling boyish impulses which had been considerably frosted in New England were, after all, my birthright. (A Tramp 20–21)

Yet before he fully claimed it, the churlish gods would toy with him yet more. Meanwhile, the job waited for him in Los Angeles. In 1885 Southern California was undergoing one of its periodic land booms, and the city was growing crazily as men made and lost fortunes overnight. In the midst of the froth, Lummis' Puritan conscience bloomed. Dorothea joined him, but, day after day, he worked through the hours, catching only catnaps, hyperactively buoyed by the excitements of capitalism's whirling wheels.

After three years of this busy turmoil, he suffered a breakdown that was manifested by paralysis of his left side. It was the first of several such collapses which would hit him during times of crisis, whether with women or boards of directors. Lummis fled to friends he'd made on his earlier passage through New Mexico. There he had yet another epiphany, or, rather, the first one fully exfoliated. Living first with the Hispanic New Mexicans and then with the Pueblo Indians at Isleta, he felt the scales fall from his eyes. He saw again, as he'd seen when earlier crossing the Mojave, that the desert was the "most beautiful place on earth" (26) and its people, living in a world of myths, were veritable angels walking the planet. "The city is more or less a disease" and "man can endure on this planet only when he has roots in the earth," he later summed up, rejecting much of his Anglo heritage (108–109).

What to do about it? Slowly recovering, he might have dug in there out in those spacious lands where the changing sun and moon ruled human life and the shaman awed his flock by filling the underground kiva with lightning, but Lummis was more of a Puritan than he realized. The seasick Pilgrims spent weeks sailing across the Atlantic with no less a purpose than to found the City of God on Earth. Likewise, after suffering his dark passage, Lummis would do something similar for Los Angeles, nay, for the entire misled nation. He would show his fellow citizens that their overly busy ways were empty and all wrong, that salvation lay in singing Spanish songs, eating chile, and wearing huaraches. The Southwest, with its climate, cultures, and exotic landscapes, was the shining Right Hand of the Continent (Gordon 190–191), and the new convert wasn't about to hide his light under a bushel. Thus, he launched a major theme in desert devotion, the arid lands as the path to redemption.

Thereafter, the pattern of his life was set. Returning to Los Angeles a new man, the True Believer threw himself into his missionary work. It doesn't matter that, as cynics might quip, Lummis became a self-made man who worshiped his creator. That he smoked and drank too much, ran through three wives, with numerous affairs on the side, and generally abused his family. Lummis was a man with a Mission—details could take care of themselves—and, whatever his foibles, as Bingham says, summarizing a life, "He got things done" (35). As the editor of *The Land of Sunshine*, Lummis boosted the careers of such budding Southwestern writers as Ina Coolbrith and David Starr Jordan; the progressive head of the city's library, he blew out the dust; he helped found the Southwest Museum, today invaluable for the region's study; saved crumbling Spanish missions; stood up for the much-abused Indians; and wrote book after book awakening "the consciousness of America" to the Southwest as the Republic's best hope (Fiske 72).

Though he'd probably chafe at the clinical observation, absolutist Lummis was but a digit, though a fairly good-sized one, in a social process having both national and regional dimensions. The Civil War was bad enough, rattling families with death, disease, and doubts about man's innate humanity. On top of that, pile the dislocations as former farmers streamed into factories; pile on repeated news of a government riddled with corruption from the top down. The agricultural country was becoming an industrial state, and it suffered through a plethora of unsettling changes. Then add to that the hammers of Darwin, Marx, with Freud soon to come, and immigrants by the millions crowding into slums and bringing a fairly placid society to a boil with strikes and blocs of ethnic votes, why, a decent person didn't know who he was or where the future was going anymore. While the United States grew powerful, its psyche tottered, trying to create a new balance in the midst of a confusing dance.

Tom Lutz maintains that such afflictions struck the upper classes especially hard. While the common man might grouse, he had more immediate concerns, such as hard plowing and grueling factory hours to occupy his mind and drain his energies. With time and money on their hands, better-off people had the means to indulge their neuroses. A newly emerging class, they didn't know exactly who they were, and, if they did, things were changing so fast that their stability often was pulled out from under them. The result was cultural freakiness, a desperate search for meaning through regimens of colonic irrigation, fad diets, and flights into spiritualism. Some people escaped into art, while others, this having more bearing on Lummis' message, fled into the arms of an idealized nature.

As to the related local situation, in Lummis' time Californians lived in a new and amorphous society, with people raised elsewhere flooding in, leaving familiar homes and values behind, jostling with one another, and facing a new place not at all like Indiana or Georgia. Southern California was a bright and exciting place, but what were they to do with all this newness?

Franklin Walker catches the response in a precise metaphor:

Having no traditions of their own in this region, they resorted to a process comparable to the agricultural device of hydroponics, the science whereby the farmer grows his vegetables rapidly without the benefit of soil. All that is needed is water and a certain number of valuable salts.

The enthusiastic embracing of all things Spanish that overtook the Southern California population in the last quarter of the nineteenth century was a result, to a very large degree, of this strong desire to establish cultural traditions in as short a time as possible. (121)

That is, since they lacked a solid culture, they assembled a new one, and it had large elements of make-believe to it. California was indeed once a Spanish colony, but historically it was but an outpost, an unimportant place populated mostly by poor, mixed-blood Mexicans. No matter. Lummis and his fellow enthusiasts turned the grubbing peons into Castilians of royal bearing with genteel manners and high-minded posture. Strolling about impressing potential donors to his projects with his costume of a Spanish grandee while strumming his guitar, Don Carlos, as

Charles F. Lummis

he liked to be called, was an actor in the creation of this picturesque, romantic, and largely fantasized past.

Swept along into this vortex of the imagination, the desert, too, took on a beneficent glow. And if it wasn't always beneficent, it sometimes was something better, a spooky place to chill the soul. Wrote a Lummis contemporary of one night camped out on the sands:

The Indians believe the whole region to be haunted. They claim that in the night-time if a man dares to walk here a peculiar light will follow him, and he will hear voices singing and talking. . . . It is a lonely region and when night falls upon us, in spite of our disbelief in the stories of the Indians, we cannot deny that we are impressed by the spirit of loneliness. . . . Even the well, standing on the roadside, ready to cheer man and beast with its vivifying water, takes on the appearance of a scaffold. (James, Wonders of the Colorado Desert 2:455–456)

Out there, the newcomer to Los Angeles, amazed by the palm trees and the blooming oleander bushes, soon learned that another strange and beautiful land lay over the mountains, weird as a De Quincey hashish dream. Just the thing to get the blood racing in the veins of umbrella-toting matrons smelling of mothballs as they glowered about in their big, flowered hats. And, of course, when such tourists finally saw the desert, they saw it in terms of the convincing exaggeration that had schooled their perceptions.

One can imagine the range of writing spun out of this gaseous atmosphere. On one end of the spectrum stands Theodore Strong Van Dyke, whose *Southern California* offers a reliable primer on the region concerning its climate, agricultural possibilities, and general economic potential. On the other, shading off into ozone, is George Wharton James, the author of the above passage on the desert well. He admirably describes scenes giving him the creeps. In Southern California's freewheeling milieu, this defrocked Methodist minister accused of unmentionable sexual acts could do much more. He hailed the very winds in the mountains for zapping disease germs with their electricity, and his Radiant Life Press put out *The Story of Captain,* the horse with the human brain who could play "Nearer, My God to Thee" (9). Such was the larger seedbed for desert appreciation.[3]

There were then, and still are, desert phonies, writers who know little about the desert and deliberately fabricate their prose to serve up the thrills desired by their readers. Lummis was not of that class. He was a doer, with years of desert experience under his belt. Besides Lummis' impressive public accomplishments already mentioned, he had lived intimately with the Pueblo Indians, rode hard with General Crook deep into Mexico to report on the pursuit of the rampaging Apaches, and built his charming and whimsical home, El Alisal, with his own hands. Lummis knew what he was talking about. The difference separating him from ordinary men was more than his successes in churning out books and inspiring the public to support his projects. A man grounded in reality, he also was able to soar beyond it, flying on the wings of a vision he held as true. What Patricia Limerick says of James applies to Lummis and many other enthusiasts; he wished himself into desert enthrallment "the way the prospector wished for riches" (123). Lummis was, then, something of a cross between the accurate Theodore Strong Van Dyke and the untethered and poetic James. Lummis got his basic facts mostly straight; it was what he did with them that produced a colorful legacy for a public often preferring the pleasing fantasy of a thing over its reality.

What Lummis preached about the region can be summed up in one word: Wonder. It was a word he used twice in his subtitles, and one thereafter so popular it began popping up in others' titles about the region, as in James' two-volume *Wonders of the Colorado Desert,* already quoted. With its very title, one of Lummis' most popular works steers readers into an exotic place. With his macaronic *The Land of Poco Tiempo,* the Land of Pretty Soon, Lummis signals that New Mexico and environs may be *in* the United States, but it is not *of* the United States. It is an "American Mystery," and it is this mysterious land that we enter on the very first page. This place of "Sun, silence, and adobe" is the antithesis of the abrasive world of time clocks, secular squabbles, and competition left behind (3). Here, we marvel in the opposite, a land pleasantly and radically different from the rest of the nation in its long sweeps and distant mountains, its Indian villages perched atop mesas, and its timeless, healing spirituality—a land so rarefied in such qualities it "cannot be adequately photographed" (9), as if we're confronting a wraith.

Given the rising sentiment of awe, astonishment, and the marvelous that might have floated him off into a never-never land of prose, fortunately Lummis had the good sense to ground his book in the particular. The book is a travelogue, but not one by a glib Pullman tourist merely reeling off prose from his poetic skein. Lummis was writing about places in which he had lived, about people he'd known, and the book gains richly from his shared intimacy of experience. After an introductory chapter setting the stage, he wisely takes us directly to the Indians, then, as now, the ethnic group accorded the most mystery by the public. Wisely, also, he takes us into Acoma, "The City in the Sky," as he temptingly calls it, a tiered city of whitewashed stone and mud rising above the desert and, according to Lummis, outdoing "one's wildest dreams of the picturesque" (61). Much better than this, therein we meet a people as intriguing as their remarkable home, their daily affairs rooted in the earth's cycles, laced with strange foods, and their lives governed not by the factory whistle but by the tempo of a mythology thousands of years old. This scene, for example, from the nearby Pueblo village of Cochití, combining paganism with Roman Catholicism to celebrate the day of its patron saint, San Buena Ventura (254), with an abandon and color startling to Eastern readers. They likely never suspected such activities were going on within the borders of their country. First, the pum, pum, pum of the drum, then comes a procession of women:

Their beautiful black hair, carefully combed, hangs down their backs, unrestrained by ribbon or ornament. Around their necks they wear a dazzling profusion of necklaces. Costly corals, silver beads alternating with silver crosses, and long strings of priceless turquoise, are a dozen strands deep on those pretty brown necks. Their heavy jet bangs wave as they come hopping along on alternate feet. Each has a bright vermilion patch on either cheek-bone, and each holds in either hand a sprig of sacred cedar. (260)

All of which—the mountaintop cities, mythology, and ruddled dancers—were revelations to the book's readers, culturally unrooted epiphytes.

In a related book, *Some Strange Corners of Our Country*, Lummis all but outdoes himself on the score. He takes us into the underground kiva, the earth-topped chamber for the Pueblos' religious rites. Here, sword-swallowing goes on, and shamans turn into wolves, bears, and dogs (86). Better than that, as the awed Indians sit in the gloom full of expectancy:

. . . they hear the low growl of distant thunder, which keeps rolling nearer and nearer. Suddenly a blinding flash of forked lightning shoots across the room from side to side, and another and another, while the room trembles to the roar of the thunder, and the flashes show terrified women clinging to their husbands and brothers. Outside the sky may be twinkling with a million stars, but in that dark room a fearful storm seems to be raging. (83)

What factory worker, what frazzled corporate executive heading for yet another session of colonic irrigation, wouldn't feel the allure of such a place?

However, the nature of wonder in Lummis' books is various, and lest we become sated by pyrotechnics, the two books take us to the Grand Canyon, discuss Navajo blankets, pass on old Spanish songs, and show us the Penitentes of northern New Mexico, so deeply devout that they flagellate themselves in honor of Christ's suffering. Back in *The Land of Poco Tiempo*, one of the most gripping chapters is Lummis' account of joining soldiers during 1886 to pursue marauding Apaches escaping deep into the desert of Mexico.

They find the wily enemy in his camp, and their ally Indian scouts begin closing the jaws of a trap:

> . . . the scouts, by infinite work and strategy, crawling bellywise all night along the rough ground, came very close upon Geronimo's camp. At five hundred yards one of the hostiles heard an unfortunate twig snap, and the stalk was up. From answering rock to rock the bullets pattered. The scouts, stripping off every rag save the G-string, crawled forward from cover to cover, firing as they went. . . . (204–205)

Such writing, for the time and for Lummis' purpose, has, if not everything, then a good deal going for it: action and danger, sloe-eyed Mexican maidens coy in the folds of their mantillas, and mysterious occurrences, all taking place in a landscape overwhelming in its space, beauty, and desolation. Though the books may seem a bit overwritten today, depending too much on primary colors, they nonetheless remain convincing as firsthand accounts.

Yet the writer gives the whole one more spin, much to his advantage. Assaulted by the white man's technology, all this is passing, the quaint customs of wooing a wife, if unsuccessful ending in a humbling gift of squashes (21), the extralegal execution of witches causing readers to suck in their breaths (24). All the better for romantics, whom "fugitive glimpses of the Land of Pretty Soon" (25) tantalize far more than the reality and to whom living out a past almost gone by re-creating it in their own lives gives a convenient license to select the features they prefer rather than deal with the unsavory aspects of what is nearly gone. Evidence of this tendency is the way Lummis picked and chose, transferring what suited him to Los Angeles, elements which glorified him and most appealed to transplanted Midwesterners prospering in the city while participating in the creation of an artificial culture.

A booster of the entire Southwest, Lummis celebrated many features of the region. Yet if New England didn't have Mount Whitney, it did have impressive mountains, and if New York didn't have oleanders, it nonetheless had its share of flowers. That is, in the new view of the Southwest, the region in large part was an amplification of features found elsewhere, features in this newfound wonderland perceived as magnified and perfected, the Divine manifestation of what lay at the end of Manifest Destiny's rainbow, in a remote and practically unknown corner of the Republic. However, the Southwest had one phenomenon setting it apart. Back East there was nothing approaching a desert.

"Sun, silence, and adobe." The desert thus became the foremost feature lending the region its distinctive character, just as today the giant saguaro cactus has become the Southwest's emblem, displayed on license plates and on advertisements even in areas where that branching, spiny mass of weirdly twisting vegetative matter is found not at all. Lummis made much of this feature. If people were to be converted to wonder, the largest converting act of all would be to stir them with a landscape widely shunned as uninhabitable and useless. Building his case, he went to the extreme. Well, it *was* horrid, so horrid that its worst parts turned Lummis' beloved Indian into a "terrible man" (163). Lummis was referring to the predatory Apaches, among the planet's fiercest guerrilla fighters. Yet this is a good example of his fudging, for he neglects to mention that peaceful agricultural tribes, farming along the riverbottoms of desert streams, lived side by side with the Apaches.

But forget about that. In Lummis' work, it's the effect that counts, and his way is all the better for striking high emotions into his armchair travelers, who didn't have to worry about being scalped by Apaches, or worry about dying of thirst, either. Out there, he pointed with his expert fescue in *Some Strange Corners*, were "freaks of vegetable life" (36), sandstorms that bury people alive (33), and sandy rivers going nowhere (35). That is, the desert as a land of sideshows, a land of curiosities, at once repulsive but intriguing for people who rouse themselves to peer into those "weird and deadly valleys" (36). Which indeed were strange to outsiders, but by Lummis' time were hardly deadly. Lummis had created the best of both worlds, a land inspiring with the echoes of danger while having no real danger present. It was the tourist's dream.

Although the tendency now is to chuckle a bit at Lummis, the passionate and often superficial extremist, if we approach him with a little forgiveness in our hearts, he still makes engaging reading. What he lacks in intellectual depth and finesse he makes up for with direct experience, enthusiasm, and immediacy, the always youthful guide at his happy best. In a more historical context, he represents the conjunction of the longings of an age with the writer giving them a voice, individualized by Lummis' volume and particular color. Lastly, and perhaps foremost, as one of the region's early, full-time zealots, he established many of the major themes for those coming after him in desert writing. What he said is what, to one degree or another, most desert authors have been expanding and embroidering upon ever since, each concentrating on filling in details already in Lummis' outline.

That can be said of few writers in any genre.

5

MARY AUSTIN

Beauty, Madness,

Death, and God

When she was five years old, she saw God under a walnut tree. When a young woman, she sat in a tree, laboring over a manuscript while dressed in what she imagined to be the paraphernalia of a Paiute Indian princess. Later, having achieved literary cachet, this hefty woman scooted about the nation in a large, flowered hat and skeins of turquoise jewelry. Standing on the lecture platform, she made ridiculous pronouncements about Indians and Hispanics, demeaning the very ethnic groups she thought she was praising. At her worst, Mary Austin is embarrassing, but at her best she wrote some of the most delicate passages ever printed about America's deserts.

That such a concoction should thrive in California—future land of the hula hoop, the skateboard, and the curing copper bracelet— should not surprise us. Just seen in Charles F. Lummis' work, the process of growing a new culture can produce some strange flowers. Yet apt as Franklin Walker's metaphor is about hydroponics, it doesn't go far enough. Nothing grows on thin air. It is not true that newcomers to Southern California had "no traditions of their own." However their thinking could get muddled in the process of transplanting themselves, with few exceptions they brought with them faith in technology and progress. This, rather than the attention-getting features of their concepts, lay at the heart of the culture. In fact, it was the former that made the latter possible. People would, in time, come to berate the very freeways and petrochemicals that made their everyday lives comfortable, while, of course, hardly eschewing the benefits. In the meantime, John Muir whizzed around the country on free passes provided by railroad magnate E. H. Harriman, a man the wilderness lover was savvy enough to enlist on the side of the conservation angels. For his part, desert lover George Wharton James celebrated the blend, boasting that he could swing out to Palm Springs for a little skinny dipping in the desert, then catch the train and be back in civilized Pasadena the same day to enjoy an evening of culture. In reality, what we have is not hydroponics but an alluring romance growing out of the fertile industrial soil in the sunny climate of California favoring experimentation. In his *The Ordeal of Change*, Eric Hoffer comments on rapidly shifting societal circumstances both as potentially beneficial and as potentially traumatic:

> As I said, a population subjected to drastic change is a population of misfits—unbalanced, explosive, and hungry for action. Action is the most obvious way by which to gain confidence and prove our worth, and it is also a reaction against loss of balance—a swinging and flailing of the arms to regain one's balance and keep afloat. Thus drastic change is one of the agencies which release man's energies, but certain conditions have to be present if the shock of change is to turn people into effective men of action: there must be an abundance of opportunities, and there must be a tradition of self-reliance. Given these conditions, a population subjected to drastic change will plunge into an orgy of action. (4)

A hundred years ago, no other part of the country had such ripe conditions for an orgy of action as had Southern California. As Hoffer warns, there was a good deal of swinging and flailing of the literary arms. The horse with the human brain is but one of its manifestations, as is the germ-zapping winds. Much of it adds up to an appealing nonsense. Said James of himself on a lecture advertisement:

> In religion I am a Methodist, with leanings toward Roman Catholicism, Presbyterianism, Congregationalism, Christian Science, Theosophy, Buddhism, Confucianism, Universalism, Free Thought, Seventh-Day Adventism. . . . (Bourdon 315)

If that is so much popular gibberish, it also arises from the same atmosphere producing our greatest desert books. If at times they were written by people who now make us blush at their absurdities, we should give thanks for the rare individuals who, out of the great sea of campy delusions, some of them their own, managed to cast up memorable pearls. That is, at the time, Southern California was full of Paiute princesses, but only one of them was Mary Austin. Such is the mathematics of lasting literature.

The woman who declared the undemonstrable "fact" that the rhythm of American poetry was schooled in the wilderness by the swinging of axes also could, accurately, beautifully, and without sentiment, describe elf owls hunting mice through the desert night as "speckled fluffs of greediness" (*Land of Little Rain* 38).

She was, she would not have liked to admit, a lucky woman, for it was her mentor Lummis who early on published this obscure but hustling writer in his magazine, the *Land of Sunshine,* and Lummis who, selflessly recognizing her talents, urged her on to national outlets (Langlois 27–28). It was a kindness repaid by several bites on the hand, but that, too, was typical of the woman.[1] Whether or not the troubles she bore were substantially greater than those of many people of the time lacking the privilege to voice them loudly and publicly in print is a moot point. She chose to think of herself as bludgeoned by the gods, yet, to our benefit, she managed to turn her victim status into a wider blessing. Perhaps, as sometimes happens with people of a peculiar psychology, it was a self-pity necessary to energize her talents. Once set in motion, she became one of those wind-up machines whirling through their escapades, sometimes slamming into walls, sometimes performing brilliantly, but in either case running according to the pattern of her own, internal mechanism.

Also no doubt not eagerly acknowledged, the outline of Mary Hunter Austin's early life shows a young person taking advantage of the new mobility for women, both socially and in literary circles, during the closing decades of the last century.[2] Though not wealthy, her father was an attorney in small-town Carlinville, Illinois. A lover of books and a gentle man, George Hunter also served as a captain in the Civil War over the area's military volunteers, and thereafter he bore the respect of the men of the town who had served under him.

Unfortunately, Mary's beloved father died in 1878, when she was ten years old. Nonetheless, her widowed mother had the resources to put Mary through nearby Blackburn College, where she published in the school's literary magazine and became the poet laureate of her graduating class. For that, finances were becoming thin, and Mary, her mother, and a brother, along with thousands of other Americans, headed west to California. There, what they held brightly in their minds as a promise of prosperity in the Golden State failed them, and Austin's life took several bad turns. The three tried homesteading near the edge of the Mojave Desert, but along with thousands of other Americans they found their ears full of the wails of dying cattle in that arid land. Briefly, she tried teaching, then in 1891 married Stafford Austin.

That only compounded her troubles. Her husband had grandiose dreams of getting rich on desert real estate in the arid Owens Valley. Time and again, along with others swept up in the craze to turn the new desert lands into dollars, he failed. As Mary's daughter, Ruth, grew, it became painfully apparent that she was retarded. Also that the marriage was failing. Adding to the frustrations, while bill collectors hounded her and the child moaned, Mary decided that she wanted to be a writer. She began by starting a new life. In 1899 she went to Los Angeles, where she became a member of the salon at Lummis' El Alisal. Profiting from the contacts, she later moved on, hobnobbing with Jack London, Lincoln Steffens, and other Bohemians in the artists' colony at seaside Carmel. In the meantime, her marriage ended in divorce, and daughter Ruth was institutionalized.

Following wide publication of her poems and short stories in such national magazines as *St. Nicholas* and *The Atlantic Monthly*, Mary Austin's deciding break came in 1903 with the appearance of her first book, *The Land of Little Rain.* This collection of essays, based on her earlier life in the desert, confirmed the nation's brewing wonder over rumors from that mysterious land. After that, Austin's career became ever more successful as Mary supported herself by lecturing and by turning out book after book, novels about the Southwest, volumes about feminism, folklore, and social reform. She traveled to Europe and chummed with H. G. Wells and Herbert Hoover. Between 1911 and 1918, ever the more successful writer, she divided her time between Carmel and New York City. In 1925, she settled permanently in Santa Fe, New Mexico. There, reflecting the pattern of Lummis, she became a leader in various causes, in social reforms, Indian affairs, and such. By the time she died in 1934, her vision of the Southwest was clear. She saw it as a region blending Indian, Mexican, and Anglo cultures into the harmony of small communes that emphasized the arts, leisure, and spiritual consciousness.

Missing in this outline is the wayward force and direction of the personality informing Mary Austin's writing. The literary establishment, then as now, is no more immune to fads and flamboyance than other sectors of society. Austin fed powerful Easterners cotton-candy dreams of the chic New Woman of the future, surfeited with Southwestern mystique and leaving repressive traditions behind in a shambles. Augusta Fink catches this scene of Austin at her height, bowling over neoteric New Yorkers:

> On January 8, 1922, she swept into the National Arts Club, splendidly attired, "to take the center of the stage" at the event given in her honor. Her gown was fashioned of an iridescent fabric, "the rose of an Arizona sunset," and she carried both a black plumed fan and a bouquet of roses. "This with a Spanish comb and appropriate touches of black and silver," in her own words, gave her attire "the effect of having been made in a candy

shop." To add to the impact of her entrance, she had chosen as her escort the young Indian painter Overton Colbert. He came dressed in embroidered buckskin and a magnificent headdress of black, white, and flamingo feathers that brought gasps from the reception committee. (203)

The prestigious editors and publishers loved this tawdry misrepresentation of the Southwest. Raved New York luminary Carl Van Doren over such spectacles, "Everybody who talked with Mary Austin knew at once that there was greatness in her." Mary Austin had learned her lesson well from the guitar-strumming Lummis.

Yet there was far more going on here than the poseur chuckling up her sleeve as she manipulated the powerful Easterners who held her literary career in their hands. Whether or not Austin saw God under a walnut tree, could predict the future, and had a preternatural relationship with animals, as she claimed, such experiences became the essence of her literary stock in trade, and she seems to have convinced herself that she was a special medium with connections to a mystic place that much of the bored nation longed to believe in—and did believe in, with no more authority than Austin's own compelling assertions. "There is something in Mary which comes out of the land," she said of herself, vaguely but appealingly, in *Earth Horizon,* her autobiography (15), and it was that mysterious something that people longed to hear about. They longed to hear that out there in the desert Indians still lived in harmony with the earth, their lives governed by chthonic ties to the planet, and that a far-off reader, even though an Anglo, might participate, feeling the power if only through Mary Austin's books.

As with many a person thinking himself a misfit, Austin found solace both by lashing out at the society that she imagined had rejected her and by identifying with groups outside the mainstream, in her case with the remnant Paiute Indians, cowboys, and itinerant miners of the Owens Valley. From these, she seized the fetching absurdities pleasing to her audience. In her short story "The Pot of Gold," an anthropologist throws off his old, rational life for a new, Edenic existence with an Indian woman in the desert. There he sees that his new life has taken on "the color of a lotus eating dream" (493). So much for the hardships of life in an arid land. In *The Land of Little Rain,* Austin creates a Mexican village up in the mountains where people are poor but happy, making up for lack of food with the richness of a culture based on earthly rhythms and fiestas (265–281). So much for the realities of dancing on an empty stomach. And for robbing Hispanics of their flesh-and-blood humanity by turning them into happy cartoon characters.

Austin's enthusiasm for her own ideas knew few bounds. Her widely hailed *The American Rhythm* claims a remarkable revelation about the creation of the Gettysburg Address:

> *Thus the rail splitter arrives at his goal*
> *with the upswing and the down-stroke:*
> > *That government of the people*
> > *For the people*
> > *By the people*
> > *Shall not perish from the earth!*
> *And the ax comes to rest on the chopping log*
> *while a new length is measured. (16)*

For, after all, she later lectured a group of enraptured English teachers, intimate knowledge of a land is more important than talent when writing about a place. Then she proceeded to bash rival novelist Willa Cather for her well-received *Death Comes for the Archbishop* ("Regionalism in American Fiction" 105–107). Austin, of course, would be the arbiter of such issues, whether they pertained to New Mexico or Illinois.

Perhaps the most offensive, wrongheaded, and arrogant aspect of all this is Austin's treatment of American Indians, the very group she claimed she most admired. In writing the preface to her drama *The Arrow Maker*, Austin shows her heart in the right place by condemning the widespread "misinformation about Indians" and joking that the popular stereotypes have as much to do with real Indians as do the wooden statues standing outside cigar stores (vii). Then, with typical Austinesque abandonment to self, she rushes in to commit the very errors she ridicules in other writers. Even when enduring lives that most other human beings on the planet would find abysmal, her Indians are suffused with joy. Austin's portrait in *The Land of Little Rain* of four old, blind Paiute women, hanging onto life in an Indian camp:

By noon of the sun there were never any left in the campoodie but these or some mother of weanlings, and they sat to keep the ashes warm upon the hearth. If it were cold, they burrowed in the blankets of the hut; if it were warm, they followed the shadow of the wickiup around. Stir much out of their places they hardly dared, since one might not help another; but they called, in high, old cracked voices, gossip and reminder across the ash heaps. (177)

This is the turning of human misery, of malnourishment and uselessness, into a saleable literary product warming the cockles of the hearts of Eastern audiences. Such things, observes Southwestern critic Larry Evers, "are probably best forgotten" (xxiii).

Behind the preposterous posings was a design. For Austin, the dominant society was wrong, all wrong, though it could redeem itself, so she implies, if the people in those teeming cities would heed her wisdom and by the millions abandon their railroads, electricity, and telephones to seek solace by grubbing in the desert with wooden hoes while voicing charming incantations to the gods for rain. The path lies, then, in becoming instant Indians, an insult both to that group and to whites. Also best forgotten on this score, cautions Dudley Wynn, is that such insights which "she frequently asserted came from observation of aboriginal life" actually derived from her familiarity with the tag ends of various romantic movements in Western thought (35). Blending primitivism, transcendentalism, and other elements, Austin's philosophy was, in fact, a glittering hodgepodge of self-serving romanticism.

And third on the list of things best consigned to Lethe are the aspects of a personality swelling into egomaniacal dimensions. Yet, even while impressed by her presence, some of her disciples, seeing the prophet in action, caught inklings of doubt. On a tour into southern Arizona to visit the land of the Papago Indians, while the automobile bumped along the rutted dirt roads, Austin held forth to her three companions about the place she had not yet seen. Writes Ina Sizer Cassidy, a member of the group:

The role of mentor is a favorite one of I-Mary's, and, with her remarkable memory for the printed word, she really is a rich source of information. Whether this role is prompted by a spirit of generosity, a desire to share her knowledge, a subconscious prompting of her old "teacher" habit, or an exposition of egotism, one is never sure. Her friends commend her for it; her enemies condemn. (205)

From her high seat of self-righteousness, Mary Austin considered herself an expert on just about any topic that came up. This is an aspect we perhaps should good-naturedly forgive in writers, unless they lack the strength to prevent it from slopping over and skewing the good sense of their writing, which in Austin's case it often did. This, much to her immediate acclaim, but much, also, to the depreciation of her literary legacy.

And yet, and yet. If the gods bludgeoned Mary Austin, they also truly blessed her. Published in 1903, her first book, *The Land of Little Rain*, retains some remnants of the sentiment found in "The Pot of Gold" but little of the squid-like bombast marring her later writing. This is the fruit of youthful risk, the work of a beginning and ambitious, but not yet self-dazzled, writer pouring the best of herself into a book and achieving, through that charming naiveté often marking fresh genius, a memorable event. Perhaps the occasional slide off into the swamps of gratuitous emotionalism owed something to her eagerness to curry favor with what she thought was the purple taste of the book-buying public. Perhaps it indicates the lingering immaturity of her writing hand in discriminating between true talent and the easy chaff coming out of the end of her pen—we cannot know which—but if we can lightly pardon such patches as mentioned in the paragraphs above, what remains is one of our great desert books. All the more to her favor because she lacked the schooling of wise predecessors. Combining authority, delicacy, and depth, Mary Austin's alchemy took the desert circus of Lummis and turned it into a deep, spiritual rite.[3]

The first literary promoter of the region par excellence, Lummis shared the ad writer's zeal for skimming off the land's arresting features, the romps after Apaches, the desolate sweeps, and curious folkways that turned his books into easily digestible travel films gliding from scene to exciting scene. In his wake, Austin refined the loud approach, appealing to the more sensitive side of her readers by softening the tones into expositions of the region's delicacies. The method is a large part of her book's charm. Our guide over mesa and creosote flat, she knows how to impress her gawking followers, pointing when the dust of the trail before our horses' hooves suddenly congeals into a lizard in flight: "Now and then a palm's breadth of the trail gathers itself together and scurries off with a little rustle under the brush, to resolve itself into sand again" (155). More than a conveyor of information, she is that best of docents, a person teaching out of infinite curiosity about her subject. Winding up into the sierra high above the tawny stretches, we join her in placing an ear to the snowdrifts to hear the "eternal busyness" of water running far below (206). And she catches the commonest desert things with a knack we bear away to mull over later in cities. Out in the calescent barrens, the mesquite is not simply a tree. Nibbling on one of its sweet, life-giving pods while wiping our brows in the relief of its shade, we notice its beautiful canopy and understand Austin's vocabulary dubbing the mesquite "God's best thought in all this desertness" (86). So she brings us beyond Lummis' verge, to a new and deeper impression, one far more flattering to our intelligence and sensibilities. However, such features would make a pleasant but not a moving book.

As with Lummis, Austin is invitational, but with her different tone, she anticipates a larger purpose. This will be no tour of Grand Sights but a tender visit to those desert features—the cowboys, Indian camps, and hidden springs—Austin holds dear in her own daily rounds. With her, we are not paying guests but instant friends welcomed to share the things enriching her private life. In fact, we set off from her doorstep in the Owens Valley, leaving "the brown house under the willow-tree at the end of the village street" (xi).

All this to an even larger purpose. Intimacy is not her goal but her method. Through taking us into her personal life, Austin wants to accomplish a shift in our souls. "Somehow," we hear her say, startled by the daring of her statement, "the rawness of the land favors the sense of personal relation to the supernatural" (120). Can she deliver on that seemingly bombastic sentence and on our tour make us feel in the land around us "the sense of purpose not revealed" (184), even see, if not God's face, then, turned transcendentalists in one excursion, His design all around us? Such is the risk of *The Land of Little Rain.* The book's success lies in delivering on a grandiose promise.

Immediately, problems swirl around her approach, difficulties that Lummis enthusiastically passes by. How is she going to make her whimsy stick, make it convincing and lasting, rather than the momentary vision created by the illusionist with words? Furthermore, though winsome, such attractions of nature are brutally contradicted by the less comforting side of nature's ways, the clawing and tearing and dying of thirst blatantly evidenced in those stony places where the scant ground cover reveals gnawed skulls and tufts of fur. And what is Austin to do about the human violence, the influx of white people, recently arrived in great numbers with their technology and remaking the very land Austin loves with houses, railroads, and irrigation ditches?

Such are problems of hard logic, and though Austin deals with them, she wisely does not try to resolve them with reason. Rather, she admits to them. With her own eyes, in piteous description of the ravages of drought, she has seen the cattle die "in their tracks with their heads towards the stopped watercourses" (48). To her, personally, such death is "squalid," and there is nothing beautiful about it: "The heavy-headed, rack-boned cattle totter in the fruitless trails; they stand for long, patient intervals; they lie down and do not rise. There is fear in their eyes when they are first stricken, but afterward only intolerable weariness" (49). As for humans with their machines, they are "great blunderer[s]" (60), and lest no one be deceived, those "speckled fluffs of greediness" floating back and forth through the gloom over a spring hardly are candidates for the nursery room but are hungry to rip up and devour escaping mice (38). Hardly naive, Austin knows full well the reality behind "the pitiful small shreds the butcher-bird hangs on spiny shrubs" (139). Yet, the violence, whether from people or nature, she accepts as part of a larger system that ultimately is unknowable and, in this, essential for the mystery it exudes. In the midst of it, surrounded by "beauty and madness and death and God" (184), she concentrates on extracting the "delicate joys" of the moment (20), rewards in themselves from the harshness. This woman looking longingly on the world around her sighs after the scurrying lizard as "pure witchcraft," whatever its ecological role, and even though in the next moment, it may be torn for a hawk's meal (155). Her love, then, her whimsy, is intuitional—her readers either will feel it or not—and she stakes her case on the ability of her prose to move with emotion rather than with reason. This is the process of courtship, and by book's end, we will not be blasted out of our saddles by lightning or brought around by Jesuitical exchanges. Rather, through the writer, we have received "news of the land . . . as one lover of it can give to another" and are slowly wooed until we, too, look on the desert with a lover's eyes (xi).

This implies no lack of substance in Austin's delivery. Though Austin comes to the land leading with her heart, her intellect is there, too. From her long treks and close observation, she knows the habits of the plants and animals of her home, and she often gives their Latin names. Attuned to ecological nuances while other settlers pursued grim schemes of turning the barren places into dollars, she considers the angles of slopes and ponders why north-facing hillsides have far more plant life than the nearby slope only a few feet away over the crest (9). This, too, is part of the land's news, and whatever her flights, the natural history blends into her prose the authority of a writer who knows her subject from the inside out. And this serves a larger purpose. The whole message of her book is that "the manner of the country makes the usage of life there" (88). That is, at least it should. Living attentively with the earth, adjusting our lives to its rhythms, brings us in harmony with nature's larger forces. If such cannot be measured by T-square or pinned to a board or a page, it nonetheless can be experienced, bringing peace and a deep, personal satisfaction not garnered from a busy society. Her method, then, in this intimate exploration is to take us to the people and places dear to the author that illustrate the thought. If in the end the book collapses logically, it pulls readers along with lush examples. Some of these are more persuasive than others, while a treasured handful almost fuse aesthetic and realistic focuses perfectly into one convincing whole.

The common, abused, and ignored things are Austin's pathways to the discovery of larger moments. She takes us to the camp of the pocket hunter, an itinerant prospector who contents himself to survive through the years by now and then finding small deposits of gold (63–80). With his coffeepot bubbling on the evening fire, his pack burros munching nearby on the desert scrub, he is a man surrounded by peace and beauty, a man content with his wide world. When he strikes it rich, he's off for a long toot in London, and the author misses him on her wanderings across the sage, but in a year or two, true to form, he reappears, happy to be back in his desert home (79–80).

If that were the whole of the matter, however, we'd have no more than a Wordsworthian cliché, the happy simpleton, so brainless he'd likely be at ease in any circumstances. What Austin needs in such scenes is the transcendental moment, the link between man and nature that manifests the connection to the larger powers beyond us. This she sometimes delivers with a low current flickering with hints of things beyond, heat lightning trembling over the horizon, but sometimes with a jolt, leaving us bewildered after it passes, though with our awareness rearranged and sure that something significant has happened. Or, to change the analogy somewhat, the epiphanies need to arise effortlessly out of nature, as if it were an ocean on which we're sailing, occasionally seeing beautifully luminescent creatures rising close to the surface.

Leaving the sands of Death Valley to explore the mountain heights, the pocket hunter becomes lost in a sudden blizzard. After stumbling around for hours, he naturally enough takes refuge by crawling into a clump of cedars bent over by the snow:

. . . he found it about four hours after dark, and heard the heavy breathing of the flock. He said that if he thought at all at this juncture he must have thought that he had stumbled on a storm-belated shepherd with his silly sheep; but in fact he took no note of anything but the warmth of packed fleeces, and snuggled in between them dead with sleep. If the flock stirred in the night he stirred drowsily to keep close and let the storm go by. That was all until morning woke him shining on a white world. Then the very soul of him shook to see the wild sheep of God stand up about him, nodding their great horns beneath the cedar roof, looking out on the wonder of the snow. (75–76)

Though the naturalist will know that such a moment with a flock of the wild and highly shy bighorn sheep, though not impossible, is unlikely, still, we'd like to believe in the meeting, and Austin allows us to, for she prepares us for it through the perfectly believable build of the circumstances. The man and the sheep, after all, are both common things, though for this moment they are brought uncommonly together, and in their conjunction lies the light, as in the flash of a chemical fusion. The remarkable thing, after the initial shake in his soul, is the prospector's rather unsurprised reaction. A man riddled with superstitions, to him the event belongs to the folklore of venomous toads, charms for snakebite, and other beliefs he carries with him (77). Yet though he makes little of this besides a puzzled wonder, we make much, seeing for a moment what we want, the meeting of an unpretentious man wrapped in myth with the emissaries of the divine existing all around us in nature.

Though less dramatic in its events, Austin's story of old Seyavi, petal-like in its fragile beauty, is not nearly as convincing (163–179). Years before, having lost her husband in one of the final battles with the whites, the Paiute woman fled with her son into the bleak desert hills. There she grew strong by learning to fend for herself, then, after the enmity between the two races cooled, made baskets for sale to the whites.

So far, so good. Then Austin goes too far, lapsing into the treacle of the Cult of the Noble Savage. She turns Seyavi into an icon of all that is good in the primitive life as contrasted with all that is bad about the money-grubbing white society. Forced to exist in this brutal economy, Seyavi remained true to her spiritual self, for she made "baskets for love and sold them for money." "Every Indian woman is an artist," Austin further tells us (168), turning out baskets that are "wonders" because the "weaver and the warp lived next to the earth saturated with the same elements" (169). That is, living close to the earth in itself is a virtue, as if no inept or mean-spirited basket maker pained by the dull labors of working with arthritic fingers ever lived. Topping off the idyllic life, now in old age Seyavi is one of the four blind but happy crones already mentioned, in their darkness existing in a state of advanced sainthood (177–179). The story as Austin tells it has charm, but it is a made-up charm, thin in its veneer and quickly wearing through to the less happy realities the writer chose to ignore while building her wish-fulfillment. In this respect, the glib construction of the piece counters the very values Austin thinks she is promoting. Fantasy has stretched beyond reality to the breaking point, and the illusion is lost.

This is not true of "My Neighbor's Field" (125–139). Here, the two work in tandem rather than at cross purposes. Ironically, the piece is one of the quietest and, at least on the surface, one of the least ambitious in the book. Blessed by its lack of self-conscious literary set-up or brightly colored propagandistic intent, it also is one of the most subtly complex, profound, and moving chapters.

Offering the best of herself, Austin abandons the sometimes cloying narrative line and drops her dependence on holding readers by presenting eccentric or exotic people to write an essay focusing on the land itself. In this case, on one field nearby, lying at the border of her village, a nondescript place most passersby would think, with a ragged irrigation ditch and overgrown by brambles. Perhaps the piece benefits from its more active, surrounding chapters, for they create a context for this most telling pause. In this humble circumstance, the land stands for nothing else than itself, its significance rubbed out against the thought of the observer. In musing on the field's history, Austin conveys the richness of the larger landscape to the attentive heart. Austin's understanding of her neighbor's field is the essence of *The Land of Little Rain.*

Because of the small stream running through the property, for years it was a campground visited by the wandering Indians, and the village children delight in finding arrowheads there. In fact, remnant Indians, unable to give up their old ways despite the crush of civilization, still pass through there and camp, wraith-like and ignored on its edges. In recent times, the place was variously nibbled down by sheep and trampled by cows, fenced, and its trees cut down. That was due to white men, whose successive owners have quite undone themselves over very little, wrangling for possession of the worthless place, one owner maniacally building a small fort with loopholes to warn off an acquisitive rival, another hiring a "one-armed lawyer with the tongue to wile a bird out of the bush" (128), who successfully bilked the rightful owner out of his title in court.

He, in turn, was outdone by another, though now the place between the foot of the mountains and the village lies mostly abandoned. But it is hardly inert. Over in the south corner, where the Indians camped, stand three scraggly hackberry trees, not native to that nook of the desert but monuments to the Paiutes, who years before probably dropped the seeds from the hackberry's edible fruit that they had brought along from elsewhere. Rotting stumps stand where larger trees once grew, though the stream brings down pine cones from the mountains, and furry saplings are beginning to sprout up unnoticed, as if stealthily reclaiming their old territory. Between three and four o'clock each afternoon, a hawk visits the field, soaring back and forth "with the airs of a gentleman adventurer" (138).

That is, the field very much has a life of its own, and now, as if recalling its own history, it is becoming all the more alive for the very fact that it is ignored and abandoned by the juggernaut of leveling civilization. With its force, living into its own remembering, it becomes a vital treasure for the one who walks there looking for intimate news of the land. The unstated message being that this little plot of wildness, however treasured by the sensitive heart, can't last, anymore than anyone can who loves those things deemed worthless by the larger, macadamizing society. For this, the chapter is all the more bittersweet.

Such would go down as a fairly sentimental portrait of the land, to be appreciated by those coming after who wistfully remember a favored suburban field rudely turned into a shopping mall. Except for one thing. Using her best technique, Austin restrains her preachy urge and, instead of saying all that she might, leads with delicacy. Unfortunately, it is a subtle point lost to many modern readers. Pretending graciousness, after reeling off the list of former, obtuse owners of the field, Austin calls the present titleholder only Naboth (128). She says this is because she envies his possession of the place. Yet apparently he's little different from the other owners, and Lord knows what *he'll* do with the place once a developer dangles a wad of bills in front of him. In the naming lies the key. Out of respect for the inheritance from his fathers, the Naboth of the Bible refused to sell his land to the jealous King Ahab. Austin's field, then, is more than a charming place, it is a sacred trust, as is all of the nature around us. The biblical Naboth went to his death rather than betray his loyalty to the land.[4] Of an entirely different sort, the modern namesake only waits for the most lucrative offer to come along before selling his birthright. This is a form of blasphemy, stemming from our high-handed treatment of the earth, an arrogant violation of our sacred matrix. Austin might have rightly reared up on her hind legs to make the point, but rather than blast her readers, she resists, embedding her message in the subtleties of the story in the Scriptures, and for that it is all the more lasting and powerful.

In another chapter, describing the old mining town of Jimville, Austin similarly restrains herself. Implying a story but allowing readers to fill in the details, she uses a deft image for her apology: "You shall blow out this bubble from your own breath" (113). By having the most important news of the land take place in her audience, Austin achieves her most lasting effects, for here the complex parts of her stories, the richest insights into the land, are knit to completion within her readers. In such a way, if Austin brings the mindset of the industrial romantic to her writing, imposing it on her subjects, it is an imposition moving readers to a new assessment of the landscape before them.

6

JOHN C. VAN DYKE

AND THE DESERT

AESTHETICIANS

The name most often mentioned when discussing Mary Austin and her desert writing is John C. Van Dyke. According to the prevailing view, in 1901 Van Dyke wrote the first book to praise the widely scorned deserts. In doing this, Van Dyke "led the way," says the usually reliable Franklin Walker, to the nation's appreciation of the arid lands for their own beauties, with Mary Austin, George Wharton James, and others thereafter falling into the route of march (185). Another critic is even more laudatory. According to him, Van Dyke saw the desert "first and said it best"; he was the fountainhead of the genre. Most scholars have gone along with the assessment.[1]

There is some truth in the view. Lummis' books gurgle over the whole wonderland of the Southwest, praising the region's forests, lakes, and sandy barrens in one all-encompassing geographical and spiritual encomium. He doesn't often deal with its deserts as ecologically separate entities. In this sense, Van Dyke's little volume, *The Desert*, was indeed a "first," for it was the earliest book printed in America focusing specifically on the topic; furthermore, the influence of *The Desert*, today in print after a hundred years, cannot be doubted. However, as detailed in the last chapter, the young and developing Austin was allied with her mentor, Lummis, along with other like-minded writers in Southern California, not with Van Dyke, an Easterner. Furthermore, in the closing decades of the last century, any number of boosters in the region were bubbling over its virtues with a fervor that permeated the very atmosphere of the place. At the time, such enthusiasts were well on their way to turning the ugly duckling of the desert into a swan. A refiner in a movement already under way, Austin was a part of this. Though Van Dyke's book preceded hers by a slight two years, the precedence was accidental. Austin was writing poems and short stories about the desert some time before Van Dyke ever put down a public word about the region. The *Overland Monthly*, for instance, published Austin's poem "Inyo" in 1899, and her short story "The Pot of Gold" ran in *Munsey's* in July 1901, several months before Van Dyke's book appeared in September of that year. Given such things, the chances are very good that Van Dyke had little or no direct influence on how and what Austin wrote in *The Land of Little Rain*, a book putting a delicate touch on the ideas of Lummis and other Californians, not on those of Van Dyke.

To point this out is not to indulge in a literary quibble, nor is it to denigrate Van Dyke's rightful place. As shall be seen, both books are similar, cataloging the loveliness of nature in dry places. And this may be responsible for the confusion, for the quality is due to the general romanticism creeping into the area like a golden haze, rather than to any copycat impulse on Austin's part. Desert beauty was the commonality shared by both authors, but the differences in their approaches and motives are the keys to their startlingly different contributions, distinct roles that have not been fully credited by their ardent readers.

Austin saw the beauty of the desert as good in itself but also as a means to a larger end. This was nothing short of society's redemption. Living close to nature, attuned to its nuances, people would be healed in a mystic way, she intuits but does not explain, of their overcivilized ills. This concept of the curative powers of nature on society was not as novel as it might first seem but part of the day's popular romanticism. When in 1858 Frederick Law Olmsted and Calvert Vaux designed Central Park, their purpose was more than the creation of a pleasant place in New York City where mothers could push their wicker baby carriages. Earlier, Olmsted had voiced the airy belief that nature, because it revealed the "mysteries of God," improved both morality and the intellect (Roper 63). Applying such ideas to the land, this Emerson with a hoe, as one wit dubbed the idealist, molded the city's former wasteland of ash heaps and pigsties into a landscape of rural, New England loveliness. In his mind's eye, Olmsted saw his future park uplifting the public with transcendental experiences. The very proportions of his hills, the grouping of his trees, and the curves of his paths would evoke tranquillity, giving the city-plagued masses the sublime peace they lacked in their crowded, noisy lives. Later, conservationist John Muir argued similarly for building more roads in Yosemite, as pathways to balm for weary souls visiting from the city.[2] Moving west, that transcendental spirit, a deep part of our heritage, found a home in the desert, too. When it came to Austin, since she was more interested in effects than in beauty's composition, she didn't trouble herself overly much about analyzing its makeup.

Other writers, however, worried the subject considerably. J. Ross Browne called the desert a "mystic" place (*Adventures* 75). Soon after him, on his way into the thundersome labyrinths of the Grand Canyon in his little wooden boat, explorer John Wesley Powell paused to climb a height for a view of the badlands. Confronted by a land spreading away in wave upon rocky wave to the horizon, he exclaimed in his *Exploration of the Colorado River,* "Barren desolation is stretched before me; and yet there is a beauty in the scene" (9). And such loveliness seeped into the soul of even a jokester such as Cozzens, who saw the peaks towering around him as "perfect models of architectural beauty" (207). But what made such landscapes beautiful, what in them caused such wonder in the breast of the observer? The questions were asked again and again, rarely indeed by hard-bitten ranchers and miners, all too familiar with hard life on the desert, but by visitors bred on the aesthetic movements that troubled sensitive, well-educated Easterners. Compiling theories of beauty and the psychological effects of it is a tempting, tantalizing, if earnest, enterprise, but rarely if ever in the history of civilizations do thinkers come up with watertight explanations that serve for all times and satisfy theorists in all cultures. Experiences of such things are too much colored by the culture in which they take place, by changing fads, and by the chemistry of the individual philosopher to result in a universal field theory.[3] Beauty does not come in absolutes, although it may seem so to the person enthralled. Whether or not what we see before us grips with its loveliness may have more to do with the state of our health (as in the famous case of van Gogh), the overwhelming brightness of a current *affaire de coeur* (witness the new lover living in a state of bedazzlement), and other extrinsic factors than with the qualities of the subject itself.

Nonetheless, such angelic wrestlings are not fruitless, and in the case of the desert, the artistic strainings have produced some of its most exquisite writing. At the close of the last century, Captain Clarence E. Dutton, out on a geological expedition, proposed one of the most developed theories about the beauty of the Grand Canyon and why the Great Chasm was "the most sublime of all earthly spectacles" (142). The world, he said, had a plentiful supply of canyons, some of them deeper, wider, and wilder than what lay before him. But what made this particular dungeon in the earth the most overwhelming was not the quality of its parts but the assemblage of the whole, its *ensemble,* as he said, using the French word and implying comparison to a harmonious musical composition (143). That is, the Grand Canyon was neither too large to elude the stretched human comprehension or too small to fail to have the impact of enormity; rather, all its features were just right, having the correct proportions to make a supreme impression. It was as if here at the beginning of the eons the Divine Hand had stirred the dough of Creation, and putting forth His greatest effort, gotten everything to come out exactly right (144). Strange words for a man with a dual career as a geologist and a military officer, though the thought verges on the formulaic proportions seen in the sculpture of the ancient Greeks, and, though, too, Dutton had studied at Yale for the ministry, which may account for the airy element that lightens his scientific treatises.

In this sense, Dutton was an aesthete. Unlike Austin, he had no notions about saving the nation's citizens by dragging them by the ears into the Canyon's desert bowels, where in the blistering summer heat they would heal themselves by hoeing corn yielding thumb-sized ears, as had the bleak Canyon's handful of lean and ancient residents. Dutton simply wanted to equip visitors to best appreciate the soul-elevating splendor of this outstanding and timeless grand event in the earth's history.

Not so John C. Van Dyke. He may have pretended to care for his large audience—all the better for the large sales he enjoyed—by leading book buyers into this wonderland, but the desert's wiliest and most misunderstood writer cared not a whit for the public that avidly supported him, thinking Van Dyke their guide to beauty—in fact, he despised it—and scorned, too, lower down on the social scale, the masses who were the objects of Austin's sympathy. He was, or at least thought he was, a doomed man. Religion, civilization, womanly love—all had failed him. And if the desert's beauty could not save him from the inevitable pit of nothingness waiting at the end of his life, it might, nonetheless, give him some sublime moments of narcotic pleasure along the way. However, even then, it was no nurturing mother, as nature is in Austin's works, but a ruddled, deceiving strumpet, luring the doomed man on with her charms and, having enticed him, grinding him up finally in her lovely but crushing maws. Whether or not he believed such things or was baring his breast, bleeding on the thorns of life for dramatic effect, Van Dyke was a marvel of romantic *Götterdämmerung.*

This should give some inkling that, again running counter to the prevailing sentiment often linking the two writers, Van Dyke had far less in common with Austin than has been thought.

In contrast to her middle-class background, John C. Van Dyke was born in 1856 at Green Oaks, a three-peaked mansion near the gingerbread edifices of other family members.[4] Here in the idyllic landscape of farmlands and wooded hills on the outskirts of New Brunswick, New Jersey, he grew up, very much aware of his Old Dutch heritage dating back to 1652, of a well-off, respected, and politically powerful lineage boasting Revolutionary War heroes, a famed mathematician, and a bevy of state and community leaders. John's father was, variously, a lawyer, bank president, congressman, and a member of the New Jersey supreme court.

In this atmosphere of accomplishment and leadership, much was expected of the five Van Dyke boys, and they didn't disappoint their elders. Four of the brothers became lawyers, one a medical doctor. John attended Columbia Law School and in 1877, at the age of twenty-one, was admitted to the bar. The curious thing is that he never practiced. The young man took flame with the movements from France then firing the hearts of art lovers in New York City. But if he had a year or two of Bohemian adventure in the city's art world, an experience that stayed with him and grew through the rest of his life, he also felt the tug of a basically conservative nature, of the moneyed salons beginning to support the new art. Returning to hometown New Brunswick, only thirty miles from America's art center, he eventually held two, concurrent academic appointments. Van Dyke served as the director of the library at the prestigious New Brunswick Theological Seminary, upon what is still called Holy Hill. It overlooks the leafy and spired campus of Rutgers College, where he became the first professor of the history of art.

Valued by both institutions for his growing reputation as a writer and for his fund-raising connections, his duties were light and his position enviable. There he sat in a house built especially for him by the seminary, in an atmosphere of servants and tinkling crystal. Gazing out from his hillside perch over the Raritan River to the placid meadows and forested slopes beyond, he turned out taste-setting articles on art for such national magazines as *Century* and *Scribner's* while publishing book after book on nature, travel, and art. Yet in this nearly pastoral setting, his was a busy life, riding the train into New York City to visit publishers and hobnob with the wealthy and serving as an art adviser to Andrew Carnegie, the richest man in America. On top of that, meeting demands as a lecturer and trying to keep up on social obligations in the bon ton, he had to keep flipping through his calendar, arranging vacations at Carnegie's castle in Scotland and scheduling tours of the world's art museums, during which he stayed in the elegant hotels along the Champs Elysées and along other fashionable boulevards of Europe's capitals.

It was a milieu about as different as one could imagine to that of failed homesteader Austin, and it is reflected in Van Dyke's views of nature. True, as a boy he had romped in the countryside surrounding his boyhood estate, hunting and fishing and swimming in nearby Mile Run, but his theories about nature came more through art than up from the ground. Along with other devotees of Art for Art's Sake, Van Dyke held that pleasure from art was life's highest good, a salving joy in a failing world. Admittedly, the tenets of this romantic movement were so hazy and personalized that they often defy definition, though one faction, to which Van Dyke belonged, held a particular, definable view. The greatest art was to be found not in museums but in wild nature itself. It was an idealized, if fey and somewhat predictable, approach, indulged in by the wealthy who, escaping their fetid cities, where they made their money, for weekends and summers in their country homes, could pleasure themselves away from the mobs by observing the shifting play of color and light over mountain vistas and seascapes.

Van Dyke's so-called nature books, then, really are treatises on art, for wherever he traveled around the world, the art critic treated the scenery before him as if he were describing beautiful paintings. When, in the late 1890s because of nagging respiratory problems he began visiting elder brother Theodore in Southern California, Van Dyke did what he often did on his trips, he wrote a book, in this case about the desert where land developer Theodore had real estate interests.[5] And thus, too, the strong visual impact of *The Desert*. This passage, for example, elevating the bane of pioneers, the much despised sand dunes through which they slogged, to a vision of ethereal grace:

The long line of dunes at the north are just as desolate, yet they are wonderfully beautiful. The desert sand is finer than snow, and its curves and arches, as it builds its succession of drifts out and over an arroyo, are as graceful as the lines of running water.

But even then, the aesthetician doesn't let it go at that. Continuing the passage, Van Dyke outdoes himself, imposing the Eastern aesthetician's view of what the desert should look like on the barren landscape by painting in prose the artistic deliciousness he sees in his head.

The dunes are always rhythmical and flowing in their forms; and for color the desert has nothing that surpasses them. In the early morning, before the sun is up, they are air-blue, reflecting the sky overhead; at noon they are pale lines of dazzling orange-colored light, waving and undulating in the heated air; at sunset they are often flooded with a rose or mauve color; under a blue moonlight they shine white as icebergs in the northern seas. (53)

Such measures the radical change in desert perception. Manly would have been appalled.

Or to choose further from Van Dyke's panoply of flitting, lilac-hued lizards and dust storms whirling up in great, golden monsters of beauty, awing the traveler below, this impressive handling of a sunset that Van Dyke describes during a side trip into Mexico:

I have seen at sunset, looking north from Sonora some twenty miles, the whole tower-like shaft of Baboquivari change from blue to topaz and from topaz to glowing red in the course of half an hour. I do not mean edgings or rims or spots of these colors upon the peak, but the whole upper half of the mountain completely changed by them. The red color gave the peak the appearance of hot iron, and when it finally died out the dark dull hue that came after was like that of a clouded garnet. (91)

That is, a sunset done in the vivid colors from a painter's palette.[6]

Both Van Dyke's *The Desert* and Austin's *The Land of Little Rain* leave such strong impressions with their revelations of the arid lands that it's easy to be overtaken by the immediacy of their surface lushness, reason enough to assume that one writer followed the lead of the other.[7] First of all, though both acknowledge the desert's desolation and dangers, a literary device to build extremes of tension, both emphasize the favorable qualities. Yet this is not simply a pretty place before them captured by the talented traveler's hand but food for the writers' very being. Each poses as the romantic loner finding here, at last, succor for his soul as he rides his horse through canyons and over lonely mesas. In their prefaces, both Van Dyke (xi) and Austin (xi) accordingly call themselves lovers. Stating it best, Van Dyke might speak for both when he says, "The desert has gone a-begging for a word of praise these many years. It never had a sacred poet; it has in me only a lover" (xi). Last, each reveals the grand sweeps as well as the curious particulars, the ways of the desert's strange plants and animals, as each moves from one enchanted place to another.

Yet on second thought, the apparent similarities are accidental rather than by design, the overlapping accounted for by two sensitive people pondering a similar landscape and their eyes, by the very nature of the country, drawn to similar features. Despite the immediate resemblances, this is backed up by telling differences in the two works. In tone and perspective, Van Dyke is more active, more like barker Lummis, hailing the grand spectacles of his country, while, as we've seen, Austin is intimate, gentle, and personal, qualities, one might say, divided between the two along traditional male and female lines. As a result, *The Desert* has the power of a sweeping panorama, while Austin focuses on specific places, a favorite field, canyon, or spring, many of them still identifiable. Along similar lines, much of *The Land of Little Rain* has a narrative sense as it tells stories, sometimes impossible stories, about the desert's humble people. On the other hand, Van Dyke, the aesthetic purist, wants to escape the human element in preference for the artistic glories of pristine nature. Hence, there are no characters, none whatsoever, in *The Desert*. It comes down to this: If Austin distorts the desert's human inhabitants for her ends, Van Dyke distorts the desert's landscape for quite different reasons.

Noting the diverging paths leads to a major watershed, that of purpose. The writer of *The Land of Little Rain* takes the position of one who cares for humanity and wants to enrich people through her revelations, to change their lives. Believing humanity damned and, in any case, not worth saving, Van Dyke writes to catch in print what we've referred to as the narcotic pleasures salving his otherwise pained existence. Austin has hope, however rationally false. Van Dyke, so he would lead us to believe, has only a string of momentary thrills before he returns to the oubliette of his blighted life back in civilization.

This may seem an extreme view, though it is supported by formerly overlooked evidence within Van Dyke's text, by his strong aesthetic position also taken in other books, as well as by what we know of him as a person. Exploring such things takes us into some dark labyrinths, but the reward is to catch Van Dyke and his desert work emerging in a new light. Seen in it, both the man and his book become more complex and rewarding than the simplistic desert-saint image of the man commonly held through the decades since his death in 1932. Though on this score, the blame cannot be laid entirely at the feet of naive readers innocently seeing the desert hero they craved. Van Dyke himself leads them into the deception. Praised as the first person to urge preservation of our desert heritage, Van Dyke is often quoted for his rousing call: "The deserts should never be reclaimed. They are the breathing-spaces of the west and should be preserved forever" (*The Desert* 59), and for such heat he draws applause from modern audiences who wish his advice had been heeded. Not only was his heart in the right place. His preface fosters the image of the two-fisted hero swinging a leg over his Indian pony and riding off into the unknown, a man perfectly capable of surviving in the wilderness while surveying its beauty (x).[8] All the more envy for the modern reader, who sees in Van Dyke not only a determined trailblazer but a sensitive man glorying in a pristine desert as no current desert lover, pained by the ravages of civilization, now can. Titillated, the willing reader goes for the bait and swallows the attractive picture, missing entirely the trick of the preface, that Van Dyke is doing nothing less than thumbing his nose at the mass of his gawking supporters. It's but one instance of several making the art professor at Rutgers our trickiest, and perhaps most fascinating, desert writer.

Readers likely are flattered when Van Dyke begins his masterpiece by addressing it directly to them, speaking with the all-encompassing "you," and inviting them to follow him into the wilds. That way, despite his many accomplishments, Van Dyke shows that he is a humble man, asking his audience to participate, if vicariously, in his adventures. What his admirers likely don't see, however, is that the "you" slowly changes. Or, rather, that there are two "you's." One is the general reader, the other an identifiable person. Yet as often happens in Van Dyke, he himself provides the clues leading to the unveiling of his own trick, almost as if he were planting incriminating evidence about himself, chuckling from the anticipatory joy of being discovered decades later and thus increasing the impact of his successful hoodwinking. In this case, the "you" begins referring to specific incidents, such as "When you are in Rome again . . ." (ix). That, however, is but slight and inconclusive. On the next page, he refers to "you and I, and that one we both loved so much," obviously a specific reference. The clincher comes in the preface's concluding paragraph, hoping that "you, and the nature-loving public you represent," will accept his book as "truthful" (xi).

Who is this person held so high in the esteem of the author? One might assume Van Dyke would have chosen John Muir, John Burroughs, or some such prominent nature lover of the day. Further, one catches a hint from the fact that the opening pages form not simply a preface but a "Preface-Dedication," with the book addressed to an "A. M. C." As it turns out, counter to expectations, this is not some figure in those early years of the conservation movement, boldly alerting the nation to the ruin of its natural heritage, but Andrew Carnegie, whose steel mills were then choking the skies of Pittsburgh with soot and whose iron-mining machines were making huge yardage chewing across the lovely forests of the Mesabi Range (Ingham and Wild).[9]

At that, doubts begin flooding in, eventually undermining the view of the book as the archetypal work of a desert lover, until it collapses. We remember that the desert at century's turn hardly was a pristine place of wolves and grizzly bears but a landscape being crisscrossed by roads, railroads, and fences, that even then hunters were shooting out the last of the big game, and huge irrigation projects were under way, transforming the wild face of nature into orderly rows of lettuce and melons disappearing into the point of infinity. With this, the factual validity of the book implodes. Much of Van Dyke's natural history is so preposterous as to be laughable. He tells us that the coyote, in fact a hunter of rabbits and other fleet prey, "seldom runs after things" (158), and that we need not fret about rattlesnakes, for they are "in fact sluggish" (169). In Van Dyke's desert, "nothing ever rots or decays" (41), all spiders are poisonous (169), and, for some strange reason not explained, the birds are "hopelessly sad" (71).

The list might go on for some length. These are not the occasional errors that can creep into any book. Instead, they are so frequent, wrongheaded, and even bizarre in their misinformation that one begins to suspect that the author didn't care about the accuracy of his pages and, worse, that he may have deliberately misrepresented his facts. Add to that the strange news Van Dyke reveals toward the end of his life in his autobiography, that he didn't particularly care for the desert (125). Still more disturbing, Van Dyke likely saw what he did of the desert not from the back of a horse but from the windows of Pullman cars and from the verandahs of first-class hotels (Wild and Carmony).

Egregious as the building case becomes, it burns calescent on two further counts. A well-educated and intelligent man, in books on art history such as *Rembrandt and His School*, Van Dyke showed himself a keen observer capable of producing meticulous scholarship. Furthermore, two months after publication of *The Desert*, a professor at the University of Arizona with ample desert experience nailed the Easterner for his glaring deviations from the facts.[10] Nonetheless, though the book went through printing after printing over Van Dyke's long writing career, he didn't bother to correct many of his mistakes. In the last reprint during his lifetime, two years before he died, the coyote still fogs along and the dangerous, lightning-quick desert rattler remains sluggish.

The truth is that the desert's most famous book is a compendium of falsehoods, a hoax. The entire volume is an elaborate joke on the writer's audience.[11]

On the surface, there seems no reason for Van Dyke to engage in such contemptuous silliness. With his large reputation, talent, and publishing connections, he could have easily written a lushly memorable yet reliable book about the desert. Why would he instead purposely bilk the public? Answering the question is important beyond the sake of satisfying curiosity or exploring biography, for it leads back to art and to one of the main reasons for the book's shape.

A personal element certainly comes into play. Aloof and dignified, a thoroughly private person, Van Dyke also could be quick to zero in on people's weaknesses and lash them with his tongue. A mossback proud of his sterling heritage, at least of what he imagined it to be, it rankled him that the values of his class, the nation's unofficial aristocracy, were under assault by millions of ignorant immigrants, by women, and the reforms of such brash upstarts as Mary Austin. For years he feuded, trying to keep novelist Edith Wharton out of the all-male ranks of the American Academy of Arts and Letters. Van Dyke, a person of power and culture, felt himself besieged, about to be toppled from his privileged status, yet instead of supporting the ways of good grace and upper-class gentility, the world kept changing, the rude masses pushing, rocking his pedestal. Whatever Freudian wounds lurked behind all this, the built-in frustration led to tantrums, sharp outbursts over both the particular and the general sorry state of the world.

This can result in some fiery and entertaining displays indeed. *In Egypt* takes aim at the New Brunswicker's favorite pet peeve, tourists, mocking those who likely wouldn't recognize him as their better as they sit gawking dully on the porch of their hotel in Cairo while sucking the paint from the handles of their canes (15). On other occasions, the peeve could be prolonged and sustained into a firestorm of calumny. In *The Money God*, Van Dyke stamps his feet and rends his garments over the nation's idiocies, and in the process he scourges professors, businessmen, various ethnic groups, and just about everyone else for their greed and stupidity—everyone, that is, except his friend Andrew Carnegie, in Van Dyke's mind a model of human kindness and philanthropy. Otherwise, Van Dyke moans, the Republic is in such bad shape that its only hope lies in return to its old, traditional ways and to renewed devotion to the Ten Commandments (vii). It is an intemperate performance by a man feeling his power slipping away. His chronic respiratory problems, possible poisoning from silver nitrate, a widely used antidote whose toxic effects weren't recognized, and the lonely bachelor's own stormy affair of the heart hardly mollified the general ire that kept biting his flesh like so many impetuous imps.

Unloved in a world of spite and greed, in a Godless, heartless Darwinian system sucking us all toward the grave, Van Dyke could get down in the chops with the existential jimjams. The very grandeur of the heavens tortured him:

The entire belt of the Milky Way is supposed to be moving as a mass through space. Wither? Whence the measureless energy that started or keeps such colossal bodies in motion? And where and what are we in this mighty scheme of things? Are we anything more than petty animalculae clinging to a cold discarded fragment of a sun? You turn over in your blankets and listen to the yap of a distant coyote. Along that Milky Way lies madness. (The Open Spaces 19)

That is, the big picture was horrible. Even the wonders revealed by science came with a massive, poisonous sting to the soul. All the better for the romantic aura, heightened by the delicious suffering of the writer, who occasionally leaps alive at beauty, like some muscle quivering at electric pricks, before he slumps back into his menopausal funk.

What, then, was left? In this bleak world in which we live, where was the succor? There were the pleasures of art—the greatest good of all in this horrid existence, maybe the only good, the only salve. Though here, too, there were features of Van Dyke's involvement that in the midst of pleasure kept rubbing him raw.

Appreciating beauty heightened his awareness of mass ugliness, for humanity preferred gewgaws to delicate joys. Proud of his Calvinistic background, his family heritage, and his powerful position in society as critic and academic, Van Dyke had a highly developed sense of superiority, harboring the notion that he was right and the rest of the world was wrong. The mass of people wanted quick thrills, movies, fast cars, and the tinsel of society columns. "The rushing world," he glowered toward the end of his life, "craves the novel and exotic, and in seeking to avoid the obvious it only too often falls into admiration of the merely bizarre" (*The Meadows* 125). As to art, the masses slavered over paintings that told stories, the easy sentiment of the distraught maiden wringing her hands under a weeping willow, not the keen joys wrested from a life of culture and refined contemplation. This further separated Van Dyke, leading him into additional storms. Damning "anything that is of popular interest" (*What Is Art?* 87), he railed against realism as "the lowest and most contemptible form of art" (*Principles of Art* 176).

Van Dyke's exclusive social circles shored up such ideas. Many of the wealthy disdained the masses as brutish and beyond help, witness, other than their poor tastes in art, their slums, bad manners, and laziness. This was the unwashed, unmovable herd, unwilling to be led by their betters. Consoling fellow art critic Kenyon Cox, worrying the realism issue yet again, Van Dyke snorted that people are so stupid they can't tell the difference between "nature and art." Summing up with a humph, Van Dyke dismissed the glutinous masses. With no doubt about his meaning, he smoked to Cox, "the public is a great ass of some booby" (Teague and Wild 108).

Hoodwinking such sorry sorts, too dense to understand his book anyway, was just about what they deserved. Instead, then, our greatest desert writer dedicates the pearl of his *The Desert* to wealthy art collector Andrew Carnegie and the small coterie of art lovers whose sophisticated tastes match the volume's finely drawn sensibilities. And Van Dyke knew, too, that as part of the cognoscenti they would harbor no mundane notions that art should reflect literal, scientific truth. Instead, joining in the joke, they'd ripple in mild amusement over his inaccuracies, appreciate them as part of his art. Urbanely complex connoisseurs, they knew the difference between nature and art, nodded over the slippery ploys of writers, and certainly understood the hint in *The Desert*, that "the reality is one thing, the appearance quite another" (109). The volume, they knew, was not meant as a lowbrow natural-history handbook but was reality transformed into a work of art between two covers. For instance, this luxuriantly exaggerated description of the moon:

After the clouds have all shifted into purples and the western sky has sunk into night, then up from the east the moon—the misshapen orange-hued desert moon. How large it looks! And how it warms the sky, and silvers the edges of the mountain peaks, and spreads its wide light across the sands! Up, up it rises, losing something of its orange and gaining something in symmetry. In a few hours it is high in the heavens and has a great aureole of color about it. Look at the ring for a moment and you will see all the spectrum colors arranged in order. Pale hues they are but they are all there. Rainbows by day and rainbows by night! (104–105)

What counted in Van Dyke's pages was not the real moon or the real desert but artistic impressions rendered through subtle gifts into prose (xi). *The Desert* is "truthful," then, not in terms of reality but in terms of art. It all made perfect sense.

In this, Van Dyke got the last laugh. He was well aware that the mass of people, following his own bent, often preferred fantasy to the literal truth, whether concerning nature or any other aspect of life. The difference was that sly Van Dyke knew art was a beautiful lie, while they didn't. In whatever heaven art critics spend eternity, he's likely still chuckling that the pacesetting book that teaches Americans to see their deserts in vivid colors, the volume most treasured by innocent desert lovers, was intended as an insult, an elevated scam. It would not be the last.

7

WILLIAM T.

HORNADAY

The Happy Travelers—

Part 2

Earlier, we saw Juan Nentvig, S.J., writing about his desert life in the eighteenth century. He describes two-headed eagles then moves on to a tarantula leaping out of the bushes to bite off the hoof of a galloping horse. Unlike aesthetician Van Dyke, his mind floating off on poetic musings while he glided across the arid spaces on a train, the good padre likely believed what he wrote to be fact. And lest we accuse Nentvig of softheaded gullibility, we should remind ourselves of his rigorous Jesuit training, of his impartial judgments in other matters, and of his skill as a geographer so accurate that his descriptions of the land remain convincing. For there were extenuating circumstances. Here he was, a learned man in a savage, crazed place, his brains bubbling with the heat, dealing with sly natives so intractable that he and a fellow missionary once barricaded themselves in a church and fought off their rebellious charges for two days. For all his pains, all his efforts over the years to civilize his rambunctious flock, now the priest suffered a head contusion. Thus bloodied, he escaped, just barely, dragging himself for five days, thirsty and torn, through the cactus, to the Spanish stronghold at Santa Ana. Such tortures, such daily fear and suffering to the very verge of death, can give a strange shape to one's perceptions.

There was a documentable progression, and one might think that over the centuries and decades, as the deserts became tamer, as technological civilization, symbolized by trains, school boards, and paved roads, spread ever more inexorably across the land, travelers' accounts would become less bizarre. That Cozzens' hilarious excesses would yield to the polite wit of Browne and in turn to ever more rational assessments as scientific knowledge of the area and safety in journeying across it grew. To some extent, this has been true. In the changing atmosphere, Cozzens was no longer believable. We now look upon his teetering peaks and exploits with Cochise as the literary high jinks of an era when public knowledge was not there to put the brakes on a writer's fancy, though to balance the picture in a world not always following logic, the more rational atmosphere also would have a counterpart, be paralleled by the florescence of appealing literary flimflams of a peculiarly modern sort.

Despite what one might think, the desert remained a strange place—continues to remain a strange place—though the quality of the strangeness was changing, even diverging into two main streams. On the one hand, things began happening there that, challenging two-headed eagles, became ever more impossible. The other developing strain concerned things that probably were explicable, though the wonder over them nonetheless prevailed.

Take this scene, for example. In 1907 a scientific expedition from New York City arrives by train in Tucson, gathers up its wagons and supplies, and heads out across cactus-studded Arizona to explore the famed but little-known Pinacate region, a desert within a desert, a great, isolated expanse of lava fields in northwestern Mexico. The excitement runs high over all the new species ahead that wait to be encountered, but the major, most puzzling surprise of all occurs a few days later as the group, threading its way through the briquette mountains, swings south to enter Mexico. Watering their animals at the little oasis of Quitobaquito, the scientists look up to behold, not a tarantula leaping out of the bushes to bite off the hoof of one of their horses, but coming out of a horizon in the middle of nowhere, five Japanese men in dark suits and city shoes approaching them across the sands.

William T. Hornaday

This, of course, was not a fantasy, not the city-bound indulging in wish-fulfillment, but a measurable, demonstrable fact. Unable to speak English, the dapper quintet accepts offers of food and tobacco, bows politely, then moves off over the desert. Whither, none of the scientists, scratching their heads as they watch them go, knows.

Whether for the willfully believing or for the hardheaded rationalist, the desert remained a reservoir of exotic possibilities. Part of this had to do with the expectations of travelers from a staid region eagerly seeing the unusual sights they desired, the sights they had borne with them for three thousand miles in their heads and by then felt almost obliged to see. After all, there's nothing innately unusual about a saguaro cactus or a lizard bleeding from the eyes for one who's seen such things from the day of birth. But part also was another psychological syndrome: the more rational society became, the more it yearned, like city slickers flocking to a circus, for a bizarre show. Whatever the impulse, the desert, by comparison to the populated, monochrome East, was so spacey, un-inhabited, and qualitatively different that it was turning into a play-ground where overdisciplined schoolboys could romp during the recess of their vacations.

Of this particular expedition, something of its tenor can be gathered from a glimpse at its makeup. Though the number in the group varied, picking up and dropping off members here and there along the line of its march, its core consisted of:

William T. Hornaday, leader of the expedition and director of the Bronx Zoo.

Dr. Daniel T. MacDougal, second in command; former assistant di-rector of the New York Botanical Garden and present head of the Desert Botanical Laboratory in Tucson.[1]

John McFarlane Phillips, a wealthy Pennsylvania banker, outdoors en-thusiast, and the group's photographer.

Godfrey Sykes, an engineer at the Desert Botanical Laboratory, who, his admirers came to believe, could fix anything.

Jeff Davis Milton, once a Texas Ranger and a renowned lawman.

Rube Daniels, a friend of Milton, married to an Indian woman, and a rough-and-ready frontiersman. At one point on the trip, he almost erupted into serious gunplay aimed at Dr. MacDougal. It is said that during one rowdy Christmas party Daniels threw at his desert ranch, his Indian guests nearly killed him.

Charlie Foster, the expedition's Mexican guide and packer. Foster nor-mally lived by smuggling Chinese aliens across the international border.

Frank Coles, another packer and desert guide of long-time experience.[2]

As can be seen from the list, the men break down into two groups. The well-educated and influential Easterners arrived in the desert, scan-ning the place with large eyes looking for excitements. The old desert rats, whose home this was, for whom survival on the desert was a matter of habit, no doubt took the trip with certain equanimity, as a paid vaca-tion during which they did their bit for science by doing what they had most of their lives, and this leads us to a larger point.

For the most part, the two groups got along well on the month-long excursion: the Easterners scurrying about collecting plants and animals for museums back home; the old hands making sure no one strayed too far as they kept the stock in line and led the way from one critical water-hole to another. Especially early on, before the going got tough, a holi-day atmosphere prevailed, with antics by day and good stories at night around the campfire. This provides Hornaday, chronicler of the trip in

Camp-Fires on Desert and Lava, the opportunity for lighthearted vignettes. On the first day out of Tucson, the men spy an anomaly coming toward them, the first of many they'll see. In this case, it's a wagon with two Indians hauling a load of watermelons. Getting to know thirst on that first day, the expeditioners swing into action and hail the Papagos:

> *The unfortunate red men took an inventory of our fighting strength, and made low sounds of despair.*
> *"Hello, there! Stop immediately!" was our command.*
> *The Indians drove out on the south side of the road, stopped their team in échelon, and prepared to sell their lives as dearly as possible.*
> *"Sell us some of those melons, or die!" shouted our war-chief; and the party held its fire, for a reply.*
> *"Two bits! Muy dulce! (very sweet), said one of the Papagoes, as plain as print.*
> *His life was saved. There was a rush to the end-gate of his wagon, and while four men selected melons, the Man-with-Silver dug up coin.*

There follows, Hornaday gibes his fellows, "a wild, disgraceful orgie [*sic*]" of feasting (29).

Yet in the midst of the general good cheer, few pondered what a delicate pivot they were turning through in the history of the desert. This is illustrated by the two groups themselves. The desert was still a wild enough place, still bearing the tang of uprisings in Mexico and memories of Apache raids, stories the frontiersmen passed on from their own experiences while the mesquite logs blazed against the satin blackness. Yet while Browne and Cozzens, surrounded by real Apaches, had to keep up their guard, the expedition had little to worry about beyond loosening wagon wheels and the camp dogs playing games of chase with coyotes across the men's sleeping bags long into night. The members, not quite yet tourists, had the delicate best of two worlds. While rumors of dangers spiced the trip, the desert then was a place where you'd want to travel about armed, though chances were good that you'd not have to draw a gun in anger. While reveling in the desert's wildness as their little train picked its way over the unsettled sweeps and up through the low mountain passes, the Easterners also complained that the forking trails were not marked by signposts, and hauling up the bloated carcasses of snakes and rabbits in their buckets at isolated wells, they grumbled that the county government should be more fastidious in maintaining a suitable water supply for wayfarers. Manly would have hooted at that.

But the grousing was rare and mild. The Easterners, especially, were in a festive mood, thrilled to learn about an unmapped corner of the world, buoyed by the joy, as Van Dyke put it in *The Desert*, of "riding into the unexpected" as they explored an unknown land (198). They glowed with the prospect of visiting occasional hamlets of Indians and Mexicans huddled timelessly beside oases and of bagging the fabled desert bighorn sheep. It should not be supposed, however, that this was a brash bunch of ugly Americans, shooting up the countryside with their rifles and leaving the natives shocked at the crude strangers. Rather, these were gentlemen in the days when that word implied a code of behavior. They also were scientists intrigued by the newness around them, and they were conservationists, deeply concerned that the Mexican government was allowing a fragile desert heritage to slip away. Through their expedition and strong political influence, they hoped to put a stop to this, especially to the slaughter of the area's unique treasure, the bighorn sheep, declining before the new, long-range rifles being fired by Indians, Mexicans, and whites alike.

Despite the atmosphere of happy play, of men working at what they enjoyed most, the leaders laid down strict rules, and they were willing to enforce them. Significantly, the one nasty incident over this was caused by a former frontiersman, Rube Daniels, of the drunken Christmas party, who had, uninvited, inserted himself into the expedition. When told that his indiscriminate killing was not acceptable, the libertine grew hot and declared, "I'm going to shoot at anything I please—any time." Then the confrontation grew hotter as Daniels' hand slipped toward his six-shooter. Fortunately, the three Easterners handled the touchy situation well, gathering around Daniels and standing their ground, until, outnumbered, the bully scuffed off cursing, saddled his horse, and rode away (171–174).

As he left, he likely was surprised at the toughness of the threesome. Though new to the country, they hardly were tenderfeet. They'd had enormous experience far outmatching his in trekking through wild country and keeping men in line. One of them particularly, a man of clipped beard and flashing eye, was known in jungle and city precincts for fixing a man with a fiery gaze and piercing his heart until it quivered.

This was the formidable William T. Hornaday, a man who could make presidents gnash their teeth and secretaries of the interior squeal for mercy. For Hornaday, such a figure as Daniels was but small beer.

The man who would become a major force in conservation was born to humble circumstances, on a farm in Indiana.[3] In 1858, when he was four years old, the family moved to pioneer Iowa. There, agape at huge flocks of passenger pigeons darkening the skies, young William became enthralled by wildlife. Orphaned at fifteen, the boy managed to attend

Iowa State Agricultural College. There he found Audubon's great works and decided to become a naturalist himself. Self-taught in taxidermy, he moved on without graduating to Rochester, New York, to work for a natural-history museum.

That launched his career. The proprietor sent his eager assistant to South America, India, and Borneo, where he waded through swamps, braved heat, cold, and disease to bring back unusual animal specimens. With the country awakening to its wildlife heritage and his reputation growing in a new field, Hornaday made a stop in his career at the United States National Museum in Washington, D.C. After squabbling with his bosses over plans for constructing a zoological park, he moved on to New York City, where he became the first director of its Zoological Park. In this regard, his great accomplishment was building the innovative Bronx Zoo. At the time, animals stood stuffed and forlorn, without context in museums, or they languished alive in barren steel cages. Hornaday took a radical approach. Creating the first of the nation's great lifelike exhibits, he mounted his subjects in three-dimensional replicas of their natural habitats and, freeing living animals from their bars, let them roam, on display in reproduced natural surroundings. At the time of his trip to Arizona and Mexico, middle-aged Hornaday was on the ascending curve of his fame.

That renown, however, sprang from far more than success in what Hornaday called museology. Being a trail-blazing professional in the field wasn't good enough for him. Studying wildlife consisted of more than presenting subjects to be gawked at by idle curiosity seekers; animals were a vital, lovely part of God's Creation, a precious treasure, and for that they demanded preservation. In a fury of activity, Hornaday became a campaigner for the cause. Inspiring a crash program to save the American bison, then almost extinct, he expanded his efforts, lobbying for game-protection laws and game preserves. He raised huge amounts to support his own Permanent Wild Life Protection Fund. So successful was he in such efforts, stirring especially the wealthy and influential to their better instincts, that he received the blessings of President Theodore Roosevelt and had the likes of Andrew Carnegie and Henry Ford reaching for their checkbooks.

Yet that is only half the story. As it happened, his Permanent Wild Life Protection Fund had but one active member: William T. Hornaday. Why would it need more? After all, he raised the money, and he knew best how to spend it. Anyone who disagreed with him in this righteous work deserved to be pursued, publicly flayed, and silenced. In this, given his effectiveness, he had many supporters, but as a zealot not always under control in his charges for various causes, lashing out at Jews, Germans, and consumers of alcohol, he could make cooler heads uncomfortable. In this respect, the titles of such books as *Free Rum on the Congo, and What It Is Doing There* and *Thirty Years War for Wild Life: Gains and Losses in the Thankless Task* give a measure of the combined conservationist and teetotaler. William T. Hornaday loved a row. In three words, Carmony and Brown best sum him up: he was "bombastic and combative" (xxxviii). Despite Hornaday's successes, which nobody denied, many a conservationist breathed easier after his death in 1937.

The remarkable thing is how reasonable and calm he could be at times, how talented and cheerful. His account of the trip into Mexico, *Camp-Fires on Desert and Lava*, seems written by a perfectly happy man at ease with his world. This owed much to the festive atmosphere, the writer's escape from the fraying daily chores back East, and the pleasurable remembrance of adventures with men who shared his enthusiasms for the outdoors. For a month, combative Hornaday was free from the daily hassles of administrative work, and, possessing the wisdom to forget what ired him, he made the most of the release he found in the isolated Pinacate Desert.

He also had the wisdom to seize the opportunity of the book, that if the land is exotic to him, a seasoned traveler, it will thrill his readers all the more. It's the character of the land that is always before him. Mexico itself, Latin, Catholic, a place of bandits in serapes and sombreros, or so it was pictured by the popular imagination in the United States, lent its own appeal, gave him a stage full of color. Beyond that, it's the character of the goal before him that pulls the reader on as the wagons creak across the desert toward five hundred square miles of black rock and sand, weirdly dotted by the cones of ancient volcanoes, all but uninhabited and so far from civilization that few Mexicans even knew what lay out there. Such is Hornaday's literary lure, one containing several goals. Collecting and discovery leaven the prose with almost daily surprises about strange plants and animals. But what keeps the men and readers looking ever forward, daily stretching their vision, is the dark mass of Pinacate Peak, rearing ahead out of that wasteland. Protected from invaders by jumbles of knife-edged lava fields and sloughs of sand, the ghostly presence almost dares the newcomers to figure out how to reach it. The outcome is by no means certain. The explorers circle the looming mass, double back, scatter, find one another. Then, a lucky break. They finally stumble across the rumored waterhole that in the nearly waterless place provides the essential liquid for the climb to the top and the success of the expedition—for the release of suspense and the satisfying aftermath. This is the book's major scheme.

The story is further flavored by the men reacting to the land and to each other as they travel, by the writer's intuitive sense of when and how to break the pace, interleaving natural-history talks with anecdotes about the travelers and moments of suspense. We've already seen the brash Rube Daniels verging on gunplay out there in the middle of nowhere. Hornaday also shows the sly bighorn sheep, acrobats on their high crags craftily leading on their frustrated pursuers. Not far from Tucson, the expedition's leader voices his disappointment at the Papago Indians. Peering into a house, he sees women's "shoes with high French heels; corsets out of commission; tin cans, and broken kerosene lamps." Is this what he traveled thousands of miles to see—more of what he left behind? Pretty soon, he quips, there'll be Indians riding around on bicycles (63). "If an Indian is not picturesque," he says, mocking his own tourist expectations, "why is he?" (67).

That leads us to suspect that we *will* see "picturesque" Indians, but Hornaday is toying with us. We don't because there were none of the headfeathers-and-striped-blanket kind living in that country. For them, Hornaday substitutes unexpected color from a land that, although appearing vacant, is full of surprises, as seen from the appearance of the five Japanese. In the crude little Mexican burg of Sonoyta, so far beyond civilization that it has no store or mail delivery, Hornaday takes us to the home of Señor Traino Quiroz, a dignified person with "a low, musical voice and the manners of a Castilian gentleman" (88). And what does the scientist find in the unusual man's back yard?—of all things, a botanical garden! (92). Take that for irony.

Varying the flavor of irony, Hornaday takes us into the labyrinths of Mexican politics. Given the isolation of the country, the expedition quite likely could have slipped across the border, explored to its heart's content, then returned, with the authorities none the wiser because there were no Mexican authorities in that part of the desert. However, trying to obey the letter of international law, months before the trip started, farsighted Dr. MacDougal made arrangements with Mexico City to exempt the expedition of astronomical tariffs for the temporary import of the horses, wagons, and other items in the little safari. Well, and good. The authorization was slow in coming, but Mexico has always shown its enlightenment by treating scientific endeavors favorably, and after a last-minute flurry of telegrams, all the details are settled and the papers are in order. Or so MacDougal thinks.

To make everything official, the physical steps in this international dance need to be walked through. Since where they cross into Mexico so rarely sees travelers that it has not even the thought of a customhouse, a lieutenant with a squad of soldiers travels a hundred and twenty miles across the desert to greet the peripatetic Americans. Brotherhood prevails at the border, with little speeches given from each side. Then, embarrassment casts its shadow. When the two parties go through the formality of checking the list of items to be allowed free of duty, they find that some bureaucratic blockhead has left out the most expensive items—the wagons.

By this time, so much to-do has been made, with the crossing turned into a diplomatic ceremony such as the desert has never seen while a handful of locals gawks on, that Lieutenant Medina can't simply wink and wave the Americans through. Now, the very picture of a wet rooster, he gives another speech:

> *"It is perfectly plain," he said with great fervour, "that my government desires that your expedition shall be admitted and facilitated; and of course you need your wagons in order to proceed. But my authority is found only in this official list of what is to be admitted free of duty! I dare not assume the responsibility of exceeding my instructions, much as I would like to do so." (96–97)*

For a while, it looks as if all is lost, that the wagons will have to turn around and crawl back to Tucson under a cloud of defeat. Then the savvy Jeff Milton, an old hand on the frontier, whispers into the ear of Dr. MacDougal, who makes another elaborately polite speech, and at that, with the swift exchange of nine dollars, the wagons move on, with no face lost on either side.

Interesting as such details are in themselves, they are but items in what amounts to a long prologue, part of a narrowing plan to funnel readers through the constricted, bureaucratic glitch at the border and out into a different awareness widening beyond. Hornaday began his account while speeding across Kansas on the Golden State Limited. Here, he nodded at the thousands of new farms dotting the land, each windmill "a monument to agricultural endeavour" (7). So the story continues across Oklahoma as prosperity moves west and Hornaday wishes "the home-makers God-speed" on what was but a few years ago a wild plain (8).

In New Mexico, the character of the land changes. Ranches begin replacing farms, and adobes, the wooden houses. He sees "naked and rocky buttes" underlined by "melancholy wastes of low mesquite and greasewood brush" (8). That is, he has struck the arid region where lack of water challenges civilization. Still, there is hope, and Hornaday claps his hands for the orchards and alfalfa fields, the blessings of irrigation brought to this "dull and hopeless" region (10). As for the rest, the desert is "dreary" (12) and "sadly desolate" (11).

One might think that such a low opinion of the desert and such high praise for the overlay of civilization is at cross-purposes in a book whose future chapters will celebrate adventure in the desert and revel in escape from well-ordered, technological society. Given the prevailing double standard of the time, however, the open spaces seemed so large that even enthusiastic irrigationists couldn't imagine a desert completely paved with alfalfa fields. Rather, in this best of both worlds, the attitude reflected in *Camp-Fires on Desert and Lava* is that we can have both, both civilized progress and the wild wonders always lying beyond.

Indeed, technology fades fast behind Hornaday when he leaves the railroad and sets out on horseback, riding beside the two wagons as he leads his party southwest into the unknown. After Tucson, the land becomes drier and drier, the Indian villages fewer and fewer, the waterholes scarcer, the plants, with their branching cacti looking like organ pipes, ever more bizarre. The incident at the border with embarrassed Lieutenant Medina is the last vestige of order and government, and at that, in this wild place of abandoned graves of travelers murdered by Apaches, where streams disappear into the sands, the meeting is a farce, a comic opera. With the incident at Sonoyta, Hornaday passes through a physical and psychic looking glass. Far behind in Tucson are the signs of progress representing the best, if the somewhat boring best, of America; ahead, as the title of his chapter "Trailing into a New World" implies, lies a twilight zone (23). It is here that the unpleasantness with Daniels occurs, a place where there is no law, a place where weirdness, danger, and beauty abound for these boys at play in a region so remote that it will always remain a never-never land. So we have reached the focus of the book, a vast land of wonders.

On the other hand, this presents a difficulty for Hornaday. He is not aesthetician John C. Van Dyke manipulating the desert into a dream landscape and in the process blithely trampling roughshod over the facts of the ocotillo, coyotes, and other features of the natural world before him. Neither is he a Samuel Woodworth Cozzens, writing still earlier and taking advantage of his readers' ignorance to feed them exciting phantasmagoric scenes of sacred flames burning in Indian caves, impossible derring-do with Cochise, and other such literary stunts. Instead, William T. Hornaday, one of the most widely read authorities on the outdoors of the day, is a scientist, has a reputation to protect in the writing territory he's carved out for himself. The director of the New York Zoological Park is addressing an intelligent, well-educated audience, which in the brief seven years since Van Dyke's *The Desert*, from books and articles piling off the presses about the subject, has learned too much about the Southwest to be hornswoggled. Furthermore, Hornaday's financial supporters include Andrew Carnegie, Henry Ford, and other men of cunning and sharp acumen. They might wink forgivingly at the antics of Van Dyke, a zealot for beauty with visions swirling in his poetic head, but Hornaday's backers would brook no such nonsense from the head of the Bronx Zoo, whose job it was to disseminate the facts of nature, then lobby in its favor. Hornaday's problem, then, is how to write a realistic account while also keeping the pulses of his readers fluttering.

As already seen, he does this by highlighting the most dramatic events, pausing for a somber moment by the grave of the Mexican mail rider slain by Apaches and recording the very conversation at the parlay resolving the international impasse with Lieutenant Medina. The events of the journey are interesting in themselves, awaiting Hornaday's keen journalistic eye to record them, and he doesn't pass up the good moments Fate provides. In a similar fashion, the land itself offers occasion after occasion to clothe reality in wonder. Interested in the natural history of this far-off place so different from the docile countryside of the well-watered East, readers pause with Hornaday to marvel at the ocotillo, a rangy plant looking like an instrument of the devil with its long, thorn-studded wands, that suddenly bursts into a mass of crimson flowers when the rains come (138). On such matters, Hornaday's descriptions may be lush, but they also are accurate; and when in doubt about his facts, he further shores up his authority by conferring with the equally respected Dr. MacDougal.[4]

His book is written "to show the Reader a strange, weird, and also beautiful country" (xliv) with "boundless space, the glorious sunshine, the balmy air, [and] the cleanness of the face of Nature" (xlv). These are perceived qualities, not aspects of an identifiable character in the sense that Van Dyke makes nature a beatific but fatal strumpet. Realist Hornaday couldn't, and probably would not have wanted to, go that far. It would have opened him to the reputation-wrecking charge that all scientists wish to avoid, that of the sentimentalist and the anthropomorphist. Yet if he can't make nature into a being, a foil off which he can play, he nonetheless finds a valid way to keep up the energy level of his pages. Rather than do the deadly thing and ascribe emotions to nature, he shows men reacting to its presence.

The goal of the trip, scaling Pinacate Peak, the dark cinder cone always looming before them, becomes far more frustrating than expected, a damper on the high spirits of the men. In that searing country of "piled-up hellfire" (230), of splintered, knife-edged lava alternating with miles of sand dunes, the water keeps running short; and the wagons, prone to miring and breaking down, are forced to take circuitous routes as they follow the most promising paths through the shadeless wilderness. The problem of the peak, then, is twofold: how to find a waterhole close enough to provide a water supply for the final assault and how to maneuver the wagons close enough to make a base camp. For days, the party circles the peak, at one point making a loop north back into the United States to fill the water barrels at Quitobaquito. As time runs short for the venturers and it looks as if they'll circumnavigate the tantalizing cone without reaching it, Hornaday moans that they're "as far as ever from Pinacate!" (163). The emotion is justified; in those circumstances even scientists are allowed to vent their spleen at the unyielding problem.

And they're allowed, too, to show their soaring spirits when at last they find a pass, slip through it, and in ideally cool weather behold the eminence before them, almost in hand:

The morning after our night in the neck of MacDougal Pass dawned gloriously across the dark-brown lava landscape and found every member of the party keenly expectant of interesting events. The morning temperature was 42 degrees and the humidity 80 degrees [sic]. It was a great relief that at last we were to cease swinging around Pinacate, at a radius of about fifteen miles, and go directly toward it. (165)

The climb, it turns out, is steep but easy enough, yet it hardly is disappointing. The slopes are all but crawling with bighorn sheep, a marvel the perspiring men trek through bug-eyed. Once they gain the top, they turn the collected tension of the previous days into "wild revels" (267). So great is the release that Godfrey Sykes, a usually reserved Englishman, stands on his head and wiggles his legs in the air in imitation of the beetle after which the peak is named (268).

Dramatically appropriate, the exuberance comes toward the end of *Camp-Fires on Desert and Lava*. However, Hornaday is too wise to stop there. A deft manipulator of emotions, he completes the cycle with a satisfying, if bittersweet, aftermath. In good time, the expedition strikes north to the railroad station in the little Arizona town of Gila Bend. It happens to be Hornaday's birthday, and to his surprise the men spring a party for him with a feast "loaded down to the guard-rails" with roast chicken, pickles, peas, and apple pie, a splendid repast for the hot, sweaty, and unshaven men after the trail fare of the last few weeks, as well as a psychic reentry point, with the book bringing us back into the world of advancing technology (353).

As Hornaday and his men clomp aboard the train, he has shown the otherliness of the world left behind, one borne away so bright in his mind that it leaves him "limp and spiritless" back in civilization; and it takes him days before he feels himself again (354). The implication being that he (along with his readers) never will be quite the same as time and again over the years he goes back to that strange world still glowing in his head.

There are more gripping accounts of experiences on the desert. Not many passages anywhere can compare with Cabeza de Vaca's hair-raising desert monster, Evil Thing, racing around at night with his firebrand and slashing people's arms. And few writers etch such a lasting picture on their readers' imaginations as does Van Dyke with his rocky shaft of Baboquivari burning like hot iron in a sunset, then glowing from within like a clouded garnet as darkness settles around it. Yet pyrotechnics aside, few works can compare with Hornaday's *Camp-Fires on Desert and Lava* as a gracious, reliable, and informative tour of the desert. First of all, as a scientist, Hornaday came to the region with enthusiasm for nature and with an in-depth knowledge of plants and animals on which he could draw to understand the new phenomena before him. And where his own background failed him, he could consult the ever-eager and experienced Dr. MacDougal or Jack-of-all-trades Godfrey Sykes. This was no Van Dyke wheedling that all he could do was give his impression.

Furthermore, Hornaday anchors his professionalism and the ready resources of his colleagues in a daily account of his experiences based on journals written in the field. When a wheel comes off a wagon, Hornaday tells us precisely how handyman Sykes leaps to the task, solves the problem, and has the wagon moving on again in good time. This is no free-floating series of visionary experiences but a rounded account, with stories about human conflicts, difficulties with stock, and the ever-critical search for water alternating with seriousness and humor, and thus giving readers as sure an account as might be found of what it was like to "be there" in the desert early in this century.

Another story, however, lies behind this one. No doubt, Hornaday's prose heightened sympathy for preserving the desert, but he was only secondarily a writer. An avid hunter as well as an avid preservationist, he was primarily an activist, and he didn't simply send forth a book and sit back resting on his literary oars. Using his political power, he dogged the government of Mexico until it agreed to protect the Pinacate's wildlife from the unrestrained riflemen he knew would soon follow in his tracks (345–346).

That brings up a larger desert issue, one having far more impact on the region than mere lovely writing about it. It would be pleasant to think that the likes of Van Dyke and Austin, winsome as their prose is, did yeoman's work in preserving the deserts they claimed to love. Unfortunately, this is not true. We can give thanks for many of the great desert preserves we now treasure, such as the Grand Canyon, Death Valley, and Joshua Tree, not to the efforts of full-time writers but to the insistent, years-long, grueling labors of lobbying by Theodore Roosevelt, Charles Sheldon, Aldo Leopold, and other hunter-naturalists. Such men often were writers, but their first love was the arid lands, not their own prose.[5]

JOHN WESLEY

POWELL AND

WILLIAM E. SMYTHE

God Smiles on the Irrigationists

"The Conquest of Arid America." Put into a slogan, the proposed national goal would elicit guffaws today. In a time when people avidly visit national parks to enjoy their desert heritage and just about everyone from schoolchildren to suburban developers at least mouths sensitivity to nature, the very idea of wiping out the treasured expanses of lava and cactus seems the suggestion of a raving madman.

And yet a hundred years ago, after some sidelong glances, the notion swept the country until the words became a catch phrase uttered by the hope-filled masses, even a shibboleth to measure patriotism. A utilitarian and expanding nation had stopped and scratched its chin, puzzled before deserts, and wondered what they were doing there, as if God had made a mistake in creating these useless places. Then it discovered that Manly was wrong. The arid sweeps were not good-for-nothing wastelands. And Van Dyke was wrong, too. Neither were they simply beautiful places for the privileged where wealthy patients suffering from respiratory problems could breathe freely as they beheld the sunset hues on bare mountains shift through delicate progressions of tinctures. As the scales fell from people's eyes, they saw that He knew all along what He was doing. The deserts were put there as a special favor to a chosen people, not only to enrich humanity but to save the very nation that once scorned them, and beyond that, to bring Americans, now glowing and united as they walked along the path of their new mission, closer to God Himself.

So the nation had a new vision, a new religion, the Religion of the Desert.

Arriving at that happy state involved a conglutinate complex of ideas, some old and some new, some going back through the centuries to our ancient roots, while others at first seemed radical. To the Greeks peering with fear and wonder out into the Atlantic through the foggy Gates of Hercules, what they saw out there was tinged with the visionary, and so the stories multiplied through the ages. Out there to the west lay Isles of Flowers and Isles of Angels, perhaps even the New Jerusalem, the Heavenly Kingdom on Earth. It was, then, with good reason that when a heady Columbus skimmed past the mouth of Venezuela's Orinoco, he declared that up that river "I believe in my soul . . . the earthly paradise is situated." [1]

So it was that, compelled by a hopeful drive, Europeans swarmed across the Atlantic to the New World in anticipation of fulfilling the dreams already swirling in their heads. Often the searchers were disappointed, as the cities they saw shining ahead turned out not to be gold but made of mud. But often, too, fantasy was stronger than reality. There were just enough Grand Discoveries—the flabbergasting Halls of Montezuma dripping with jewels and the bright news of gold in California—to keep the nation moving westward in a high state of anticipation. Faith in science also had a great deal to do with the fervor. Married to hope, the two became a winning couple. As summed up by the seventeenth-century English philosopher Francis Bacon, science and optimism working together could do just about anything, delivering man from his old, outmoded ways into a world of limitless possibilities. And so the nation, not without suffering the drag of old superstitions, arrived on the desert.

The changes of history, however, are embedded in the particular and often in ways that give little hint of their outcome. Most immediately, in the spring of 1869, ten men push back from the table at Ah Chug's little eatery in the frontier town of Green River, Wyoming, and troop down beyond the railroad bridge where four rowboats bob in the gentle current. With little ceremony, they throw off the ropes and pull out into the main channel, wave their hats at a few curious bystanders, and disappear around a bend.

The last great exploration in the continental United States has just begun. However, it didn't begin auspiciously. The leader, John Wesley Powell, is an amateur scientist, a self-taught, former farmboy, and now a professor of geology at an obscure college in Illinois.[2] Only five feet six, he's also missing an arm, smashed by a minnie ball in the battle of Shiloh Church. What supplies he has were begged from friends and private institutions. Worse than what little the men have is what they face. They are about to enter the unexplored bowels of the Grand Canyon, a venture from which no man has been known to return. Some of the idlers trudging back up the bank to town are shaking their heads. The Eastern-

John Wesley Powell & William E. Smythe

ers are crackpots. They face roaring waterfalls higher than Niagara, walls so sheer there will be no place to land the boats, and mammoth cauldrons that eat boats and spit out splinters. The fools might just as well be casting off into hell.

Beyond the momentary tongue clucking of Green River's citizens, hardly anyone cares or even knows about the expedition. When the men die in that raging hole of nature, they'll die unknown.

After weeks go by, a man named John Risdon appears back in civilization. Wracked by grief, he weeps when he tells his story to reporters—how, leaving the explorers to go hunt, he watched helplessly from a height as hundreds of feet below Powell and his brave men sped into a maelstrom, were ground up in its fury, and utterly lost. He himself is the sole survivor of the expedition.

Then, despite the tragedy, at the close of August, Powell and his little expedition come shooting out the other end of the earth's Great Chasm—victorious![3]

Risdon was a fraud. But a fortunate one for Powell. Moved by Risdon's morbid tale, the nation has taken fire from his accounts published in dailies across the country. Now the telegraph wires sing with the astonishing news. Powell is alive! The newspapers go wild.

The man with the missing arm has become an instant celebrity.

That fact would have a huge impact on the future of deserts. Unknown as he was, the professor had a vision, and as a practical man he seized his new fame in a grand attempt to change America. To do this, he realized two things: He would need the power of the government behind him, and to effect this he would need popular support. His *Exploration of the Colorado River of the West* is one of America's great exploration accounts, at once accurate and dramatic. As page after page turns, Powell sweeps his readers along as the lonely men, at times doubting they'll ever return, speed irrevocably into nature's boiling maws before them.[4]

For instance, this masterful engagement of the reader with the leader's psychological churning over the difficulties ahead. As each day civilization slips farther behind and the canyon walls close tighter behind them, the amateur explorers begin sampling hardships from dwindling food supplies and boats overturned in icy rapids. Such trials they know will become worse the deeper in they go. Then, down in that gloomy place they reach the point of no return:

We are now ready to start on our way down the Great Unknown. Our boats, tied to a common stake, are chafing each other, as they are tossed by the fretful river. They ride high and buoyant, for their loads are lighter than we could desire. We have but a month's rations remaining. The flour has been resifted through the mosquito net sieve; the spoiled bacon has been dried, and the worst of it boiled. . . .

We have an unknown distance yet to run; an unknown river yet to explore. What falls there are, we know not; what rocks beset the channel, we know not; what walls rise over the river, we know not. Ah, well! we may conjecture many things. The men talk as cheerfully as ever; jests are bandied about freely this morning; but to me the cheer is somber and the jests are ghastly. (80)

The moving prose and the profound heroism of the venture sent high voltage surging through the country, and Powell used the electric fame to his advantage. Combining it with growing friendships with scientists and members of Congress, Powell obtained funding for further explorations of the West. He served as head of the Bureau of Ethnology in the Smithsonian Institution and convinced Congress to establish the U.S. Geological Survey, of which he soon became the chief officer.

All this, not in the spirit of the power-grabbing Washington hustler but to gain knowledge of the West. Powell knew two great truths. First, the West was an arid place. Second, the nation was badly botching western settlement because people refused to recognize that overriding fact. Believing the myth that rain follows the plow and similar nonsense, farmers rushed westward from the greenery of the East only to find that the fable of the West's abundance existed mostly in their dreams. Time and again they failed, by the thousands, by the tens of thousands. So much so that newcomers crossing the plains often stopped bewildered as their predecessors passed them going in the opposite direction. Now battered and broken, returning in ghostly, dispirited wagon trains, in bitter mockery some of them had nailed banners to their rickety vehicles: IN GOD WE TRUSTED, IN THE WEST WE BUSTED.

Yet growing ever more colorful over the centuries, the myth of abundance became so powerful that a public figure who questioned its truth was damned as anti-American. Such can be the power of fantasy over reality.

Powell, however, was a brave man. He had an agenda, as we'd say today, and he put it to work three years after gaining widespread fame with his *Exploration.* Showing the results of his further studies in the West, he handed Congress his *Report on the Lands of the Arid Region.* An eminently reasoned volume with few of the literary flourishes of his first book, it was meant to give the country's leaders a sobering jolt with a realistic assessment of the West. Instead, the book fell like a bombshell in the middle of Washington, D.C. Settlement was failing, said Powell steadily, rationally, and clearly, because what worked in the well-watered East wouldn't work in the water-short West. For instance, the Homestead Act of 1862 granted 160 acres to each westering family. That might be ample land in Kentucky, but out where a hundred acres or more might be necessary to support a single cow, it was an absurdity. Instead, Powell argued that each rancher should receive at least 2,560 acres and that each homestead should be guaranteed access to water. Noting that constructing large irrigation works was quite beyond the means of individuals, he recommended settlement by colonies, whose members could pool their money and labor together on community projects. And he argued here and elsewhere that large corporations were stripping the land of its timber and minerals, making huge fortunes while leaving the land blighted for generations to come. Average Americans were being robbed of their heritage.

This was blasphemy. Rather than thank Powell for one of the most perceptive books ever written about the West, members of Congress all but hooted him out of their halls. Badly stung by the arid-lands volume, the exploiters and their friends—who were building mansions in fashionable Newport with profits shipped east across the Mississippi—went on the attack, accusing Powell of being everything from a quack to a socialist. Unfortunately, they were joined in hurling brickbats by well-meaning congressmen who'd never seen the West but who knew as an article of faith that it was a natural garden. As a result, although Powell battled through the years, his enemies progressively cut his appropriations, until, realizing he was being rendered ineffective as a reformer and government scientist, he resigned.

Wallace Stegner sums up the accomplishments of the man hounded out of government by an irate Congress. Not only did this farsighted public servant add new names to the map and tell the West about itself:

Before he was through, he added whole new branches to science, revitalized others, and created federal bureaus dedicated to practicing them in the public interest. He was the man who began and carried part way to completion the systematic mapping of the nation. He developed a comprehensive knowledge of western resources . . . , the irreplaceable resources upon which a continuing society in the West would have to be built. To conserve these resources from the wastage, folly, and graft that were already threatening them, he conceived what he called the "general plan" of governmental control. . . . What he proposed was rendered absolutely essential by the nature of western terrain and western climate . . . (Introduction xiii–xiv)

Yet despite the litany, hardly matched before or since in its vision and boldness, "wastage, folly, and graft," along with the appealing myths of the West, won out. Powell was pushed aside, and what all his accomplishments pointed to, reform of the nation's relationship to the earth, fell through. When John Wesley Powell died in 1902 at the age of sixty-eight, he looked like a failure.

Such might have been the judgment of history except that, in the very year that Powell published his arid lands volume, a seventeen-year-old boy from Worcester, Massachusetts, became a journalist. For some years, William E. Smythe, the son of a shoe manufacturer and a youngster with deep concerns for social problems, floundered, moving from one newspaper to another until he reached Omaha, Nebraska.[5] As it happened, Powell had been only an apparent failure, the pioneer who is bloodied while breaking a trail, for Smythe the young idealist arrived in the offices of the *Omaha Bee* in 1890. It was the year of a severe drought in the West; and not only would that lead the youth to take up where Powell had left off, he would do it with doubled verve, rocketing himself into the leadership of a movement that soared into nothing less than the Religion of the Desert.

Along with other plains states, Nebraska had flourished during wet years that coincided with early settlement. Then, its deep, dark, loamy soil had yielded astounding wheat bounties. On the margin of the arid Western lands, Nebraska was a place where rainfall could be unpredictably skittish. Only a few inches difference from one year to the next could spell disaster for farmers. With the area experiencing a dry cycle, day after day Smythe joined his worried friends in bib overalls. Each morning they watched as the huge sun rose to sail through the brassy skies. Hour after hour, the crops drooped ever more toward the friable earth. Neither prayers nor cannons fired at random moved the heavens.

Why, this was silly, thought Smythe. Running down from the distant Rocky Mountains, water flowed all around the state, with the Missouri, the longest river in the United States, forming part of Nebraska's northern boundary. Yet all that water flowed through the state unused. Wandering in New Mexico, an even drier state, Smythe had seen a similar problem, but one handled successfully. There, for centuries Hispanic and Indian farmers had tapped the rivers, running water into their fields and growing fine crops of fruits and vegetables regardless of an endlessly blazing sun. Why not do something similar here? The young reporter approached his boss with the idea. The editor, however, was cautious. The concept of irrigation was not unknown to the nation, but it was thought a method used only in lands deemed barren. So strong was the myth of abundance that to admit the need might sound libelous and offend the state's boosters. Still, Smythe persisted, and the editor finally agreed that the youth might write a series of articles about irrigation. If, that is, they appeared under Smythe's signature, thus deflecting criticism from the editor should tempers flare in response.

In this, Smythe was fortunate. By the time his articles appeared, the drought was so severe that desperate farmers were open to just about any suggestion that might rescue them. And Smythe's, radical as it was, made excellent sense. With their own eyes, the farmers, a conservative lot, could see the water in rivers running past them, going to waste. Within months the state was abuzz with Smythe's new possibility of salvation. Irrigation would save us! On top of that, Smythe discovered new and valuable talents within himself. A sincere, well-spoken, and fair man, he had the organizer's skills to smooth ruffled personalities and get men with varied notions to cooperate in a common cause. As a result of his articles, and now backed by a surge of popular interest across the seared West, he led his enthusiasts to an irrigation congress held at Salt Lake City in 1891.

Subsequent years led to larger conventions in Los Angeles, Denver, and in other Western cities, growing still larger and now attended by representatives from as far away as Russia and Peru. Whether men drive history, or history drives men, can be a question of endless debate. Certainly, nationwide sympathy for farmers and for the irrigation idea in particular had precedents, as seen in New Mexico and in men like Powell and as illustrated by a little-noticed irrigation convention held in Denver in 1873.

Furthermore, the concept of cooperative farm communities went far back in America. Beginning with the Pilgrim Fathers, much of the Colonies was settled by groups working together. More forcefully, seventeenth-century religious sects arriving from Europe strove to create ideal communities in the wilderness and there live in harmony with God, and, more difficultly, with each other. Added to this, in the developing agricultural nation, the farmer took on a near sacred status as the nation's best hope as, heroically beating back wild nature, he replaced swamps and tangles of trees with an expanding progress of civilized homesteads. Comparing the plow to the magician's wand, none other than Thomas Jefferson declared, "Those who labour in the earth are the chosen people of God" (290). Concerning Smythe's particular spin on the notion that the nation began to hold dear, already convincing with their success were such California examples as Riverside.[6] Here, in the early 1870s stalwart Tennessee farmers colonized a rocky sheep pasture, siphoned water from the nearby Santa Ana River, and turned the dry land into thousands of blossoming orange trees.

Whatever the disparate forces at work, their energy came to a head in

William E. Smythe. The once obscure newspaper reporter now found himself leading a national, grassroots movement, with politicians and bureaucrats in Washington, D.C., taking note. Smythe now boasted support so strong that he founded a periodical and hailed the sunburst of the new enthusiasm by calling his magazine *The Irrigation Age*. A new day was dawning. Even as Powell, battered by his enemies, was descending, Smythe and his new religion was fast rising. Buoyed by Smythe's optimistic message, his audience grew larger and larger. Soon evangelist Smythe was promulgating his gospel in the pages of *Land of Sunshine*, insistently, in lavish prose, and so often he was second only to editor Lummis himself in the frequency of his popular articles (Bingham 144).

Religion? To sum up the ideas rapidly evolving from Smythe and his followers hardly catches the calescence, the brisance, of their belief in the Divine Hand at work. In a simple word, Smythe adopted Powell and then some. He pushed for reform of the water laws so that monopolistic land-grabbers couldn't seize a water source and effectively control tens of thousands of surrounding acres. He believed in settling the land by colonies and in cooperation among landholders for the common good thereafter. He believed not only in irrigation as the key to success, he wanted the federal government to fund extensive irrigation projects. And he believed in much more. He believed not that Nebraska or Colorado or some other marginally deficient state in terms of rainfall was the best place to initiate the irrigation idea on a massive scale, but, in a seeming reverse of the triage system, he looked to the desert, yes, that expanse of broken rock and shiny spines, as a region ordained by God. There, waiting all these centuries for the experiment to begin, the sands would soon give birth to the planet's New Jerusalem, one thriving beyond measure with a Brobdingnagian eruption of vegetables, sweetness, and light.

Conversions breed extremists. Basically, the settling of the West had been a free-for-all, a looting of resources as frenzied men broke into nature's treasure trove and happily carried off gold, coal, and timber. In the words of another of America's radically insightful books, we were wrecking our own home: ". . . we are, even now, breaking up the floor and wainscoting and doors and window frames of our dwelling, for fuel to warm our bodies and seethe our pottage, and the world cannot afford to wait till the slow and sure progress of exact science has taught it a better economy" (Marsh 52). Sounding the alarm, Powell had failed to rally sufficient support, as held true of George Perkins Marsh before him. But by the time Smythe came along, some common sense had begun to sink into the national consciousness, and people began listening to the reformers. Surely, if people felt any obligation beyond satisfying their own greed, gluttons frantically stuffing themselves, if they owed anything to their children and the children coming after them or cared aught for the welfare of their country, something was wrong, and something needed to be done about it. Surely, if we were to have a future, we could find ways to live more rationally and harmoniously with the earth instead of tearing down our earthly house around us.

It was the age of the incipient conservation movement, of concerns for disappearing birds, the setting aside of national parks, the creation of the U.S. Forest Service. An evangelical Gifford Pinchot stood on his government pulpit and sternly warned that we would run out of trees if we didn't mend our ways, while the sonorous John Muir urged city people to find good health and mended spirits in the wilderness.

There was a larger psychological and economic context behind this readiness for change, this new caring for nature. Like a horse emerging from a burning barn, the nation came out of the Civil War rattled, and it would never again be the same. As the United States earnestly entered the Industrial Age, people flocked to cities. There they encountered a milieu radically different from their lives on the ordered and predictable farm. For the first time, they faced crime, pollution, and millions of immigrants crowded into slums, their new neighbors. Corruption reigned in government; traditional religions faltered, reeling especially from Darwin's theories; and general values were collapsing. In short, society seemed to be falling apart as bewildered people watched. Then the Panic of 1893 hit, pulling out their financial rug. As often happens in times of rapid change, people thrown off balance grabbed at whatever was available. Adrift in turmoil, where could the concerned citizen turn? Radical movements proposing new answers to the mess began to draw followings (Lawrence B. Lee, Introduction xxxiv).

Finding a focus for their ills, many people turned to a new relationship with nature as their balm. As part of this, Smythe's *The Conquest of Arid America* offered not just an aspirin for temporary relief, as did Van Dyke, but a Complete Cure. To pick up Smythe's book is to enter a religious service where good feelings, sanctity, and order combine into one overwhelming uplift of body and soul. Not only that. As with the best of religions, this was no one-hour Sunday jolt of elevated spirits diminishing as the week wears on but a complete plan for remaking one's life along with the life of society. Furthermore, Smythe offered no foggy-headed gaze through pink mists to a vague promise of an afterlife far in the future but holding out little for the confused to grasp onto in the roil of their daily lives. No, Smythe's Complete Cure promised nothing less than new health, prosperity, artistic pleasure, and familial harmony, along with all the other comforts of faith—and best of all, all occurring in the present life. If Smythe's religion was airy, then it also was practical. And, with the best of religions, it made perfect sense—or at least seemed to.

It was nothing less than the final fulfillment of the ancient Greeks' dreams particularized in America. The agrarian ideal haunted pioneers as the apparition shimmered before them, powerfully pulling them ever westward (Foote). And they found it, just as Manifest Destiny had promised all along, as if first they needed to have their characters burnished by stumbling across a continent to be made worthy of the goal. There, after all that pain, at the end of the rainbow they had been following, there it was, in the nation's western extremity. The scenario couldn't have been better for high drama. Although William E. Smythe painted the picture in its brightest, most panoramic colors, he was but one among millions who saw it. In 1890 California writer Theodore Strong Van Dyke, one of Smythe's supporters, had a vision:

Even more striking was the change that had come over the broad slope of gray sand that ten years before had excited my sympathies for the poor hare that fate had condemned to live on it. Near its outer edge I found what seemed the same old hare, sitting in the same old aggravating shade of the same old emaciated bush. But he now looked happy and fat. . . . Half a mile beyond where he sat lay a long stretch of bright green, above which rose the gables and cupolas of hundreds of houses, mingled with the spires of churches and the bell-towers of imposing school-houses. Up to the very edge of it the land lay sad and gray as ever, then suddenly changed into a maze of green as I crossed a cement-lined ditch in which sparkling water from the mountains was winding its eddying way. (27)

Note the cement-lined ditch.

This pleasant picture, and much more, was exactly what Smythe would tell America how to achieve.

A master psychologist attuned to the workings of human nature, Smythe expertly sets up his potential converts in his book's first pages. He knows that only the dissatisfied are willing to change their lives. Like the ad for the ninety-pound weakling in the old weight-lifting come-ons, the unspoken assumption in *The Conquest* was that prospective converts already are unhappy with their lot and open to doing something about it. Who should go West? Only those ready for the challenge of building new lives, who love to be in a place of activity "where things are being done" and who are willing to roll up their sleeves to "found cities and states" and "carry railroads through unheard-of mountain passes." Thus, Smythe not so much persuades as reinforces his readers' incipient longings, holds out challenges to them, and enlists them in a patriotic brotherhood (xvii). Those plagued by smut and social disease in fetid cities in the East should know that a "new era is dawning" in the West (xxvii), and "if you are the *right* young man," this is your big chance to play a role in the success already under way (xxviii).

Smythe next takes a surprising turn. After all, he does not want enthusiastic boys of the guts-and-glory sort but men of sober habits and substance, entire families enlisted in his cause to build the New America. He goes back over the Republic's history, showing that it was settled by a race of empire builders, nobly "taming the wilderness" to build civilization (8). All this to an end. Americans are a good people, loving their homes, wanting only the opportunity to provide comfortable lives for their families (12). And with such accomplishments behind us, we all can be proud. Few in Smythe's day would have disagreed with that. He's shown himself a patriot, a man of traditional values, and by now he has his readers eating out of his palm.

The problem is more than that the process is incomplete; more so, all that progress took place in the wrong half of the United States. Smythe, however, delivers that shocking news softly. Meanwhile, playing, always playing, in the background are the social frustrations and fears enumerated above, the message that the East, with its unsolvable problems, is failing. However, it is ominous music already there, and Smythe need touch on it only occasionally to remind his readers that the present system, as contrasted with the one he's about to spring, stymies the best efforts of honest men (31).

He next elaborates on what his readers undoubtedly have already heard, that the West is a pretty fine place, huge, open, shining, so full of timber and minerals that it's "the nation's treasure-house" (27). And the climate out there is so healthful that it's one, vast, outdoor sanitarium (24). Just the place to start a new life. The problem is, he keeps inserting lightly, that it's mighty dry, and that's the one feature holding the region back.

Confidence is built between two people by showing that they share similar values, and this so far Smythe has done. Having gained that advantage, the point of establishing trust with the reader long behind him, he is ready for his revolutionary message.

You see, aridity is only a perceived problem. In fact, lack of rain is a huge advantage. The most promising spot of all in the United States is not Iowa with its fertile soil or the palmy California coast but the stony, bone-strewn, and nearly waterless desert (30). Realizing that at this point shock will occur, devastating any good his later rational arguments might do, psychologist Smythe inserts a full-page photograph opposite his statement. It shows a full watercourse with lush trees and grass and a well-dressed man looking on. The caption reads in part: "Two Years and Four Months Prior to the Taking of This Photograph, Neither Water, Tree, nor Man Existed in This Place . . ." The picture wins the day with its visual impact, though the logic still reels.

In a trice, having convinced the eye, Smythe addresses the mind. The world, you see, has had its values backward. People in the well-watered East only *think* they're lucky. They depend on the rain to water their crops, but rain can be fickle even there. And if it fails to fall when their crops most need it, the farmers suffer (47). The better way is to forget about rain and have a steady supply of water coursing past your fields for use whenever you need it. That is, irrigation, the means to set farmers free from the slavery of dependence on the unpredictable weather.

That was, however, only the most obvious advantage. Smythe was writing no mere handbook on successful farming methods but a treatise on reforming the entire United States. Though irrigation should be instituted nationwide, it works best in the desert, where the thirsty land, waiting through the eons for water to be piped out of rivers and down from the mountains, was most fertile. Desert soil, Smythe assures his readers, contains "three times as much potash, six times as much magnesia, and fourteen times as much lime" as soils east of the Mississippi River (38). But that was only the beginning. What mattered was what kind of society would arise out there in the desert, an example for the entire country—for the whole world!—to follow.

The Big Blessing of irrigation, it turns out, is not what it does for people's pocketbooks but what it does for their souls.

Admittedly building on Powell, whom he thought the hero of the cause and called the "First Scientific Explorer of the Arid Region,"[7] Smythe argued that irrigation would create an ideal society of happy individuals. By its very nature, the technique favored the small, family farm with members working together. Furthermore, they would be part of a larger societal context. Because of the extensive waterworks required, deserts fostered cooperation and democracy among men. They would settle the land in colonies, and once the irrigation system was in place, they would continue the communal spirit, not only to maintain the system but to run their own community affairs, including the creation of cooperatives to market their produce.

The vision got rosier the more Smythe detailed it. With its wealth of water, irrigation in the warm desert meant a great bounty, intensive farming yielding several abundant crops a year. Therefore, only a few acres could support an entire family, and the consequence of this was enormous. People could cluster in what Smythe saw as a typical "thrifty and beautiful hamlet" of orderly, tree-lined streets studded at regular intervals with comfortable homes. There, since their workday was healthy and not onerous, people could indulge their intellectual and spiritual sides at night in their local libraries, schools, and churches. Better yet, Smythe envisioned the harsh domain of the Gila monster and cracked rock turned into "a long series of beautiful villages," all connected by electric trolley lines. And they would be linked to the nearby cultural center of a city. Happily tending God's crops by day, at night the grower and his wife could whizz into the urban center to enjoy an opera or concert before returning to God's bosom, their peaceful, idyllic plot of home and garden (46).[8]

And lest anyone think that Smythe was an idealistic dreamer, borne on the wings of his own fancies, he cited example after example where the very plan he advocated already was in place and successful. Take the before-mentioned Riverside, settled by colonists but a few years before. Here:

> . . . at least ninety per cent. of the total population live in homes which front on beautiful boulevards, presenting to the passer an almost unbroken view of well-kept lawns, opulent flower-beds, and delicate shrubbery. Newspaper carriers canter through these streets delivering the local morning and evening dailies. . . . Their schools are of the highest standard, and are housed in buildings the beauty and convenience of which bespeak the good public taste. A well-patronized institution is the club-house and its reading room. There is but a single saloon, and it is considered decidedly disreputable to frequent it. (102–103)

A little stodgy perhaps, but given the fetid cities, then as now, one hardly could attack the scene as a goal to be shunned.

Our far more cynical age might give Smythe considerable ribbing for the airy theological cast he gave to his particular combination of science and poetic vision. As men turned the desert's "grey barrenness into green fields and gardens," like the Israelites of old they were following God's plan for America, recently discovered by Smythe, converting the Republic into "the Promised Land" (xi). And they were doing it, not through prayer but through irrigation, which now was "a better way to pray" (328). Yet while scoffing, we might also envy Smythe's bright hope. Bustling with energy, he helped nurture several agricultural colonies in California and Idaho and, as a sideline showing his versatility, wrote the reliable *History of San Diego* while working for the city's newspaper, the

Union. Envy him, too, that, the year before he died in 1922, he was still glowing with happy expectations that his plan would solve the nation's knotty problems. His *City Homes on Country Lanes* is just what it sounds like, a handbook further laying out how to make the dream of *rus in urbe* come true. Its frontispiece, a young, elegant woman taking a break from her satisfying work to smile out at readers from her sumptuous garden surrounding a comfortable house, should give our easy cynicism pause.

The truth is that there was nothing wrong with Smythe's idea, not in itself. Given the conditions then prevailing, it was perfectly workable. Then what happened to Riverside and Redlands and other pleasant, tree-shaded communities built along Smythe's lines? And what madness that, at the urgings of the irrigationists, the government took up the cause, then became so carried away with dam and canal building that it wrecked the West's rivers, diverting them into giant plumbing systems piping water thousands of miles around the arid lands to grow surplus crops and support burgeoning, desert-wrecking population growth. Starting out with high hopes, the irrigation idea evolved into a monstrous disaster for the desert (Reisner; Worster).

Like most men, Smythe was not blessed with perfect foresight. The fatal flaws lay not in the campaigner's plan but in what it left out, for the real, ragged world refused to conform to Smythe's rosy vision. Moths creep into almost all idealistic schemes. Because by nature they simplify the world and cannot predict the future, when put into action they often metastasize into freaks. Men were not nearly as virtuous as Smythe had hoped. He'd underestimated the culture's deep streak of individualism and the influence of greed, particularly as embodied in powerful special interests, both working counter to the cooperative, idealistic spirit. But most of all, as we'll see in the next chapter, he along with others of the time all but ignored huge population growth combining with new, leaping developments in technology. Together, they would take on their own wayward life to overwhelm beautiful boulevards and sedate homes set among well-kept lawns.

John Wesley Powell & William E. Smythe

9

J. SMEATON CHASE

Our Araby

When Pandora released the world's ills from a box, one of the fleeing essences, making it only halfway out, clung trembling on the rim. It was hope, and it still clings there, vacillating between evil and good, a symbol of yearning but also of the potential for self-delusion in human affairs.

By the time the United States was becoming well acquainted with the new turmoils of the twentieth century, the culture, turning multifarious and demanding interlocutor, was insisting that the desert be many things at once. The desert was supposed to be a land of horror as well as a land of ecstasy, a mineral bonanza, a place of vast eucalyptus plantations, stuff to be spun into romantic novels, a hunter's paradise, salve for individual's psychic wounds, as well as balm for the nation's social and political ills; lush alfalfa kingdom and fruit ranch, outdoor sanitarium for tuberculars and the mentally deranged, Boy Scout camp, and movie set for romping cowboys and inscrutable Arabs.

An accommodating if sometimes bedraggled quick-change artist, it also soon would be called upon to serve as tennis court for starlets and staid retirement community where block after block of low-slung, brick-faced ranch-styles, each propped up by a blooming bougainvillea bush, crouched still lower under the punishing knuckles of the summer sun, while inside the aging inhabitants listened for a message in the interminable hum of air conditioning. It would be a gambler's paradise, the eternal beacons of Sin City flashing so brightly through day and night their lure was felt as far away as Chicago and Los Angeles. Appropriately lectured and humbled, schoolchildren would come there, approaching a pool reverently, on tiptoes through the mud and rushes, answering an ecological sacring bell, to peer drop-jawed at rainbow wisps of desert minnows as if beholding Lilliputianized dinosaurs. And there would be that Flash out there. About to witness the miracle of intense neutron bombardment, scientists would hold their breaths, some fearing that the very oxygen of the earth's atmosphere would rip into flames and race around the globe in a worldwide conflagration, as in the next second—too late now—they beheld a preternatural brisance the world would never forget.

Yet, still, used up, mined, maligned, driven over by military tanks and its colored sands shipped around the world in little vials, the same peaks were there, crouching Sphinx-like, in the sunset stretching out the same impenetrable shadows as they had for eons.

The confusion occurs because, like lovers enjoying a new affair that brightly promises to change their lives, people project their needs on exotic landscapes. To Smythe, the arid lands held the golden key to solving the nation's ills, while Austin presents desert subtleties as salve for the harried soul. We have come to the desert as tourists expecting therapeutic vacations. Such was not the case, as best as we can tell, with the native peoples living there. They may have charming stories about how the Devil Himself lives up Tahquitz Canyon, emerging now and then to snatch up an unfortunate Indian, or about how a winsome girl sprouted out of the ground and turned into a saguaro cactus. But the desert was their home, not at all an exotic place, and, being practical people, what they wanted from it was not psychic healing but the means to survive. Where to hunt rabbits, where to collect seeds, the dependability of a certain spring on a long mountain trek, these were their essential reference points in the first business of staying alive.

A technological people in many ways released from nature's harsh strictures, we may indulge in the folly of imagining the virtues of what seems to us a simpler life, but we would not want to endure the everyday realities lurking behind our pleasant imaginings: the thirst, sickness, and boredom of grinding corn for hours by hand. What was needed was an Apollonian man who could approach the desert with educated wonder yet see it clearly, without romantic lenses. We nearly had him in J. Smeaton Chase, yet he, too, though with the best of intentions, ended up erecting huge signs saying FOR SALE and GET IT WHILE YOU CAN across the desert.

That we know relatively few details about the life of J. Smeaton Chase is not the drawback it might at first seem.[1] He was born in London in 1864, the son of a publisher. Though he apparently did not attend a university, his writing, made bright now and then with a Latin phrase or the flash of a classical allusion, shows an educated mind about its happy

J. Smeaton Chase

work. At the age of twenty-six, he came to the United States and for years was involved in social work in the Los Angeles area, then served as tutor to a rancher's sons in the nearby San Gabriel Valley. At some point unknown came a change in his life. He shook loose of the city and began wandering up and down California on horseback. At least as much is indicated by his first book, *Yosemite Trails,* a backwoods guide published in 1911, when Chase was forty-seven. Thereafter followed a number of similar books combining footloose travel, local lore, and natural history. Chase settled in the tiny desert village of Palm Springs in 1915, two years later married a banker's daughter, then died in nearby Banning in 1923.

Scholars have here and there scraped together other tidbits. His house, Marjorie Bright, local historian of Palm Springs, tells us, was "the former second home of the McCallum family near the present site of the Tennis Club" (52), and he's buried beside his wife, Isabel, in the "grassy cemetery at the foot of Mt. San Jacinto," their rarely visited graves "guarded by sentinel palms" (Lawrence Clark Powell, *California Classics* 206).

Other than that, we know very little, except that Chase seems to have been an amiable man involved in community affairs. His photograph opposite the *National Cyclopaedia* article shows a handsome, intense, but affable writer, if anything can be made of character from the pose for a portrait. Two further things. As noted, he didn't begin publishing until later in life, and he waited until the age of fifty-three to marry. But of what to make of any or all of this one has little inkling.

Perhaps, as we said, it doesn't matter much. If anything, we should know a writer through his books, the part that lasts, whatever he was like in "real" life. Although in his volumes Chase goes lightly on biographical details, keeping the riches of lonely and sometimes dangerous travel to the fore, with all its botanical and aesthetic excitements, an inner core nonetheless comes through, and it is not that of a tortured Van Dyke bringing baggage to the land or of evangelist Smythe with a divinely sanctioned plan to renovate the arid places. Instead, with Chase we see a remarkably open-minded wayfarer, full of joys, and sometimes doubts, even-keeled though inwardly churning in the face of troubles, during lonely desert stretches verging on depression and even hallucination, while suffering from thirst pained more to see his horse suffer, sensitive and curious about his surroundings, worried about the future of all this beauty. In other words, a man much like us — at least, the best of what we'd like to imagine we could be — at once human but potentially heroic.

And through it all, accepting the struggles, rising above them to catch the passion he found in the desert's heart. Here he plods with his horse deep into the night across the desert because there was nothing else to do, vaguely lost, both man and horse fagged from hunger and lack of water. Still, he can appreciate the otherness of the glory around him:

Daylight had gone but the moon was well up and afforded aid and comfort. Except for the discomfort of doubt I could have revelled in the charm of the scene. The uncouth Chuckwallas rose dark behind and to my right. Moonlight whitened here and there the angle of some buttress, touching with charm of fancy the leagues of shadowy mountain. Our shadows marched before us, mingling with filmy pattern of creosote or skeleton of cactus or ocotillo. To the left the horizon line was a procession of dusky shapes, shifting and vanishing like monsters seen in a nightmare. (California Desert Trails 352)

Yes, the "uncouth Chuckwallas." Monsters beautiful to a distraught man. Yet, despite Chase's writing talents and Apollonian virtues, at the last he, too, badly bungled, and that also should give us a chill pause about ourselves.

Chase saw California in its heyday, as the nineteenth century pitched into the twentieth. Capital and new industries were flooding in, and fruit ranches were reaching for the foothills. No longer were Los Angeles and San Diego dusty relics of the frontier. They were growing into previews of sophisticated cities. Along with the happy financial eruptions in real estate, oranges, and culture, tourism also was experiencing a boom. But it was tourism with ragged edges still available for those few who enjoyed roughing it. If traveling any distance between coastal cities, most tourists, along with the general public, went by boat or took trains on the expanding railway network. Where busy State Route 1 now follows the California coast, Chase would find an intermittently disappearing track threading around swamps and over dramatic headlands that reared in the fog ahead above the Pacific Ocean. Along that way, he encountered people in isolated ranches living essentially the life of the frontier. Though it has nothing directly to do with the desert, then, Chase's early *California Coast Trails*, published in 1913, and his account of his horseback trip of two thousand miles from the Mexican border north to Oregon, serves as a key to his later writing as he responds to the mixture of civilized enclaves, characterized by the clang of trolley cars, surrounded by wildness.

A visionary Austin or a Van Dyke, plagued by the sounds of gnashing teeth within, à la San Juan de la Cruz, likely would have turned such an adventure along the wild coast into a search for the soul or some such related quest for profundity. Chase is not so afflicted. His writing does not take on the burden of pretense, to distort nature in order to display literary genius or to work out personal travails. Rather, Chase is the preeminent wanderer in that continuously moving line where the calm traveler meets nature and, full of equanimity, rather than himself, keeps his focus on the landscape around him. This because he believes that the scenery needs no "purple-patch" writing; it is dramatic enough to speak for itself if honestly presented (x). Yet, upon further consideration, Chase's prose is more complex than that. If anything, one issue is uppermost in Chase's mind, and it serves as the background for the entire work. Though he is traveling with "leisure," Chase is aware of the larger society everywhere lurking beyond his placid horizons that will soon flood into this "vast quiescence" (2). A man from the city preferring the country, rather than indulge in the histrionics of breast-beating, he is of a divided mind, vacillating between his daily pleasures and the knowledge that the scenery before him giving such joy will soon pass. In this he becomes a kind of Everyman, but an Everyman armed with the awareness that so many Californians of his time, frothing with prosperity, lacked.

Yet, having made the observation, Chase puts the somber moment behind him as he swings a leg over Chino and gets on with his trip.

For a traveling companion on the southern leg of the journey, Chase had the good company of Palm Springs artist Carl Eytel (1). Traveling light, with their Spartan camping equipment packed on their two riding horses, the pair started off from the then-idyllic Los Angeles suburb of El Monte, a farming village of bowered cottages with marigolds flashing their startling gold from the deep-green lawns (5). Traveling along the coast, where freeways now roar, the two visited San Juan Capistrano and other missions in various stages of disrepair, accepted hospitality and strong coffee at Mexican ranches, and poked their noses into collapsed boom towns. Five weeks later, long-haired, unshaven, and stained with travel, the two drew puzzled comments from San Diego's citizens as they clopped up the city's streets. It was a thriving place of forty thousand people, an "energetic" town, notes Chase (52), though he also notes that they had difficulty finding a livery stable for their horses, so great had been the recent impact of the "all-usurping automobile" (51).

All in all, it had been the jocular excursion of two schoolboys out on a holiday.

The next year, Chase set out again, heading north with faithful Chino, and this part of the trip forms the bulk of *California Coast Trails*. Here, the writing changes. Chase was alone this time. In contrast to the palmy southern coast, the land was less populated, rockier, and more difficult to travel, with clothes-soaking fogs and frequent worries about missing the way. In fact, the trail became so rough that Chino played out, replaced by Anton (182–183). Such factors lend a more sober tone to the writing, and though Chase has many a "heavenly" day (64), on the beach of Malibu, for instance, observing a world "created within the week" (66), the bone-weariness and exertion could get to him. At the end of a particularly difficult stretch up in Humboldt County, threading though an endless mountain forest on a hot afternoon thick with humidity, Chase sighs, "I fear I was not much alive to the beauty of the sunset-lighted forest through which we passed, though I recalled afterwards that the scenery had been particularly fine" (288). The arduousness heightens the reality of the account. Yet all in all, this is a Whitmanesque narrative of a footloose man camping his way up the lonely beaches, plucking trout from mountain streams with his rod, and occasionally charming farmers' wives into offering him a home-cooked meal. This is not really a travelogue or a nature book but a combination of the two—or, rather, the writings of a man on the trail recording what interests him, which fortuitously also interests his readers.

Written about California's now populated coast, *California Coast Trails* is J. Smeaton Chase's best-known book. With the tug of nostalgia, it has the advantage of telling us what a long stretch of coast, varying from palmy beaches in the south to chill and craggy northern headlands, was like before freeways, fences, and foothill ticky-tacky sank their claws into nature. To this day, enthusiasts with an equestrian bent mount their horses and, Chase's book in hand—braving No Trespassing signs and clomping across shopping-center parking lots—retrace his route for a taste of the land's former glory. Sometimes they are richly rewarded, finding the mossy base of the very tree where Chase says he lay his head one night; his writing is that accurate.

Yet despite its pleasant, ever-changing prospects, charming anecdotes about eccentric country folk, and the prose of a man working at his intelligent ease, *California Coast Trails* may be his best-known, but it is not his best, book. Maybe the problem lies with the ease. People are like tea bags, goes the old nostrum. They have to be dipped into hot water to reach their full strength. That is, though a crisis can break a writer, it also can push him beyond old, familiar boundaries into areas of talent he didn't realize he possessed. This is what the desert did for J. Smeaton Chase.

We don't know why, two years after publishing the account of his coastal trek, aging Chase moved to Palm Springs, eighty miles due east of Los Angeles over the rain-wringing mountains. It's not unfair to guess that his boon companion and desert wraith Carl Eytel filled his ears with the wonders of the desert and encouraged him in this direction. We do know that, in one of the curious connections that often link desert writers, in April 1915, Chase, who illustrated the coastal book with his own photographs, was writing Scribner's with a novel idea.

Pleading the "well-known pecuniary disabilities of authors as a class," he offered to sell the publisher a selection of his photographs to illustrate a reprint of John C. Van Dyke's "classic" *The Desert*. Chase explained, graciously but meekly, that he was working on a volume about the Colorado desert and had a great number of high-quality pictures to spare. Would Scribner's be interested in using fifteen or twenty of them for, say, one hundred dollars? (Teague and Wild 43).

They would, indeed. Somewhat strangely, the bargaining went on for a good while, with Scribner's aping the caution of a world power negotiating a delicate international treaty with this impecunious desert writer who was all but offering to give his photographs away, but, in any case, the 1918 edition of Van Dyke's book, along with most reprints the publisher issued thereafter, bore "With Illustrations from Photographs by J. Smeaton Chase" on the title page. Given the cost to Chase of obtaining the photos, it was one of the sharpest deals Scribner's ever cut.

And by cost we mean not only the expense of taking—in those days far more expensive than now—what must have been hundreds of photographs. Nor even the time and labor and the upkeep of a horse involved in stumbling for hundreds of miles through a sandy, roadless furnace, while lugging along a heavy camera to boot, to record the image of a favorite cactus or a certain clump of *Washingtonia* palms growing far back in a canyon on a sheet of photosensitive cellulose, though those costs in themselves were large. For certain they would have scotched the project for the stingy Scribner's if they'd had to pay *that* price. Rather, we're talking about the psychic cost that arose partly from the physical exertion but also from the mind-boggling, sanity-upsetting horror, especially for a man who never stopped loving the misty green hedges of England,[2] of confronting what sometimes struck him as a hideously bare landscape. And not only confronting but then writing something that made sense about the senseless. What was the meaning of all this rock and sand jumbled into madness? At times, Chase was shaken to his pins.

All of which he chose to endure, for some unGodly reason that Chase explains only in the lamest terms, at the most punishing time of year— in the middle of blazing summer, when even the desert animals have sense enough to hide from the unnerving heat (84).

Yet, as we said, it was a good kind of shaking, a blessing to his talents, bringing out the best of them.

In structure, *California Desert Trails* is similar to the earlier travel account. Whereas the latter details a trip along the coast taken in two separate stages, the desert book recounts four months of continuous travel in one great, plodding circuit of hundreds of miles over nearly uninhabited basin and range. To generalize about a journey with many side trips, Chase left Palm Springs in June. He rode south to the Mexican border; east to Yuma, Arizona, on the Colorado River; north to the little farming town of Blythe, also on the Colorado River; and then completed the circle with his westward return home in September.[3] Though he opens with several chapters introducing readers to the little-known geography, botany, and Indian lore of the area, after that his method pretty much reflects that of the coastal book. The pages follow his itinerary, describing the country, offering tidbits of history, and presenting the people he bumps into along the way.

There, however, the similarities end. This is not simply another trip moved a hundred miles or so inland to a different landscape. And it is not, one sometimes thinks, even the same man taking it. For the most part at ease on the coast, here, at least in places, Chase drops the disguise of the well-tempered traveler. Then we see not only the phantasmagoria of a surreal landscape. For it is horrid, beautiful, and dangerous all at once, yet also beyond the capacity of Chase's well-ordered mind to comprehend. Then we have glimpses into another, perhaps more frightening, phantasm, that of a psyche verging on disintegration. It is not only the weirdness of the land that does this, nor the lonesomeness of days trekking without company; neither is it the constant, grinding worry about reaching the next waterhole and perhaps not finding water enough for himself and his suffering horse, and the very real dangers of getting irretrievably lost on top of failing with thirst, and in the final stages, as the desert raconteurs Chase met loved to recite, running about turned babbling lunatic before collapsing onto the hot sands to die. All these, yes, and understandably. One wonders at times why Chase didn't simply throw it all up and run screaming out of the desert vowing never to return.

Along with everything else, an intellectual crisis rattled him. In that stark landscape, questions about his own values and about the direction of the entire nation, perhaps half hidden by comforting greenery elsewhere, here thrown into sharp, looming relief and demanding answers that he was unable to give—or, also a possibility, did not want to face. Out in the desert, Chase lost his faith.

We might not know that except for one long, tortured passage toward the end of *California Desert Trails*. Other than that, we have a gentlemanly book. Showing his contemplative side and ability to make his wonder convincing, Chase studies the palm trees growing in the mountain canyons around Palm Springs and notes that they seem "to have a conscious air," almost an intelligence and awareness of their own, as indeed they do to visitors today (32). Yet Chase will go only so far with the poetic and the speculative. When one stormy night a flash flood roars down a canyon, almost drowning Chase where he's taking refuge from the rain in a cave, he makes light of the near disaster in what must have been a Walpurgisnacht, describing the "wild uproar as huge boulders began to come down from the upper cañon," roaring past his perch and "thundering and bumping along like barrels tumbling down a stairway" (25). More significantly, early on he joshes himself along with others in society yearning for desert appreciation. Grown fat and bored from our technological ease, we now turn to the desert with "a zest for things rugged and wild." Thus, "the desolate, gaunt, and dreadful" of the desert is beginning to have their day with people like himself. Such he compares to "those funny fellows," the futurists and cubist painters yearning for the bizarre as an antidote to ennui (3).

Following in a similar vein, though he doesn't belabor the point, he shows he's of a divided mind about progress. As a nature lover interested in "God's desert, not man's" (xi), though he depreciates the get-rich-quick boomers avidly selling off the desert around the new agricultural towns, he has to admit that the arrival of irrigation water to the desert is a miracle resulting in "really remarkable agricultural developments" replacing sandy sweeps with melon fields and dairy farms (x). Thus the desert lover shows that he is of two minds, not only about weighing the value of the wild desert against the advantages of civilization; he also airs doubts about his own need to think such a desolate place beautiful. Is he forcing his appreciation out of loyalty to a romanticism rebounding from the straitjacket of modern society? Maybe, or maybe not, is the implied response. All of this so far he states merely in passing, the idle musings of a traveler through a strange country, and if Chase had let it go at that, we'd have yet another adequate, but hardly complex, book about desert touring.

In *Desert Solitaire*, a usually swaggering Edward Abbey shows himself as vulnerable as the rest of humanity when his craving for adventure nearly gets the best of him. Hiking on the Supai Indian reservation of northern Arizona, Abbey becomes curious about a steep side canyon where a little stream runs intermittently. In the course of exploring, excitement gets the best of him, and he foolishly drops over a series of dry waterfalls. At the last one, he swims across the stagnant water at the bottom to the lip of the next drop-off to see what fate will offer him. Then he looks over the edge amazed, into an eighty-foot abyss. Gazing at the sheer walls all around him, he realizes that he is trapped, unable to climb out in any direction. For once, Abbey's braggadocio fails him, and he begins to disintegrate as he realizes what a hopeless spot he's in (201–203). "Somehow," he says, after gathering his nerve, "with a skill and tenacity I could never have found in myself under ordinary circumstances, I managed to creep straight up that gloomy cliff and over the brink of the drop-off and into the flower of safety" (204–205). For the disturbing interlude, *Desert Solitaire* is a far more frightening, memorable, and revealing book about man and nature.

In a way, Abbey was lucky. His near disaster was physical rather than philosophic. Once he tore his fingernails in the process of clawing his way out of that natural hole, he laced up his boots and sauntered down the trail, answering the splendid sunset blessing the outcome of the day by bellowing the *Ode to Joy* (205). The scrape with nature's heartless ways behind him, he could pick up where he left off and go on about being the badboy of the Southwest.

A more earnest Chase hardly was so fortunate. His trial also was physical, but it brought him to a new level of awareness that shivered his outlook not only about the desert but about the whole raison d'être of humanity in regard to nature. The crisis—more accurately, a series of clustered crises—began when in a marshy place near the Mexican border Chase bumps into a prospector named Wellson who has a yen for visiting strange places. Would the desert wanderer like to see something truly unusual, spend a few days poking around in a curiosity, "a remarkable gorge, known as Split Mountain Cañon"? Up for seeing the most on his excursion, Chase eagerly agrees (250). The adventure, begun with high expectations, will turn out to be Chase's crossing of the River Styx, with Wellson serving as his taciturn Charon.

In a couple of hours, the two rein up, beholding before them a rocky, endless maze below sea level, a sunken labyrinth so confused with a lacework of passages that Chase wonders if anyone plunging in there will ever get out. Yet in they go, spending the day sliding and scrambling through the badlands as the sun beats on them. Such a punishing progress of all-day going is hard enough on men and horses. When long after dark they finally find the sole waterhole in that vast hell, the spent horses crowd eagerly around as the bucket goes down. But when it comes up the water is putrid with the bloated bodies of dead animals (261). The four spend a night of torture without water for man or beast. The next day as they drag on, Chase notices an old shoe lying under a bush. Hardly encouraging, Wellson tells him that it belonged "to a man who, the year before, had gone crazy for want of water" (262). Hours later, they find relief at a mining camp. In a mockery of civilization, it's called San Felipe City, population one Norwegian and an Irishman, and the first thing the shirtless workers do, recognizing the distress of their unexpected guests, is to thrust a waterbag at them (263). But the relief is only temporary. The worst and also the best—Chase is beginning to have trouble distinguishing the two—lies beckoning beyond.

On they go, into a land of sand and gravel and clay thrown into grotesque shapes, a place so barren and shadeless that even flies are absent (265). On they go farther still, lost and again waterless, two men turned addicts, seemingly crazed for otherworldly landscapes, until, suffering all the more, they reach an expanse so hallucinogenic that one wonders if Chase's description owes more to the writer going around the bend into a dazed dream state than to reality:

Every quarter-mile brought some novelty to sight. In crossing a bench of reddish clay I noticed numbers of bullets of some heavy metallic stuff, the size of marbles and perfectly round. Then came a tract covered with pebbles, various in color, but as even in shape and dimension as if carefully sorted. Again, plates of clear gypsum, as large as small window-panes and nearly an inch thick projected from the sides of a gully. (276)

In the midst of this, the horses are so weary that they want to lie down and die, but the two men keep pushing them through more tortures until the little party makes it out.

The strangest thing is the reflection of Chase, a man well into his fifties, on the sapping adventure. By the end of the trip, the two men are so exhausted that they can't eat; so far we've had the picture of one cursing the desolation yet fevered by its beauty. "With all my weariness," Chase declares, "I do not think I have ever been so charmed as that evening by the sunset coloring" (280). He feels like one, quoting the Psalms, who has seen "the Vesture of God" (281). Surely, we think, this either is the excess of relief after prolonged strain or that this is no normal man but a crazed aesthetician, a man gone daft. And we might repeat on this score that Chase was not a man given to exaggeration for dramatic effect.

On the other hand, a dualistic approach to the desert as both an attractive and a repellant place also is understandable and perfectly rational. Echoing John Wesley Powell's earlier exclamation about the Grand Canyon as a place of desolation yet beauty, Chase has observed: "One here sees Mother Earth scalped, flayed, and stripped to the skeleton. Yet there is a strange beauty in it all" (275). That is, the approach to the desert as a region you might want to visit but certainly not where you'd want to live.

The problem compounds when Chase encounters civilization again, this time in the newly irrigated desert stretches in the Imperial Valley of Southern California. The beauty of orderly farmsteads with trees and well-kept buildings he approves, but such is rare in this boomland. For the most part, he finds a place even more repulsive than the harsh lands he has just left. Having viewed the tawdry ugliness at Coyote Wells, its "half a score of board-and-canvas shacks," his spirits sink so low that he leaves the little settlement feeling "almost suicidal" (282). Still worse, if that is possible, is his descent into, not a natural, but a man-made hellhole. Stepping across the international border into Mexico, Chase winces:

A pimply youth with a megaphone was inviting the public to enter the widest of these numerous gates into the broad way to Destruction, and made me, as a stranger, the particular object of his attentions. . . . A dozen or so gambling-tables at which you lose your money at faro, monte, roulette, or what you please: a thriving bar: an incessant racket of "rag-time" from a quartette of tenth-rate musicians at the rear: three painted girls, or rather children, in dirty pink. . . . (291)

J. Smeaton Chase

Is this what results from irrigating the desert, a suppurating wound? Apparently so. On the other hand, the desert, Chase concludes on his very last page, may be fascinating, but ultimately it just sits there, Sphinx-like, offering no answers (358). Chase, then, is stuck. Unlike the desert enthusiast who swings off into one extreme direction or another, well-modulated Chase is neither a desert lover of total commitment nor a celebrant of technological culture. He has nowhere to go.

We rebound from confusion into strange places. Chase's solution is an escape into hope in the face of crisis. Though serving him well at the time, the handy rationalization led him into a deadly trap, and most of the nation has since followed him into it.

J. Smeaton Chase's next and last book, *Our Araby: Palm Springs and the Garden of the Sun,* is a revealing oddment. Self-published in 1920, this pocket-sized volume with the unctuous title, brief enough to be read in a sitting or two, and with a map tucked in an envelope glued to the inside of the little brown book's back cover, obviously is a guide intended for tourists. But it is a guidebook with a difference. To find this little book moldering on a library's shelves, perhaps not checked out in decades, is a special treat in desert reading. Few works in the genre have the warm intimacy and sincere desire of this desert dweller speaking personally to readers in his wish to share the charms of his desert.

To read about Chase's home in the tiny village of Palm Springs is enough to make today's desert lovers weep. In fact, flying over the area, one wonders what Chase was talking about. Yes, Mount San Jacinto, for much of the year shouldering snow, still rears above the desert floor. But for mile after mile, not only Palm Springs, but much of the wide Coachella Valley surrounding it, has been replaced by condominiums, acrylic-green golf courses, and the surreal, aquamarine kidneys of artificial lakes. Home of movie stars and wealthy retirees, Palm Springs now is a pleasant city of palm-studded boulevards, gourmet dining, and racket clubs, an up-beat, up-scale place of ready smiles and Bermuda shorts. It's enviable evidence of technology's cornucopia mated with societal privilege. One is left wondering, however, what this accidental overlay of wealth has to do with the desert.

Yet to read Chase's little book also is to see how good the early desert newcomers had it. They were caught in a brief moment, charmed in a balance of rustic living and the modern conveniences relieving residents of drudgery. The latter benefits were few but essential for the milieu: running water, mail delivery, a railroad station nine miles to the north (80). This in a healthful climate, a spectacular setting, streams pouring out of the nearby mountain barricade to the west, and best of all—just swing your arms around—all the space one could possibly hope for. Saddling his horse in the early morning, Chase knew he could ride for days if he chose, exploring sand dunes and cracked mountain ranges— so much space, he joked, he felt he might indulge a whim, pick a trail, and ride all the way to New York (26).

And it wasn't only space itself that made the adventurer's heart leap but what it contained. Indian artifacts in caves, trout fishing, quaint Mexican villages—such were the exotic lures that would make the heart of a person turning his back on the narrow, pinched, clock-watching society over the mountain ranges dance with newfound romance and freedom. That, and a desert going crazy with colors in the spring excess of flowering (30), while each day, for daily thrills, the sun thundered down, consistently turning the snowy peaks blood-red (35–36). Talk about escape from sunken-chested civilization—why, in Palm Springs a person experienced not only authentic life lived close to the rhythms of the earth but wandered dazzled, surrounded by the "spirituality of color" (35).

Even the mesmerized wanderer longs for home, and this probably was the best part, coming home to the little community of Palm Springs itself. Picture Chase returning with the satisfying weariness earned from a day's successful excursion out to the Garnet Hills to the north, where he picked jewels from the sands, or south to the waterfall in Tahquitz Canyon, where Indian spirits dwell. As Chase noses his horse into a lane overarched by trees, out of the gathering gloom come the sounds of Indian drums from the nearby Cahuilla village, while, closer still, the kerosene lamps wink on in his neighbors' houses.

And what neighbors!—not riffraff but soul-mates of the desert, a select handful of scientists, musicians, writers, painters, people after his own heart "who love quiet, thoughtful things and whose . . . enjoyment lies in natural instead of artificial" pleasures (20). Chase might, to round off the day with good talk, light his lamp and pad on over to Carl Eytel's place, home of the talented painter whose canvases slip past clichés to capture desert mysteries. The way Chase tells it, the people of Palm Springs enjoyed an isolated and enviable harmony.[4]

As did John Muir in encouraging the building of more roads into Yosemite so that more people could enjoy wild beauty, Chase wanted to share nature's buoying effects. Yet he had more caution than the expansive Muir. No doubt eyeing the sensitive bonhomie and mutual self-respect of his fellow Palm Springs residents, Chase wanted no caravans of automobilists yahooing out from Los Angeles for weekend thrills, but visitors of "the discerning few." They, blessed with a taste for fragile subtleties, would speak in hushed voices while viewing the desert, then depart treasuring their delicate memories. And at that, he didn't want too many even of these people, for if they came in large numbers, Chase recognized that the desert's "charm would be lost." But no worry. Like flypaper luring flies, lowbrow places such as Palm Beach will continue to attract the rude hordes. The arid sweeps, requiring a delicacy of temperament, are safe from the masses and likely will remain a rare province for Houyhnhnms (7).

So began Palm Springs' slide into Babylon on the slickened rails of wishful thinking.

Chase knew better, or at least should have, for the signs of threats were all around him, threats he himself lists. He knew that the local Indians, considered by tourists to be living "close to the earth," had been Hispanicized, Catholicized, and were being Anglicized to such an extent that the significance of their ceremonies were but dim memories (24). That great bird, the California condor, was gone from the skies of Palm Springs (54), as was the once plentiful antelope from the vast stretches around the village (34). The reason was clear to Chase. Automobiles were proving "the worst foe of wild game," allowing "sports" from the city to invade the desert and blaze away with their repeating rifles (35). Yet what does Chase do? He provides a guide for automobile trips in the area and includes a section, "Hints for Motorists," to ease their way (82–83). Did he think for one moment that only fine-minded people would take advantage of his good advice for desert travel?

Did he think that the folderol of film companies, their fake cowboys and fake Arabs, that periodically turned the village into a movie set to the delight of the villagers (28) would not have a lasting impact, that the Hollywood types with their large purses would not want modern accommodations, with cocktails served up beside the swimming pool by locals turned into lackeys? One day Chase saw an airplane winking overhead, and the next he swelled with the possibilities, envisioning scheduled flights whisking visitors in and out of the desert. This, he calculated, without a thought of anything ominous, was all to the good. "The American tourist," he realized, "expects to have Nature served up in up-to-date fashion" (27).

Sarcastic as we might become, there's no sense in turning moralistic and laying the blame at Chase's door. Blinded by hope, by his own obsession with Palm Springs as a redeeming place set in amber, he clung to his comfortable double standard, refusing to consider the consequences. Such an indulgence has meant the ruin of many a place once thought inviolate. Furthermore, if Chase had taken the braver, more painful path, acknowledging the dangers, surely he, no more than King Canute shouting against the rising tide, could not have turned back the invasion of America's natural treasures. Despite our fondest wishes and staunchest activism, the cancerous growth of overpopulation combined with the spread of uncontrolled technology may, like Frankenstein monsters running amok and deaf to our calls, well have lives of their own beyond human control.

10

JOSEPH   WOOD

KRUTCH

The Pronuba Moth and the

Modern Dilemma

It remains a mystery. Travelers across the Southwest with an eye for stunning natural beauty, but perhaps bored by the dun regularity of the desert hills, can't help but gasp at the sudden flowering of the yucca. The plant is, for most of the year, a large clump of craziness, a mass of sword-like leaves spurting out of the ground, minacious to hikers and impressive in itself. Then in early summer the yucca all at once goes aerial, shooting up a long spike of perhaps twelve feet or more, and for a brief period some areas of the desert for the lucky sightseer are crammed with thousands upon thousands of such stalks marching off into infinity across the landscape, each holding erect a huge, heavy cluster of creamy-white blossoms. It's as if an atheist has suddenly turned religious.

Impressive, indeed, for the tourist who hasn't seen the spectacle. Yet behind the immediate, visual delight lies something even more amazing: How that wonderful mass of blossoms is triggered to bear fruit.

Science abounds with mutually beneficial relationships. In getting its nectar, the bee carries pollen from plant to plant and inadvertently fertilizes the flowers on which it feeds. Birds eat berries, and in return, but the best we can tell quite without any purpose in mind, help distribute the plant that provided the fruit by spreading the berry seeds in droppings. Concerning the relationship of the Pronuba moth and the yucca plant, however, it appears that the night-flying insect knows what it is doing in assuring the survival of its eggs by purposely fertilizing the plant. And for its part the yucca is very fortunate, for it is constructed in such a way that only this particular species of moth can get the job done. Neither plant nor moth could live without the other, and through its actions, the little, nondescript moth seems aware of its role in this vital but delicate relationship.

This is how it happens. At evening, and on the one very night of perfect bloom, the female Pronuba moth flutters from yucca flower to yucca flower collecting pollen. This she tucks in a ball under her chin and bears to yet another flower of her choice. Here, she penetrates the pistil with a tube on her abdomen and inserts several eggs. However, as if looking to the future, before leaving she moves her head back and forth on the stigma, rubbing in the pollen she's carried and thus assuring that the flower is fertilized. The resulting fruit will be the food on which the larvae from her eggs will feed, though not destructively. Hence, both plant and insect benefit, although prescience on the side of the moth, if supposed, would be inexplicable.

The revelation is typical of Joseph Wood Krutch's *The Voice of the Desert.* Here, in what is a list of wonders, this recent settler in southern Arizona goes from item to item, showing how what might seem drab and commonplace, or go entirely unnoticed, in nature actually reveals intriguing adjustments to survival in an arid land. The retired professor from Columbia University points out that the giant saguaro cactus, emblem of the region, is more than a weird-looking curiosity covered with spines. Designed to take advantage of the sparse rainfall, the saguaro is a vertical and expandable water tank. In the brief rainy season, the plant's extensive root system sucks up huge amounts of water. To store its treasure, the cactus expands its girth via its accordion-pleat construction, swelling and growing large, and then living off its watery hoard through the long, rainless months.

Along with scientists, Krutch investigates the body chemistry of a little creature that never drinks. In "the most triumphant" example of solving the water problem in a dry land, the kangaroo rat takes the Zen approach (99). Rather than confront the constant concern head on, the rather charming, mouse-like creature detours around the difficulty, manufacturing its own water internally from the dry seeds it eats. Then there's the desert tortoise, "the camel of our deserts," who gets his water from the vegetation he eats, then takes it with him, storing water in a bladder under his upper shell (111). Or the seeds of some desert plants. They might lie dormant for years waiting for the most beneficial combination of moisture and temperature before they sprout. Or the sex life of the scorpion, who, dim though his mind might be, has panache, taking his partner by the claw and dancing off with her to his nuptial bower during the mating season.

The desert is, indeed, a place of natural wonders.

It was a message entirely accommodating to the times. The local authorities had heeded the grousings of William T. Hornaday and J. Smeaton Chase about the lack of road signs and the putrid water in badly maintained wells. Or perhaps the county commissioners hadn't even read such men, but they were heeding the message from a larger force. Politicians likely dismissed the urgings of desert writers and a handful of grizzled prospectors with no political clout, but they were quick to recognize the changing times. From San Diego, Phoenix, and Yuma, Model Ts were chugging out into the desert ruts, and with the multiplying automobile came massive change. It had two points of origin. Not only did automobilists, wet behind the ears about the workings of the desert as they lowered their goggles and sallied forth on weekends in their new playthings, demand better roads, but businessmen with their hands on the levers of local politics envisioned the influx of tourist dollars. From the two converging forces, Better Roads societies sprang up across the desert, as they did elsewhere.

That meant the spread of paved roads and all that usually implies: the growth of cities, telephone lines strung across open spaces, and the general ease of desert life, matched by the reciprocal corollary, the shrinkage of desert wilderness. By the time that Joseph Wood Krutch first arrived in the desert, in the 1930s, he came, not in a horse and wagon or even in a passenger train speeding across what were otherwise still wild expanses, but driving with his wife in his own automobile, as if on a prolonged Sunday outing. True, there were still rumors itching the ears about Seri Indians south of the border who snatched up the unwary traveler in those rarely visited lands and cooked him up for a rare meal. On this side of the international line, vast stretches of Indian reservation remained roadless, accessible only to the inveterate outsider. Yet for the most part, the desert had become civilized for the majority of those visitors likely to see it. It was no longer the place of fantastic adventures with Cochise or even of standing on one's head and waggling legs in the air to celebrate the conquest of a peak. Krutch wrote about what mystery was left to him, and that was the innate exoticism he saw in the everyday life of experiencing the desert. Therefore, his focus on the mouse that never drinks and on the amorous dallyings of an arachnid.

In the course of such revelations, *The Voice of the Desert* sometimes turned mildly petulant, reminding readers that "our boasted control of nature is a delusion" (132). And in his penultimate chapter, the writer allowed himself a sermon, glumly speculating that the unprecedented growth of the human population in recent years was driving wild animals, even in the apparently vast desert, into smaller and smaller corners of what little was left of the natural world. Few people, the author scowled, seemed to care about this "reckless laying waste of the earth" (191). Yet he followed the bleak moralizing with the eupeptic concluding chapter, "The Mystique of the Desert." Here, all was not quite well with the world, but Krutch praised both the "mystical overtones" (216) one senses in the arid lands and humanity's ability to transcend its problems, many of them of its own creation (217–218). In the main, then, *The Voice of the Desert*, along with such companion volumes as *The Desert Year*, is a hopeful book, the secrets of the desert explored in an informative, gentlemanly, and at times breezy, manner by a desert enthusiast. It was as if Krutch were writing a long letter to the friends back East he had recently left, and as the city-bound folk oohed and aahed at the surprises their writer itemized, in the main his readers must have deemed him a happy man.

One might receive a similar impression from surveying Krutch's life as a whole. Raised in a solidly stable, middle-class, and pleasant family in Knoxville, Tennessee, Krutch later joked warmly in his autobiographical *More Lives than One* at a mildly eccentric aunt addicted to camping in an age when neighbors considered such an activity risqué (10–11), and he chuckled over Uncle Charlie, a church organist and painter of water-colors who, though no one ever saw him take a drink, "was never quite sober" (12). People in this modern age might find it difficult to believe, mused Krutch, but life in Knoxville for a boy busily making money from his paper route was very suggestive of "a Norman Rockwell magazine cover" come alive (8).[1]

However, even solidly hometown boys have their itches and inklings. In 1915, after graduating from the local University of Tennessee at the age of twenty-two, right on schedule for an ambitious American boy, Krutch hied off to indulge in the mysteries of New York City while attending graduate school. There in 1923 he married Marcelle Leguia, a French Basque immigrant nurse, and received his Ph.D. in English the next year from Columbia University.

Thereafter, his life is a success story springing out of the buoyant 1920s. Writing as the drama critic for *The Nation*, teaching at Columbia, young Krutch took his place with Mark Van Doren and other notables of the period among New York's literary crème. He turned out book after book—on Edgar Allan Poe, on Thoreau, and on Samuel Johnson—had a home in the country over in Connecticut, and traveled on multiple occasions to Europe. Having toured the Southwest several times with Marcelle and liking what he saw, in 1950 Krutch took an early retirement and settled on the edge of the desert outside Tucson, Arizona. Though his New York friends of the city's bon ton were aghast at his plunge into

The Opal Desert

the wilds—What on earth would he *do* out there?—Krutch hardly went to seed. Turning amateur naturalist, he poked around in his new and strange home, feeding the roadrunners and quail that came up to his patio out of the cacti, and writing volume after volume of delightful explorations to enlighten the doubters back East about the pleasures of his new desert existence. Before he died, Krutch could look back and take satisfaction. He had written many books. He had traveled and had a happy marriage. And he'd topped the whole off with twenty years of active, fulfilling retirement.

He had, in brief, lived what academics call "the Good Life."

Although in one sense it is true, behind that glowing impression lurked a darker side that served as the engine for many of Krutch's books and gave a peculiar variety to the shapes of his desert volumes, a side that captured a developing dilemma beginning to form in the consciousness of the nation in the 1950s and one, furthermore, that would take surprising, if not shocking, turns after Krutch had made his contribution. In other hands, the genteel desert art that he sculpted would fly off into weird shapes of intractable jinni after it had leapt out of his. That, however, lay in the future, and to go back and pick up on the long development in Krutch's life, the conflict can best be said this way: Despite all of Krutch's informative brightness, for decades a worm had been eating its way through his soul.

It began in gladness. When the young Krutch arrived in New York City and gracefully slipped into the nation's powerful circle of literary moguls, far more than the finesse of putting words on paper in delightful ways was involved. The 1920s in America's largest and most sophisticated city was "an era of novelty and adventure," as he talks about the times in *More Lives than One.* Then, "it was possible to hope that next week might reveal something nearer true greatness than anything that had yet appeared" (136). It was, Krutch further describes it, an intoxicating "Gaiety on the edge of Wickedness" (59).

This had social as well as long-range political ramifications. It was a time of sexual freedom and the Bohemian naughtiness of going to speakeasies. The banners of H. L. Mencken and Van Wyck Brooks, the deconstructionists of the day, set the direction for America's disaffected but adamantly hopeful young intellectuals. The Great War of 1914–1918 had, once and for all, so it was believed, solved that international problem and brought peace to the planet, a peace that many viewed as permanent. The rather large issue settled, all that seemed necessary among the anti-establishment youth was to throw off the shackles of tradition, the religious restrictions and social taboos that had repressed men for centuries, and then the people of the world finally would arrive at their new, luminous, and lasting destiny.

It may have been George Orwell who quipped that some ideas are so preposterous that only intellectuals, creatures whose eyes can go large over fads as readily as those of anyone else, will believe them. Krutch's burden, at once also his distinguishing intellectual virtue, lay in his ability to penetrate the tissue of the prevailing wisdom and see the complexities behind. Taken up in the ferment with his fellows, he gradually saw that to think Utopia could be so simply won was but more human folly. The concept touted by his friends was based on the idea that humanity was measurable and manipulable. But Krutch noted the darker potential to this. In the triumphs of science and, more specifically, psychology, Darwin and others had reduced man to a digit in a vast machine, and Freud had explained him away as but a bundle of desires and traumas. Excited as his colleagues might be about future prospects, their ideas were jejune, the frothings of affluent people who in their enthusiasm for the whimwhams of social engineering had lost contact with human underpinnings and diminished people to amoebas under a microscope. Human beings needed religion and mystery, the very things the new enthusiasts wanted to eliminate; yet Krutch had to admit that he had no answers in return. The shackles of tradition also were anchors, but they were false anchors. As much as he desired to believe in absolutes beyond science, he could only turn away in disgust at the gimcrackery of traditional religions, and the harsh light of science, he acknowledged sadly, had all but eliminated love, replacing it with mere lust.

Camped out on the desert, earlier writer John C. Van Dyke, similarly afflicted, had gazed up into the stars swirling over him and suffering a parallel bout of the shakes had cried out, "Are we anything more than petty animalculae clinging to a cold discarded fragment of a sun?" (*The Open Spaces* 19). A slumping Krutch shared Van Dyke's vertiginous doubts.

Such gloomy thoughts he put into a book, *The Modern Temper*, published, significantly, in 1929, on the eve of the Great Depression. It was not at all, as one might guess, a happy book. "Why don't you go out and hang yourself?" was the response from many a reader (*More Lives* 209). In something of a wonder, Krutch didn't. One can speculate that his pleasure in teaching and writing and his great love for his wife kept him going. Nonetheless, much of his life thereafter was "an attempt to climb out of the pit" (210–211). And the route of his escape led to the desert, though even there, saving as the place was, Krutch eventually saw an even larger pit yawning beyond.

It's not easily said how one claws oneself out of a psychic funk. Krutch was, he carefully warns, basically a city man, certainly no "romantic primitive" (312). Whether it was the kindly hand of nature slowly lifting him as a result of his long interest in Thoreau or some other factor in his life that lightened his burden and shifted his focus positively onto nature he himself couldn't explain.

Whatever the circumstances, no doubt a combination of several factors, Marcelle had succeeded in luring him out of the city to a cottage in Redding, Connecticut, whose country ambiance the commuting Krutch enjoyed well enough. Then, after he finished his book on the penetrating eccentric of Concord, the writer had something of an epiphany:

> One winter night shortly after I had finished Thoreau I was reading a "nature essay" which pleased me greatly and it suddenly occurred to me for the first time to wonder if I could do something of the sort. I cast about for a subject and decided on the most conventional of all, namely Spring. (293–294)

He narrowed his subject, however, from Spring to a little, inch-long New England frog that after the long winter snows melt rises out of the mud to announce to all New Englanders the renewal that comes with warmer weather, the little creature shouting an antediluvian joy, a massive outpouring, a wild abandon of choral chirping that seems in itself, as in some primitive rites, to tug the sun northward. The result of Krutch's appreciation, published in 1949 in *The Twelve Seasons*, surprised the scholar as the words flowed from his pen with a force he hadn't known:

> Surely one day a year might be set aside on which to celebrate our ancient loyalties and to remember our ancient origins. And I know of none more suitable for that purpose than the Day of the Peepers. "Spring is come!," I say when I hear them, and: "The most ancient of Christs has risen!" But I also add something which, for me at least, is even more important. "Don't forget," I whisper to the peepers; "we are all in this together." (13)

For those who feel more comfortable when pondering human change to put pen to calendar and fix a date, that winter night was Krutch's turning point. Throughout the process, Krutch was becoming increasingly disenchanted with the city's crowds, grime, and bad air. Added to that, the couple already felt the pull of a freeing alternative, already had visited the Southwest and knew the "sudden lifting of the heart" at the seemingly endless expanses blessed by a sky so blue that each day it appeared to be freshly made. "It seemed almost as though I had lived there in some happier previous existence and was coming back home" (*The Voice*

And then there was the clean, dry air opening up the Krutches' respiratory passages, often clogged in the course of the drear, northern winters. Why not go? The reasons in favor kept adding up, with no compelling rebuttal in response. A year after "The Day of the Peepers" appeared as the first essay in Krutch's book of gentle ponderings on nature, the Krutches "piled our car high with all that could be imposed upon it," drove to Tucson, and started putting down new roots in the desert (*More Lives* 309).

Due to the fortunes of geography, Americans have been a westward-yearning people, though rarely has that westering led them to the Promised Land of their expectations. The gold-seekers, rarely finding the glitter they saw abundantly in their dreams, often traded the rocker for the humbler hoe, and even present-day job seekers, packing up the family for a new start in Wyoming or California, may well face the frustration of a discouraging job market and a family beginning to disintegrate in the course of the uprooting. As to deserts, it's no blotch on travelers' records if upon their arrival, shocked at a bleak reality far different from colorful postcard depictions, they're glad when their airplane closes its doors, rolls down the runway, and takes them back to a greener, more comfortable place.

Such was not at all the case with Joseph Wood Krutch and his wife. Built to their specifications, their new home looked out across several miles of cactus and mesquite to the dark green islands of pine-topped peaks of the Santa Catalina Mountains rearing thousands of feet above the desert floor. A bit worried at first about not having a regular income, the writer found that his literary connections served him in good stead. Sizing up the market, publishers guessed correctly that Krutch's readers would jump at descriptions of life out in what was still regarded as an exotic and far-off land. In fact, when Krutch arrived in Tucson, he already had just such a contract in his pocket. More would follow, at the rate of one, sometimes two, a year. As Krutch drove off with Marcelle to explore the massive, rocky tablelands of the Navajo country to the north, striated with colors, or back home sat in his study chucking his pet kangaroo rat, a high-strung but fetching little creature, under the chin, one might feel that all, or almost all, was placid in the writer's soul. In fact, it was, at least for a while. "Neither Marcelle nor I have ever regretted for a moment the move." He added with convincing confidence, "The ten years since we came to Tucson have been the most contented (and often the happiest) of our lives, and never since adolescence have I been physically so well" (312). Krutch had found his métier.

Besides the buoyant nature essays Krutch was turning out about his adopted homeland, other and more serious writing serving as its under-pinnings confirmed that he was well on his way out of the pit. In 1956 Harcourt Brace reissued *The Modern Temper* with an updated preface by its author. Krutch reflected on the gloom of the original edition:

More than a quarter of a century later I find myself asking three questions: (1) Do educated people continue to believe that science has exposed as delusions those convictions and standards upon which Western civilization was founded? (2) Is the ultimate cause of the catastrophe with which that civilization is threatened this loss of faith in humanity itself? (3) Is it really true, as I once believed, that there is no escaping the scientific demonstration that religion, morality, and the human being's power to make free choices are all merely figments of the imagination? (xii)

To the first two questions he answered yes, but he rejected his ear-lier pessimism that man is but a wind-up toy staggering meaninglessly through the universe, his hopes, his spirit, his free will all "merely fig-ments of the imagination." For the details of the change in his thinking, Krutch referred his readers to a book he'd written two years before, *The Measure of Man.* This, he claimed, not only was a reply to the downbeat *The Modern Temper* but a refutation of its hopelessness (xiii).

It is not necessary to pick one's way through all the philosophical labyrinths of *The Measure of Man* to follow the main drift of the change. Krutch rejected the mechanistic and deterministic analyses of life that had infected Western civilization. The result, he saw, was absorption with materialistic trivia by the masses and retreat into nihilism by the intellectuals. Krutch praised science for what it could do, but he also warned that its authority and glittering accomplishments had their limi-tations. Amplifying in *More Lives than One,* he reminded readers of the nineteenth-century scientist who scoffed that "he did not believe in 'the soul' because he could not find it in his test tube." Should we limit our lives to such nonsense? Fine as it was, science could be blind, denying the existence of anything lying beyond its own methods (324). Humans, Krutch asserted, are more than that. They have consciousness and curios-ity, and they keep asking impossible questions such as "What is Beauty?" In such a way, Krutch asserted traditional values and showed himself the classical liberal and consummate humanist of the Western tradition. In this, the mystery of the Pronuba moth and the other desert wonders that he popularly wrote about were reflections of his new optimism as well as responses to more widespread doubts churning in the culture. Neither science nor the desert, Krutch seemed to say, can save us from our fate, whatever that might be after death, but the desert can lift us, making the spirit hum, as science cannot, blessing us with wonder and a fascinating existence while we're on this earth. As he summarized, "One must live now or not at all" (370).

Given the widespread applause for his desert books, that cheery view of this marriage, of a man joyously writing away in his study about his desert encounters, likely is the one to prevail. Paul Pavich reflects this in the summary paragraph concluding his study of the writer:

> Krutch found in the desert a model for life's purposes, tenacity, endurance, and vitality. There he found both the spiritual and physical latitude necessary for reflection. The desert environment allowed him to find a sense of community which completely overwhelmed the estrangement he had felt in New York. In Tucson he became revitalized by his interest in the incredible panorama of nature. His writings completed in the shadow of the Catalina Mountains indicate that Krutch was not a tired, cantankerous hermit but a rejuvenated individualist who eschewed the intellectual exhaustion of many of his scholarly colleagues. His life in the Southwest brought him a rare gift indeed—a sense of joyful participation and delight in the miracle and mystery of existence. (46–47)

Much truth lies in Pavich's statement. In the desert, Krutch indeed displayed the active absorption of a man revitalized. However, though sanguine, the view also offers a single dimension of the man and his situation, a partial, if popular, truth. The remainder of it takes us into the complexities of the man and, more importantly, through them to the nature of the modern age's relationship with the desert, one, yes, of bright hope, but one also, like that of most love affairs, tangled with inconsistencies, double standards, and intractable frustrations. If the desert brought Krutch out of his pit, he faced a deeper one beyond. Loving the desert was not as simple as Krutch first proposed.

Concerning the man himself, underlying his felicity with words, his wit, and perceptive powers, was a dark and heavy streak weighing him down. At bedrock, he admits in *More Lives than One*, he was an apprehensive man (61) finding it difficult to trust himself (63), a person plagued by fears (91), and basically melancholy by nature—characteristics fortunately balanced by his wife's rosy spirits (128). Such aspects, though painful, often are the true intellectual's lot and are much to the good for a man who strives to be a careful thinker, though they also prevented Krutch from taking comfort in the absolute values that were the search of his life, a life he perhaps took much too seriously.

That is to say that there were some rather large chinks in Krutch's philosophy, and there are strong indications that the man, so yearning to believe, was aware of the damning flaws in his thought. Back to the image of the peevish scientist who couldn't find the soul in his test tube, a person of Krutch's perception must have known that his mockery of the man proved nothing. That science does not accept the existence of anything lying beyond its own methods may be a limitation of that branch of knowledge, but it does not follow, as Krutch argued in maintaining the nobility of the human spirit, that anything unperceived by science therefore necessarily exists. Krutch knew that. His belief in man as more than a machine was just that, a belief, and therefore unprovable, and, in Krutch's case, skeptic that he was, one unattached to a specific, bolstering theology or organized philosophy. But "it is as far as I have been able to go. I doubt that I shall ever be able to go further." Krutch confesses the shakiness of his position in *More Lives than One.* Then he adds in a resigned sotto voce, "At least I have lived by [my beliefs] for some years now more contentedly than I had been able to live before" (326). In terms of logic, that's little more than the faith of a drowning man clinging to an imagined plank. Unfortunately, Krutch could not accept his beliefs for what they were, intuitive compulsions beyond reason. Criticizing logic for its limitations, Krutch continued to be disturbed by the ill-logic of his own position.

The churnings in Krutch's soul, howsoever lasting and dire, would be of little concern to this study were it not for the brown colors they lent to his engagement with the desert. On the desert, Krutch found health, and he found a constant fascination with the things about him. That is much for a man to find. But chucking a pet kangaroo rat under the chin and chuckling at his antics is not a redeeming faith but a palliative, an engrossing entertainment, what one does, as the sardonic expression goes, "while moving between here and there."

As we shall see in the next chapter, following generations, reveling in inconsistencies and abandonment as Krutch could not, blithely threw off the logic that Krutch took on as his burden and bypassed the problem with a great, glad romantic leap. Meanwhile, Krutch faced a dilemma ever more unyielding and damning than his own painful grapplings with reason. Beyond them rose a worse horror: Beyond them he stood before the very dragon's bad breath. And this one followed perfectly from his desert premise.

If the desert was the thing yielding what was the closest Krutch came to mystery, what he calls "the mystical overtones which the observation of nature made audible to me" (*Voice* 216), this great, good thing, this reservoir of blessings, surely should be not only cherished but preserved in its pristine state to gladden men's hearts. It was not to be. As mentioned, the Krutches settled in Tucson in 1950. Though the house they built was only a few miles from town, they could revel in a sense of isolation. At the time, Tucson was a small city of 45,000, fairly well concentrated around its downtown district, with its Sears and Roebuck and movie theater, in short, a downtown where on Saturday afternoons people likely would recognize many other shoppers.[2] If Krutch scaled one of the nearby mountain peaks, as he likely did, he could pick out the roof of his house below sheltered by a clump of trees. Then his eyes would move across the cactus sweeps to the little city beside the Santa Cruz River, a small patch of civilization in a great, apparently uninhabited valley rimmed by half a dozen mountain ranges of serrated lava, their masses approaching a transparent vitreous blue in the intense desert sunlight.

The person who treasured such an idyllic picture, however, soon was in for a wrenching change. It was not only that Tucson was about to grow along with other U.S. cities as the nation's population increased, and not only, too, that the automobile would wreck the synthesis, sprawling cities outward in unrelated suburbs while the hearts of the communities left behind died. That, but much more, for Tucson. Along with the Krutches of a few years before, Americans were discovering the Sunbelt, discovering that the slush and ice of winters were nuisances they needn't put up with. In a few years after the Krutches' arrival, Tucson began not only to grow, it grew mindlessly and monstrously, spreading out until it threatened to fill up the great loveliness of its own desert valley and spill over into other desert valleys beyond. From the comprehensible city of 45,000 Krutch saw in 1950, Tucson swelled into a giant amoeba of 263,000 by 1970, the year that Krutch died.[3]

Krutch was no fool. His house lay directly in the path of urban sprawl, and year after year he saw the engulfing ugliness of fast-food joints and gasoline stations chewing across the desert toward him. "He was heartbroken to see it," says his widow (Wild, *Pioneer Conservationists of Western America* 132). His saving desert was being ravished like a lover with spreading sores.

The noxious phenomenon, Krutch knew, though applauded by most of the city, was but part of a larger surreal picture, and this confirmed the voice from the gloomier side of his personality that said, "The future of mankind is dubious" (*Voice* 216). The destruction of the desert was but a symptom of a wider madness rolling over the earth, the inability to solve the problems of overpopulation, technology, and human differences. Sometimes, people not only rushed lemming-like into the arms of disaster, they rejoiced at the chance. For instance, this deftly put bit of acid irony from the early 1960s:

Only a few months ago the military authorities announced that Tucson had been selected as one of the expendable cities to be ringed with bases of Titan missiles. It was frankly admitted, not only that a direct hit [by a nuclear missile from the Soviet Union] would of course annihilate us all, but also that, due to the prevailing winds, a near miss would blanket us with fallout. A small minority protested that it might be wiser to locate such bases in the still available areas not so dangerously close to any large community. But the protest got nowhere. In great alarm the city fathers begged us to say no more lest the army should, in a huff, decide to confer its blessings elsewhere. Said the mayor: "It will be a fine thing for the community." Said the president of the Chamber of Commerce: "It's something we have been working for—and hoping for—for a long time." (More Lives 360–361)

Such was men's foolishness. The happiest words Krutch could muster on the invited potential for Tucson's nuclear crisping in exchange for more mad growth was the quote from a maverick radio commentator. He quipped that the project seemed to him "a disaster with fringe benefits" (361).

Krutch, no enthusiast for speechmaking, recalled how as a favor to a friend he'd given a talk to the local Rotary Club on "Tucson as a Place to Write." The city, he told the assembled after lunch, still was a pretty amiable place for a writer, but it was fast losing its charm. Why not have a new slogan, suggested Krutch: Instead of "Help Tucson Grow," they should adopt "Keep Tucson Small." According to the newspaper the next day, "most of the audience assumed that Dr. Krutch had his tongue in his cheek" (360).

What could one do with such an obtuse world?

Remembering her husband, Olaus, a leader of the Wilderness Society, an organization responsible for preserving millions of acres of wildlands despite the odds against success, Margaret Murie wrote: "He believed that even with the very worst forecast possible for the future, it was more fun to take part in the battle for what you believed in than just to stand on the sidelines wringing your hands." Krutch couldn't do that. Had he been an active conservationist, he might have worked off some of his frustrations by channeling his energies and joining the growing movement led by the Sierra Club, the Friends of the Earth, and other grassroots organizations in their effort to combat the self-destructive insanity spreading around the world. Though Krutch sympathized with the work of environmental organizations, and they readily gave him awards for his books about nature, he couldn't join the scalers of barricades (205). He was not one to roll up his sleeves and, mounting the stump, tour the hustings making firebrand speeches about the world's dismal future unless people mended their ways. He was too introspective, too cynical about the irredeemable mass of humanity, for that.

His direction lay elsewhere, and though it once again brought him excitements, it, too, ultimately came with a heavy note of despair. He would see what he could of the desert before technology gobbled it up entirely. Through a chance meeting with avid traveler Kenneth Bechtel, a family member of the construction firm then in the process of busily building roads and dams around the world, Krutch began exploring Baja California, that long, finger-like peninsula separating the Gulf of California from the Pacific Ocean.[4]

As the writer's *The Forgotten Peninsula* reveals, Krutch found what he wanted in this part of Mexico, an extension of his own Sonoran desert far from the main tourist track. Resource poor but rich in scenery, Baja was sparsely populated. Down there, threading through the maze of desert and mountains in their four-wheel drive, Krutch and Bechtel could bounce for days to their hearts' content over the dirt roads, meeting hardly a soul except for the occasional ranchero and his huaracheed family clinging to survival in their adobe hut. The two could revel over pristine beaches that went on for miles unblemished by nary a beach umbrella and gaze in wonder at the weird forest of boojum trees, huge, upside-down carrots growing across the desert.

Yet a man as perceptive as Krutch couldn't help but see the blot spreading over the horizon of Baja's future. Once, Bechtel's pilot pointed to an airstrip below newly scraped across the land, eight thousand feet in length and ominously intended for jets (275). Besides the hotels beginning to sprout along the beaches, Krutch acidly noted that one automobile club in Southern California already was distributing maps showing members "where various large animals not quite extinct may be found by those eager to do their bit toward eliminating them completely" (236). Baja was being prepared for the ubiquitous hordes of Baja Buffs that have since swept across the once almost unknown region:

One after another the most accessible mountains and beaches are turning into Coney Islands of horror to which the hordes come, not to make contact with natural beauty, but to invade it with radios and all the other paraphernalia necessary to transform mountain or beach into a noisy slum so little different from the slums of the city as to make one wonder why they bother to come. (275)

Did it have to be that way? No, it didn't. But that's the way it would be, given the worldwide pattern reflecting people's limited vision. Man might be a noble creature, as Krutch had struggled to convince himself for decades, but nobility was an individual, not a mass, phenomenon. In the end, Krutch was defeated by that realization, and the best he could do was shrug his shoulders as he ended his book on Baja, slumping: "I am glad to have had the opportunity to enjoy what, in another generation or two, it may be almost impossible for anyone to find anywhere" (277).

On such a hopeless note, Krutch had summed up the modern dilemma. A rationalist might think that would be the end of desert writing.

11

EDWARD ABBEY

Ned Ludd Arrives

on the Desert

Each carrying a giant pair of golden shears, the governors of Utah and Arizona strut toward the center of the new bridge that links their two states by spanning the chasm of the Colorado River. The long speeches finally over, the band starts up, the multitude cheers, and the two dignitaries, in cowboy hats and pointy-toed boots, josh each other as they approach the ribbon:

"Go ahead, old buddy. Cut the damn thing."
"Me . . . ?"
"I thought you said . . ."
"Okay, I gotcha. Stand back. Like this?"

Then an amazing thing happens, something not on the program. All at once the center of the bridge rises, followed by the noise of an explosion and a great plume of smoke. Then the jaws of the gathered thousands drop as they behold the loose ends of the structure writhe and Cadillacs slide down the twisting, sinuous roadway. Flying off into space, the shiny limousines slowly revolve as they float toward the rocks of the canyon far below.

It's the opening scene of Edward Abbey's *The Monkey Wrench Gang* (14). The literary fireworks will be followed by gutted bulldozers, a blown-up train, and wild chases across mesas and plateaus as the law pursues the ragged band of perpetrators, mad but mad in the right way in their fight to stop the mindless spread of industrialization across their beloved desert.

When Joseph Wood Krutch died in 1970, the *New York Times* remembered its old friend for his "cultured" manners and his "prescient" books. Noting dual phenomena, the growth of the environmental movement and the impatience of the day's youth, the newspaper recommended that young people turn to Krutch's pages for "delight to themselves and profit to the world" ("Joseph Wood Krutch").

Such was not to be. It was not the well-measured words of a genteel professor retired from Columbia University that would be on the lips of young Americans but those of a rebellious hillbilly, an at times crude, often rabble-rousing, and certainly iconoclastic maverick who liked nothing better than to bloody the noses of authority, especially those of the wrong-headed, nature-destroying government and its minions, the industries and businesses hauling in profits from paving, mining, and chopping down wild America. Thoreau had preached that "in Wildness is the preservation of the World" (275), and Abbey took him literally, then even took the advice of the New England nature lover a step further. Reminding his readers that the likes of Robin Hood and his band flourished until the refuge of their forest was cut down, Abbey, as had Thoreau, pegged the very idea of individual liberty to wild nature (*The Fool's Progress* 47). Yet if the government was denying that essential human benefit, citizens had the right, nay, the obligation, to rise up against their oppressors. If that meant blowing up bridges or pouring Karo Syrup into the bowels of road-building bulldozers, so be it. Freedom was too precious not to fight for, even to die for.

The upheavals of twelfth-century England had created scofflaw Robin Hood. Something similar in societal turmoil rocketed Abbey to fame. The docile 1950s, with their crew cuts, neckties, and deference of teenagers to their betters—all this was wiped away in the next two decades. Replacing them was the Now Generation, of illegal drugs, bounding sexual freedom, miniskirted girls running away from home, and riots in the streets. Sociologists and historians will struggle for years trying to explain the phenomenon. Much of it had to do with rapid changes that caught the 1950s off guard. Despite the aura of sensationalism about this, at its heart lay a clinical fact of demographics. As often happens when a bulge works its way through a population, the sheer size of the generation coming of age rudely bulldozed its own, new path through society. Or perhaps it had something to do with the stars, as the Age of Aquarius dawned and the growing popularity of astrology joined other "alternative" beliefs becoming the yeasty rage.

Suddenly, the mass of impatient young people was calling everything into question. And often with good reason. The unpopular Vietnam War being fought halfway around the world, the civil rights movement, and "the Pill" all threw doubts on traditional ways and then damned the values of Krutch's aging generation. Now Youth, steeped in its own, instant Counter Culture, would rule, and it did so with a vengeance seared into memory by pictures of mass love-ins and burning buildings on college campuses. All but overnight, to be anti-Establishment was de rigueur, not only for young people but for many of their elders who, joining them on the flight into neo-romanticism, sensed that something indefinable was wrong in America's soul. Part of the upheaval was the stunning growth of the environmental movement, a return to nature and to the supposedly simpler ways from which the nation had strayed and created a queasy mess of itself. And part of this was the radicalization of the movement, the feeling that such organizations as the Sierra Club and the Audubon Society had been much too timid, too polite, in defending the earth. As in the case of protesting the Vietnam War, patience was at its end. The time was ripe for direct, if at times illegal, action. Abbey's message of revolt fit the complex and often contradictory cravings exactly. And often, the more contradictory the better. "If it feels good, do it," was the watchword of the day—a message much to the liking of youth, their juices at high tide.

The prevailing authority, whether parents, police, or university officials, was deemed corrupt, stuck in old-fashioned ideas. A sneering youth, claiming a position on the side of the angels, disdained the Establishment. In the flipflop of values, stealing became justified as "liberating," and irresponsibility was considered a form of self-fulfillment. Often, whether burning one's bra or screaming obscenities before television cameras at tumultuous mass rallies, the goal was to shock. Outrageous behavior was its means. Abbey's modus operandi, both in his writing and in his public performances, nicely matched the swing of youth's new attitudes.

Not only did he advocate tweaking the nose of the military-industrial complex by blowing up bridges; when this tall, bearded, and craggy man stepped up to the lectern, there was no telling what the self-declared anarchist might do. One of his many targets was ranchers. Traditionally enjoying a proud image of independence, actually, railed Abbey, they were on the public dole. Grazing on the public's land, their cattle degraded the environment and competed with wildlife for forage. Up in Missoula, Montana, in the heart of cow country, the visiting speaker didn't mince words:

Abbey opened his talk by pulling a .44-caliber revolver from his briefcase and waving it around, saying he'd be pleased to answer questions. It was unloaded, but his audience didn't know that. Thus armed, he proceeded to accuse ranchers, who made up most of the audience, of being "welfare parasites." Then he referred to their cows as "ugly, clumsy, stupid, brawling, stinking, fly-covered, shit-smeared, disease-spreading brutes." (Bishop 43)

It was typical Abbey fortissimo. Wilderness advocates, especially those of the impatient, more radical stripe, greeted such performances gleefully. Abbey had become an "environmental guru" (Slovic 113).

All of which makes Edward Abbey sound like the Bad Boy on the fringe of the conservation movement, an exhibitionist who enjoyed creating fusses. Above all, whether writing or lecturing, Abbey was out to have a good time. A great deal of truth clings to the statement, but the larger truth is that Abbey was far more complex than his public image. In some ways he was akin to the gentlemanly Joseph Wood Krutch, though a Krutch who had taken fire.

And yet Abbey was royally, boastfully inconsistent. The adult writer who hailed preserving wilderness also took a teenager's perversity in rolling car tires down into the Grand Canyon; the wistful romantic who spooned up sugary dotings about women often treated them as sex objects; and the rebel making a shambles of such icons as ranchers next advocated the very down-home, biscuits-and-gravy ethos he so terribly seemed bent on destroying. He wanted Americans to wake up and escape into the wilds, where they'd find their true souls, then he groused when too many people blighted his wilderness escapes. He advocated free love, then praised faithfulness; he mocked academics, then became one himself.

Facing such puzzles, we're often tempted to turn to biography for an explanation. If this tack doesn't make complete sense of Abbey, it nonetheless yields a telling pattern. Though he was born in 1927 in the mountains of western Pennsylvania,[1] not in Vermont during colonial times, something of the wayward, radical, unwashed craziness of Revolutionary War guerrilla Ethan Allen and his Green Mountain Boys clung to Edward Abbey throughout his life.[2]

It was not that the successive homes of the Abbeys in the area were all that different from other ragged farms dotting the hills and valleys of the Allegheny Mountains. In that part of Appalachia, life was a root-hog-or-die sort of affair. Along with his neighbors, Abbey's father did whatever it took to support his family during the raw years of the Depression. Adding to the larder from a few cows and chickens, he did a little logging, trapped, hunted, and drove a school bus. Whatever it took. One thing, though, set the Abbeys off. Like their friends, the Abbeys were hillbillies, but they were different from their conservative, church-going neighbors. Not only did the Abbey household ring with music, readings from Walt Whitman, and earnest debates about politics. Head of the household, Paul Revere Abbey, though not well educated, was well read; he also was an anarchist and agnostic. Not that he was an outcast, a pariah in the community. Friends would drift in and out on Sunday afternoons, eating cheese and crackers and peanut butter snacks while spinning yarns. For his part, now and then Paul would wax candescent about the virtues of Communism, but his wife, Mildred, a schoolteacher, knew how to oil troubled waters at such times by bringing the conversation back to talk about pigs and crops.

If there is any key, real or imagined, to Abbey the rapscallion adult writer, surely it must be his father, bubbling with anarchism but pent up on a dirt-poor farm and constrained by the responsibilities of a family. Son Edward felt no such restraints. After his junior year in high school, he got a taste of wanderlust by playing hobo and riding the rails west. Drafted into the Army upon graduation, he just missed the action of World War II, but he created his own excitement. While serving as a military policeman in Italy, he wracked up his government motorcycle, and he kept getting into trouble for not saluting officers. After two years of quirky disobedience, he left the Army as he had entered it—as a private.

If Paul Revere Abbey, chafing in the traces of family obligations, had any notions of someday achieving vicarious bloom, surely he was pleased at the continuing performances of his eldest son. Majoring in philosophy at the University of New Mexico, Edward Abbey developed his talents for appalling officialdom. When editor of *The Thunderbird*, the normally tame student literary magazine, Abbey blazoned his own article, "Some Implications of Anarchy," with an epigram actually by Voltaire but perversely ascribed to Louisa May Alcott: "Man will never be free until the last king is strangled with the entrails of the last priest" (McCann 7).

That stunt nearly got him expelled, but Abbey was well on his way to developing into a picaresque radical. Thereafter, his life settled into a pattern of the outdoor writer/transient/bad boy. There were a few attempts at fitting into the system: a stint as a social worker in the New York City area and, later in life, a teaching position at the University of Arizona. For the most part, though, Abbey divided his time between summer jobs with two government agencies, the U.S. Park Service and the U.S. Forest Service. The part-time work as a lookout and ranger piled up grubstakes for winter months of writing. Also, as his novels and essays celebrating the freedom of the outdoors tumbled from the presses and his fame grew, he found that he could make a good extra income by lecturing at universities. Here, during the frothy Vietnam War era, while delivering wry, anti-Establishment tirades, he was greeted by overflow crowds of effervescent youths who wildly applauded his confirmations of their own rebelliousness. And all the while, he kept getting married, married, married to younger women. And divorced. By the time Abbey died in 1989, quipping, "Well, at least I won't have to floss anymore," he had had five wives (Bishop 5). Into whatever heaven provocateurs soar, behind him Abbey left the career of a man who, despite his graying beard, never lost his "romantic and sardonic zing" (16).

The brief, biographical excursion describes Edward Abbey, but it does not explain him for those of us who, judging ourselves normal, yearn to grasp people radically unlike us. Here's the dilemma stated in a vignette about youthful Abbey, familiarly called Ned by family members. By this time, Abbey has long ago told his Sunday School teacher that she was full of beans in promoting Biblical stories of miracles, and now the rascally teenager is branching out on his own:

A few years later, he was walking with his brother Howard toward a busy intersection in a nearby town. When the light turned green for them, a car pulled up and blocked the crosswalk. Howard started to walk around the narrow space left by the car, as the average person might do. Not Ned! The lean youngster strode toward the car, and with his long legs bounded onto the hood, leaving a large dent. Leaping to the street on the other side, he continued on his way. (12)

The incident should give us pause. The world has its surfeit of rebellious teenagers who delight in performing unexpected antics. It's part of working immaturity out of their systems. If they don't grow up, however, what we wink at as youthful folly becomes wearisome in adults. Usually, such people bounce from job to job, dismissed for their petty, nonproductive goofiness; their unmown lawns mar neighborhoods; and/or they become expensive repeat cases in the overburdened mental systems. That is to say two things. Springing from the same environment, Abbey's three brothers and one sister hardly followed in his eccentric tracks. Here, then, biography has failed us. One thing we can say, however, is that Abbey's success as a writer gave him cachet; without it he simply would be another kook. Working from this, perhaps we can find what is most important about him in his books. After all, the best of a writer should be found not in his life but in the words he leaves us.

Most cranks are driven by weakness. They are victims of flawed psychological chips. Hence, their goal is exercising their problems rather than accomplishing change. Obstructionists and nitpickers, they turn meetings into prolonged sessions of torture. Not so Edward Abbey.

Whatever churned in his soul, whatever his absurd, sometimes clownish, performances on college campuses, he was among the most disciplined of writers, painstakingly keeping his journals, enduring the years of obscurity that is the common lot of the writing tribe. In his case, added to the persistence that can propel even a madman, all the while Abbey was honing his native talent into a skilled, serpentine prose, at turns lashing out with sarcasm, then going silky with pathos. And, like John C. Van Dyke before him, he had luck. Rendered into books, his own private turmoils artfully mirrored the turmoils of his times.

If a person has read but one novel by Edward Abbey, it's likely to be *The Monkey Wrench Gang*, supplying the events for this chapter's opening paragraphs. Abbey biographer James Bishop gives as neat a summary of the zany book as has ever been penned:

> *Drawing on the lives of real people, Abbey created a wealthy Albuquerque physician named Doc Sarvis who burned billboards for a hobby; a sexy, philosophizing exile from the Bronx named Bonnie Abzug; and George Washington Hayduke, a deranged ex–Green Beret whose love for dynamite and beer was equaled only by his hatred of helicopters. Abbey teamed them up with an outcast, polygamous Mormon riverboat guide named Seldom Seen Smith.*
>
> *Next, he mobilized this gang of fun-loving anarchists against power companies, logging conglomerates, and Glen Canyon Dam. The gang was unified by a single theme, allegiance to the earth, and the war cry: "Keep it like it was." Their goal: the murder of machines. (125–126)*

Fun-loving anarchists is precisely the term. Having placed the madcap characters on his stage, Abbey sends his unpredictable outcasts off on their midnight raids of eco-sabotage, twisting the tail of the law, then effecting hair's-breadth escapes into the refuge of the great desert. If this eco-farce, this slapstick on the side of the angels, is not profound, it is skillfully done, sometimes colorfully exhilarating, especially for battered environmentalists who, in the real world, badly outspent and politically outgunned, found joyous wish-fulfillment in Abbey's romantic fantasy of dragon slaying.

The Monkey Wrench Gang also had a perhaps unintended effect. It scared the bejeezies out of corporate types who, glancing from the book to the long-haired, unwashed, pot-smoking rabble chanting on their corporate lawns, protesting a timber sale or a new highway, feared the book might unleash a real revolution. By comparison, proposals by members of the certainly washed, mostly polite Audubon Society and the Sierra Club seemed the soul of moderation. Through his up-on-the-toes radicalism,

Abbey helped tug at the boundaries, moving the stakes and expanding the dimensions of what seemed reasonable demands. Give them a wilderness here or there, anything to keep such as the wild ones in *The Monkey Wrench Gang* from leaping out of its pages into real life. In this view, the book was literature turned into a weapon of fear for political ends.

To the misfortune of Abbey's readers, the multilevel literary successes of *The Monkey Wrench Gang* were not typical of his other novels. His first attempt in the genre, *Jonathan Troy*, recounts the agonies of a Pennsylvania teenager. He keeps longing for the Southwest, but his self-absorbed, messed-up personality stymies his dreams. In *The Brave Cowboy*, Jack Burns, another anarchic dreamer type, insists on living what Abbey seems to imagine to have been the old, free days of the West. Flying in the face of a modern bureaucracy, the suburbs and fenced land blocking the footloose rider, Burns and his horse are flattened by a truck loaded with plumbing fixtures. Worse is *Black Sun.* A nymphetic Sandy appears from nowhere at the desert lookout tower of ranger Will Gatlin. Her thighs go like threshing machines and her breasts are pink-tipped; she salves Gatlin's world pain. The message is clear: good sex cures all. Then, just as inexplicably as she appeared, she disappears. Gatlin is heartbroken; his winsome lass gone, now all he wants to do is stare into the sun until his universe goes black.[3]

In other words, for the most part the novels, heavily autobiographical, contain too much of the immature and schlocky side of the self-proclaimed anarchist. They may have easy appeal to sentimentalists wanting quick dunkings, but the truth is that in the main his novels offer thorough soakings in Weltschmerz.

Despite this, Abbey had become such a heroic outdoors figure that many of his loyalists, buoyed by their enthusiasm for his environmental advocacy and his books of truly fine writing, often praised anything he wrote.[4] Yet whatever the accolades of his uncritical admirers, the unevenness of his prose remains. It may be a reflection of his personality. One need not believe that Newton's Third Law of Motion operates in the human psyche as it does in the physical world to see a marked set of opposites in the writer. The man who took pleasure in being devastatingly sarcastic, even snide and threatening, to strutting governors, ranchers, sheriffs, highway surveyors—in fact to anyone in a position of authority—often glided to the other end of the spectrum and into an emotional swamp. Sometimes it was soft, warm, pink, and fuzzy-wuzzy down there; at others, but an adolescent pool of murky stump water. He never shook loose of enjoying large doses of sentimentalism, and, indeed, his indulgence in what at times can be called nothing less than bathos may well have been partly responsible for his popularity among a self-absorbed youth culture with similar tastes. When he took for his text Thoreau's bright but glib "all good things are wild and free," how could the fans of Debby Boone not scream and stamp their feet? (287).

Besides gonadal stimulation, much of this involves a yearning for a lost, idealized past. Coming back from climbing Guadalupe Peak, a spire rising from the corrugated desert of West Texas, Abbey stumbles on an abandoned homestead:

> *The house is a one-story stud-frame shack with windows boarded over, its sides creaking in the wind, cracking apart splinter by splinter under the sun. We investigate the disintegrating corral, the rabbit hutch, the chicken house, a rusted water tank, the remains of a flatbed wagon with oaken tongue and iron-rimmed wooden-spoked wheels. Relics from the 1920s and 1930s.*

So far, so good. This is an apt, even journalistic, description of many such ruins scattered across the desert. It's what Abbey does with the scene emotionally, however, that is particularly telling. The next paragraph takes a plunge into something else entirely:

> *Standing here amid this dereliction, one contemplates (maybe recalls) that former style of life. Many miles by dirt road to the nearest town. Saturday afternoon at the moving picture show. Return by starlight to the homestead. Unharnessing the team, forking hay into the manger, milking the cow. Inside the shack, Maw trims the wick of the kerosene lamp.* (Beyond the Wall 135)

Now, most of us who stroll around America's outback have come across similar dolorous scenes. The weathered door hanging by one hinge, a child's toy half buried in the sand. And it is not to our shame that considering the wreckage we twitch with melancholy for the past life and laughter of the place. Those often are immediate and perfectly understandable reactions. However, good writing offers more than the cliché of immediate reaction. Life might not have been as rosy as Abbey fantasizes. Living in that dry, blistering place of unremitting loneliness may have been miserable, the unrewarding routine of farm life a killing, soul-sucking grind. Day after day until she finally screamed, Maw may have hated the way Paw slurped his soup after the dolt came clomping back in from milking.

None of such possibilities for Abbey. Reminded of his own childhood on the Pennsylvania farm, remembered in idyllic terms from the safe distance of adulthood, he takes the easy way out, escaping into a comfortable nostrum (Cahalan 99–100). And that it is one made of the old agrarian ideal is to assume the power of a Longfellow or a James Whitcomb Riley. Attempting to revivify a fantasy, much of Abbey works off a life that never was. It is a secure method, this reaching out to push both his own and the public's button for sentiment, and it tends to work over and over again with an industrialized people yearning for easy romance.

As to the gonadal ploy, it, too, follows Abbey even into his finest work:

> *For my own part I am pleased enough with surfaces—in fact they alone seem to me to be of much importance. Such things for example as the grasp of a child's hand in your own, the flavor of an apple, the embrace of friend or lover, the silk of a girl's thigh, the sunlight on rock and leaves, the feel of music, the bark of a tree, the abrasion of granite and sand, the plunge of clear water into a pool, the face of the wind—what else is there? What else do we need?* (Desert Solitaire xiii)

Not to discount such exhilarations as the grasp of a child's hand or the silk of a girl's thigh, yet if we stop there we have little more than one great undifferentiated bowl of warm mush. If that's all there is, we are indeed to be pitied.

Abbey, however, can give the lie to himself. He hardly is the wilderness bumpkin overflowing wherever he goes with the warm and sticky. In the *Journey Home*, he recounts his first view of the Rocky Mountains: "An impossible beauty, like a boy's first sight of an undressed girl . . ." (2). If this is yet another dipping into the sexual barrel, it is nonetheless a worthy, appropriate, and fairly sophisticated trope; and it furthermore— thank Goodness!—is a happy indication that, despite what he often says about himself, Abbey offers far more than a diet of gooey emotions.

This brings us to a curious feature in the body of Abbey's work. The strain of sentimentalism is most prominent in his fiction. Here, as in *Black Sun*, the novels tend to be heavily autobiographical, yet in a particular way. In the novels, we tend to see the defeated, bathetic side of the man. Even in as late a work as *The Fool's Progress*, published in 1988, the year before Abbey's death, he offers a thinly disguised version of himself. Antihero Henry, a failed anarchist, a failure in marriage, in his finances— a failure in just about everything he's put his hand to, wanders the country in his battered, 1962 Dodge Carryall, drinking too much, occasionally violent, and in a menorrhagic funk. Considering his ruined past, the best Henry can do emotionally is escape into a brown, oceanic nostalgia for those who once wept and rejoiced, now lying in the graves all around him. Such thoughts, of course, are but goads to his own disturbed soul (273). It is a lugubrious performance.

This note often dominates Abbey's novels; and it is to say, in literary terms, that, because of such indulgence, the books suffer from limited range. However, this is not the case in the best of Abbey's nonfiction. Here, we get more than a battered, alcohol-soaked, failure-haunted man using words as vehicles of therapy. We get a writer, yes, certainly drawing on his life, but by manipulating such material, flying up and down the scales in a great range of tone, transcending Abbey the troubled man and showing that he is an artist at work. In doing so, Abbey offers a tour, not of his own psychic swamps, familiarly comfortable as that might be for readers who get pretty much what they expect from such sad excursions: a vicarious venting of their own psychic wounds. They get, in addition, challenges as Abbey skims ahead of his readers, an acrobat of words, daring them to follow him through the breathless performance of his widened emotional range, to make sense of his ever-changing wit. The sentiment is still there, but Abbey shows that he can put it to use for a better and higher purpose than self-ventilations perhaps best reserved for discussions between a patient and his therapist.

A good example is *The Journey Home: Some Words in Defense of the American West*. The very places where these essays first appeared give some idea of their tonal sinuosity: *Audubon Magazine*, *National Geographic*, and *Playboy*. Often on the losing end of the stick in defending the earth, watching the land they love chewed up bit by bit by a modern age that sees open spaces as mere opportunities for development, environmentalists can get down in the chops about themselves and the future. The world simply is not the way it should be. Accepting that condition in *The Journey Home*, Abbey next rises above it. If he can't save the world because of humanity's own stupidity, he'll at least have fun along the way. "I found myself a displaced person shortly after birth and have been looking half my life for a place to take my stand," Abbey ruminates (xiii). It's a statement that might come from the blue lips of Henry in *The Fool's Progress*. But in *The Journey Home*, Abbey refuses to get stuck. Now that he's found his home, in the desert, he's going to defend it against the madness of humanity. Given the blind power of the government, the public's lack of concern for nature, and just plain human greed and perversity, this may well be a losing battle; but since the planet will crisp in a few million years anyhow, the happy existentialist will fly in the face of the odds, choosing joie rather than gloom, whatever the outcome (xiii–iv). "Joy, shipmates, joy," is Abbey's repeated cry before the teeth of the storm.

Ironically, nothing better illustrates the buoyant attitude of the book than Abbey's self-portrait in pen and ink on the back cover. With the scowl of a fierce, large-beaked curmudgeon, Abbey clings, a slope-paunched vulture to a dead branch, surveying from his high perch his beloved, desiccated desert landscape. Here is a man who can mock himself and have healthy fun in the process.

Joseph Wood Krutch sat grinding his molars as the plastic and asphalt monster of consumerism chewed its way across the desert toward his Tucson home. Abbey, in his latter years living near the mountains at the other end of the same town, was no less melancholic about the steady advance, but as far as his nonfiction was concerned, the situation energized him. Krutch was crushed. In contrast, the role of the rebellious underdog was right up Abbey's alley. Faithful to the spirit of his youthful antics, Abbey avoided the pit of refined Krutch by channeling the emotions of depression into action, irrational as it could be at times. This necessarily involved a share of victimization, but *The Journey Home* turns it to good and revealing ends. If Abbey is bludgeoned, his nonfiction deals with it as a means not to exhibit personal distresses, but, through the glass of his experiences, to show the larger picture of a society gone mad.

If all he can do is turn a railing Ezekiel, so be it; he'll rail with a righteous, stirring fervor over society's sins: "I've said it before and I'll say it again, we've got to close the parks to private cars if we want to keep them as parks. The parks are for people, not machines. Let the machines find their own parks. Most of America has been surrendered to them already, anyway. New Jersey, for example. Southern California" (53). Four things about Abbey in his caustic mode. He sounds radical. On the other hand, he makes perfect sense. He puts into words the frustrations of many other Americans privately rending their garments over a nation badly out of control. And, as with the best of prophets, he rails in an arresting, interesting, and bounding way.

He also deepens his stance by showing he is neither a sadsack nor an insane, street-corner babbler, but a perceptive human being with cares far wider than himself. Abbey remembers his first trip west when he was arrested in Flagstaff, Arizona, for vagrancy. After leaping off a train to find something to eat, the seventeen-year-old gets his first, inside glimpse of a heartless system:

Ah, one other thing, most weird and marvelous, like something out of a dream. Did I really see it? Perhaps it was a dream. As I write these words a quarter of a century later, I am no longer certain what was real, what was unreal.

There was a cage within the cage. Yes. And the bars of this inner cage were painted yellow. And inside the inner cage—alone—was one giant, gleaming, half-naked Negro, mad as the moon, who howled and bellowed and sang and jabbered all night long. (8–9)

Abbey spices the shocking picture with foreshadowing. With that horror before him, even still wet behind the ears, the next morning the youth outfoxes the judge. We begin to see Abbey, not as the common man beaten down, but as a wily Robin Hood prepared to do combat with a system, brutal whether to man or nature, in his own sly ways, and this stirs the rebel in us all.

With Abbey, it often is a happy rebel who, despite the odds and moments of despair at the state of the world, finally laughs in the face of death. Laughs, that is, with a rascally, impish, and sometimes bombastic humor wrought with literary skill, yet one, since mankind shows its immunity to reason through continued abuses to the earth, playing over larger issues.

The rednecks of Utah, xenophobic and often believing in their narrowness that God has given them the land to be turned into dollars in whatever ways they deem fit, make a good target for sophisticated Abbey. They have over the years adamantly resisted efforts to save the desert through wilderness preservation, viewed activist members of the Sierra Club as dangerous, anti-American radicals, and openly, eagerly invited polluting industries to their state. What can you do with a bunch like that? Talks about passing on a preserved natural legacy for their children won't move their shriveled hearts, and one more tirade to the choir about their willful ignorance surely will reveal nothing new.

Well, then, when all is lost, turn to humor. Avoiding the obvious, Abbey takes an arresting tack. He puts himself in the shoes of a redneck rancher, J. Orrin Garn, a man with no love in his heart for Sahara Clubbers, as he calls them. That Garn's name has a Mormon ring to it is no accident and neither is the bold title of the essay, "God's Plan for the State of Utah: A Revelation." A religious people dominating the state and living largely by what they think are divine dictates, the Mormons are about to be skewered by Abbey's version of revelations. In fact, like the wayward Israelites of old, the people of Utah have drifted so far from God's will that they've riled His wrath. Now prophet Abbey is going to set them straight by showing them what God *really* wants.

Effectively, old cowpoke Garn himself speaks, in his down-home way telling about a strange occurrence in his life. One day while he was out riding the range on Old Diablo in the heat of July, he came upon a stranger sitting on a rock. He was dressed like a California tourist, "short pants, a shirt with palm trees all over it, tennis shoes, great big sunglasses." Plus, durn fool, he "didn't even have a hat on and he was bald as a hen's egg" (103). Despite rising suspicions about the human anomaly before him, Garn gives him badly needed water. While the stranger drains Garn's canteen, the native son of Utah's soil squints at him and asks, "You one of them there Sahara Clubbers" (105)?

Well, not exactly, but close. As Garn gasps, the stranger announces that he's the angel Nehi, and he's come to earth with a message for Utah. God is angry at the state over its perverse treatment of nature, and with no more ado, Nehi seizes Garn's hand and flies off with him to show him why. See that strip-mine down there? Clean it up. That smog spreading over the desert from Salt Lake City? Get rid of it.

Hidebound ignoramus Garn is shocked at such radical suggestions. Why, we've been doing things this way for years, he protests. "Well, sir," he lectures the angel, "your director he's crazy as a jugful of crickets" (109).

The angel doesn't like this and, performing some astounding acrobatics in the ether with the bewildered cowboy in tow, soon has him quivering and begging for further instructions. Playing off Scrooge's airy tour with the Ghost of Christmas Past, "God's Plan for the State of Utah" is at once a masterpiece of slapstick, a catharsis for frustrated environmentalists, and a putdown of their enemies.

The pieces in *The Journey Home, Abbey's Road,* and similar collections tour the arid lands. As he travels, Abbey condemns the glitz of vacationers' dreams californicating Telluride, Colorado; drives with his honey into desert hinterlands over roads whose ruts and boulders offer little promise of escape; and whizzing along a blacktop into the chiaroscuro of northern Arizona's tablelands blithely tosses his empty Schlitz cans out the window. "Beer cans are beautiful," he assures us; "it's the highway that's ugly" (*The Journey Home* 159). In such ways, Abbey is both the bad-boy rebel and the environmental journalist at work, the sardonic desert lover alternately pained and rejoicing as he celebrates the landscape and damns a development-mad culture gone gaga over technology. It's sacrificing nature, he grimaces, "on the greasy altar of industrial tourism and mechanized recreation" (129).

By turns happily manic and wittily tearful, the essays are alexipharmic tours across the Southwest. They are intelligent pennings by a long-term excursionist. In *Desert Solitaire,* however, Abbey changes once again, entering the deepest parts of himself and writing the heartfelt musings of the lover for his homeland. The zaniness is still there, the rebellious stance, and the radical shifts in tone; but the book is more complete, not a glass of Abbey's wit but a lens of his soul. Through it, we see, not Abbey, but the land as one man loves it. *Desert Solitaire* is moving rather than titillating, and in its complexity, intensity of emotion, and artistic depth, the book may well replace John C. Van Dyke's *The Desert* someday as the most profound book on America's arid expanses.

Besides the enormous talent and discipline brought to bear on this work, ten years in the making, is the compelling focus of *Desert Solitaire*. The book telescopes three seasons Abbey spent as a temporary ranger in the high desert plateau of Arches National Monument in southeastern Utah into one experience. Rather than take the easy route and skim across events, here Abbey realizes that the smarty-pants approach is too easy; instead, he confronts the land, applying the whole of himself to it with in-depth attention. This is not a series of one-night stands but a deep affair, leavened with light moments, but mostly worthy of the best of himself the writer can bring to it. Doubling the poignancy is the disaster that, since his stay, the "progress" of mass tourism has arrived at this once out-of-the-way treasure and has ruined it forever. His book, Abbey tells us, as if writing about the one grand lost love in his life, "is not a trail guide but an elegy" (xiv). Rather than a revelation of natural history, the book is an evocation. From this stance, of a great love lost, the work gains much of its power.

As Abbey wanders the wild country—far wilder then than it is now—he embeds his experiences in one great truth: This is not an explanation of nature but the overwhelming exhilaration of living with nature. Contemplating a juniper tree, perpetually posed in ragged symmetry, Abbey confesses that its essence eludes him. He thinks, though, that it might be mad (27). Out on an excursion and probably hallucinating from the heat, the ranger looks for a legendary, moon-eyed horse said to be living high up in the rocks and scrub, finds him, has a long conversation with him, then leaves. But not without misgivings about what has happened. As he walks out of a canyon, having failed to catch the tall, weird beast in that lonely spot, Abbey thinks he hears the horse following him, but when he turns and looks back, he sees only rocks and scrub (150).

Heightening the drama of the desert is its danger. At times an overly enthusiastic wanderer, the writer gets stuck in a deep canyon. Its steep, dry waterfalls prevent him from climbing back out. Slow death through starvation seems Abbey's sentence for his folly. Almost miraculously, through superhuman effort, Abbey claws his way up the rock and swings on happily home down the trail "with an enormous fire in the western sky" (205). Better than summaries, such chapters are best read and experienced for their impact. The point is that the desert brings out the extraordinary in a man: extraordinary efforts and extraordinary responses. If this is romance, goes the unstated assumption, so be it; it is a compelling, chromatic romance.

One genius builds on another. To a large degree, Abbey follows the tack of his mentor, John C. Van Dyke. Abbey also has written a desert book with a love theme and about a love so intense that the writer is both wracked by despair and buoyed into a realm where reality blurs with fantasy. But Abbey has done Van Dyke one better, and it adds up to a large difference. Whereas Van Dyke gives his impressions of a generic desert, a mystic region generalized into a never-never land so ethereal at times it seems beyond ordinary reach, Abbey evokes the mystery of very real and particularized places that we, too, might visit and experience. Such is the much different allure of the book and the greater power of the evocation for the reader.[5]

Abbey's volumes had yet an added boost. In the emotive issue of preserving nature, which had people by the thousands rallying in the streets, much of the power lay, too, in what readers brought to his books. A brilliant literary Quisling, Van Dyke had hoodwinked his audience into thinking their mentor of the arid wilds was an ideal man, a combination of the robust frontiersman and the delicately souled aesthetician—an image striking a ready chord with none other than President Theodore Roosevelt himself, who then was blustering about the nation regaining its pioneer vigor by leading The Strenuous Life. In contrast to Van Dyke, Abbey was the real thing, a tough loner and a man of endurance on treks into jumbled lands far beyond where trails petered out. Added to that, his aggressive disdain for authority struck yet another loud note with middle-class, would-be rebels of the seething Counter Culture. There he was, waving his pistol on the stage, defying hidebound, redneck ranchers, a sight that made the youthful heart leap, and one not easily forgotten.[6]

As often happens, the enhancement of a writer's image through perceived heroics brought some long-term distortions. In an age of Guru This and Guru That, Abbey's fans inflated him into a figure larger than earthly life, into a spiritual leader. Though he didn't necessarily refuse the mantle that felt so good on the shoulders, it amused him somewhat that people simply wouldn't believe that he was what he said he was: a country bumpkin with a curious mind and considerable writing talent who came down out of the hills to stir things up. Bishop quotes a forthright Abbey speaking in one of his last interviews:

I like provoking people. I've been willing to be dismissed as a crank and a crackpot simply for the pleasure of saying exactly what I really do believe. Then I leave it to others, you see, to take up the more moderate approach. I lead the attack and then once contact is made with the enemy I quickly retreat, and let more moderate people start compromising, explaining, and maneuvering while I go off and do something else. (12)

Yes, he was different. A bit distant, intellectually sufficient to himself and his mental whirlings. In remembering Abbey, his last wife, Clarke, said, "I used to tell him he was married to his mind, he lived in it so much" (13).[7]

Such a person lends himself to speculations. Joining the public, critics made much of Abbey, spinning his work into the literary complexities that are critics' stock in trade. The former farmboy was a splendid reader, and as we've seen in "God's Plan for the State of Utah," he often, having fun with words, playfully and effectively echoed the Greats who had gone before him. The result was a medley of styles roguishly thrown together, an appropriate match of the erumpent atmosphere of the times with his erumpent purposes. This led Scott Slovic to declare that the abrupt shifting of literary gears was a conscious device on the writer's part to jar readers' complacency and effect "consciousness-raising" (100). Slovic presents his case well. However, the truth might also be that Abbey was simply having his usual, scurrilous fun. A rebel with no answers, he swung from the poles of an expansive Walt Whitman celebrating inconsistency to the concentrated, self-studying Henry David Thoreau, and that allowed Abbey a tremendous range in between.

No answers, that is, except the desert is a lovely place, so lovely and so soul stirring in contrast to the mechanized mass of doomed humanity that it deserves preservation in its pristine state. That was, of course, an old message, going back at least to Van Dyke. It also, given the insistent sweep of technology that had already badly bludgeoned the desert by Van Dyke's time, was a preposterous message. In a day of nuclear bombs, vast armies, police forces, tangles of transmission lines, and cancerous urban growth, our shrunken, much-abused deserts hardly can serve as refuges for eco-guerrillas any more than they can as pristine places for urban dreamers. Yet in the contradiction was the very essence of Abbey's revivified romantic appeal. Once again, in the face of all, contradicting odds, the fantasy desert was serving as a vehicle for the exercise of the imagination's most colorful wishes.

Beyond the heat of his message, what *was* new about Abbey was his Robin Hood prose. Abbey had effectively and perhaps permanently wounded the dominance of nature writing in the classical tradition of rational, gentlemanly Joseph Wood Krutch. Abbey opened the doors and windows of desert writing and let the wild winds blow in. Just how lunatic they would become once they took over perhaps he himself didn't realize.

12

ANN ZWINGER AND

CHARLES BOWDEN

Pondering These Things

in Her Heart;

Tacitus Flips Out

Following the instructions of his master, the young, would-be sorcerer spends the night rolling around on the rickety porch of a desert shack trying to find his spiritual spot on the floor.[1]

Not far away, another writer takes us to a strange, colorful land where "The water smells like oranges but has no taste. Nothing you do here makes any sound."[2] On the other hand, the perpetually bewildered visitor can hear the hoofbeats of horses from ten miles away.[3]

Yet a third writer tops such wonders. Not only does his desert have owls that speak to him and headlights dancing on the horizon that have no cars behind them.[4] When he's in a funk about his civilized life generally, he goes to Mexico and consults a folk healer. Her ministrations are so powerful that the evil spirit troubling the patient leaps out of his body and flees from the house, slamming the door behind it.[5]

How much better he feels then! Almost good enough to return to the boring and repressive civilization north of the border responsible for his woes.

As we've seen, desert writing has sawed back and forth between fantasy and reality, often within the works of the same writer. Edward Abbey might be seen as successfully combining the two impulses. A case can be made, however, that in terms both of national influence and literary brightness, the point of desert writing's most recent culmination, with the publication of Abbey's *Desert Solitaire* in 1968, also represented, if perhaps not the death thereafter, then the severe etiolation of the genre. Since Abbey, as we shall see, the mainly realistic tradition has continued in the books of such as Ann Zwinger, though, despite her large talents, she hardly is a household name in well-read America as were Abbey and Krutch before him.

That is, the stream of the genre has radically split. Its other branch consists of the fabulists as represented in the opening paragraphs above. At times, it seems, they are bent on denying the very reality of the desert. Instead, they compete in outbidding one another to create psychedelic deserts, creations, furthermore, not with nature as the focus, but, as in the vignette from Gary Nabhan above, the tormented writer himself. The desert, as a spiritual and mystical place, now becomes secondary, but a means of salving, if temporarily, the real or imagined neuroses of its visitors. In this sense, then, the second stream is but the guise of desert writing, therapy in an arid-lands setting. And, furthermore, it is an ersatz desert writing gushed over by a few cult followers, mainly the academics who have turned nature writing of late into their own, largely exclusive bailiwick, one touted in seminars and at conferences but one largely ignored by the wider public.[6]

Nonetheless, the phenomenon is worth studying because it is part of the evolution of such writing, and, secondly, it reflects impulses in the larger culture. Though Americans, quick to throw out the old and replace it with the new, tend to feel that history began on the day they were born. As a culture, we may have more of the ancient Romans in us than we think.

In the first century A.D., Roman historian Tacitus, much like the Gary Nabhan of earlier paragraphs, was in a blue funk. To Tacitus the Roman Empire, then at the height of its power and sophistication, was overly civilized, overly wealthy, corrupt, and lacking in natural goodness. A terrible place for a sensitive man to live. But there was hope. Gazing north into the misty forests, the disillusioned, breast-beating sophisticate fixated on the wandering, barbaric Germanic tribes he saw slipping through the fogs. Why, it was obvious. They had no greed, no corruption, no evil in their hearts. Instead, they were at one with nature, loving their wives and treating each other as equals. In other words, they were the very embodiment of what we'd today call Political Correctness.

Fortunately for Tacitus, he did not live long enough to see these good-souled people of tender sensibilities come raging out of the northern woods to sack Rome. It is to say, however, that every now and then over the centuries, Western culture goes through periods of self-doubt. To victims mired in their blue moods and self-pity, just about everything once valued now seems dross and whatever lies outside the mainstream offers escape from their beleaguered selves.[7]

According to Robert N. Bellah et al. in *Habits of the Heart*, we've been going through just such self-induced schwarmerei since the 1960s. More and more creatures of the Counter Culture, we've turned our backs on reason and, becoming ever more self-centered, seek solace for our supposed woes in alternative this and that, as if sitting under crystals, eating tofu and sprouts, or listening to owls in Mexico will lead us out of our self-created swamps toward a brighter destiny. Bellah and his colleagues illustrate this with a picture of Sheila:

> *Today religion in America is as private and diverse as New England colonial religion was public and unified. One person we interviewed has actually named her religion (she calls it her "faith") after herself. This suggests the logical possibility of over 220 million American religions, one for each of us. Sheila Larson is a young nurse who has received a good deal of therapy and who describes her faith as "Sheilaism." "I believe in God. I'm not a religious fanatic. I can't remember the last time I went to church. My faith has carried me a long way. It's Sheilaism. Just my own little voice." (220–221)*

It's what happens when a society gets fat and bored and has too much time to think about itself.

Though something of a fabulist himself, the sterner side of John C. Van Dyke saw it coming: "The rushing world craves the novel and exotic, and in seeking to avoid the obvious it only too often falls into admiration of the merely bizarre" (*The Meadows* 125).

As goes the nation, so goes nature writing. And writing about the desert. It has, at least one main branch, given itself over precisely to that, the "novel and exotic" and the "merely bizarre." In the case of a pained Gary Nabhan, he may well be sincere in willing himself into the wish-fulfillment of a fantastic landscape, while a crafty Carlos Castañeda chuckles as he cashes his royalty checks at how easily people can be duped. Yet sincerity, or the lack of it, has nothing to do with art. What counts are the books themselves and what they say, regardless of the authors' intent. In an ideal world, that is. A romantic age considers an author's work a projection of himself. Playing off this, coloring the projected image to match readers' expectations becomes an opportunity for some authors to strut their egos, while other writers, feeling this below the dignity of their art, nonetheless feel the pressure to please the market. And here we see how mightily the books have warred in their two-sided battle. Whatever the furor and the dust, the participants divide rather neatly into old-fashioned naturalists who would prefer to keep their private lives in the background and the freewheeling exhibitionists.

Ann Zwinger certainly belongs in the former group. "I am a naturalist," she declares in "The Art of Wandering" (6), "my focus is nature"

(Rea 25). By this she makes clear that she admires those writers of the nineteenth century who enjoyed exploring the nature before them, hardly for the celebration of their egos, but for its own sake, much as Joseph Wood Krutch continued the tradition into the twentieth:

Naturalists find out about what goes on in the natural world through observation, which over time becomes, perhaps unconsciously, quite disciplined. Soon it is not enough just to look. One needs to identify, and then with the magic of a name in hand, begin to put together some of the facts that make up a world. ("The Art" 6)

In fact, they do it for the very "joy of learning" ("A World of Infinite Variety" 41). To Zwinger, "Research is what books are all about" (Rea 35).

As to a writer's prose honestly reflecting, rather than exaggerating, his life, Ann Zwinger's modest, self-effacing stance serves as an exemplum.[8] She was born Ann Haymond in 1925 in Muncie, Indiana, into a solidly traditional family emphasizing the work ethic and good sense. A sensitive man, her attorney father fumed when an ill-considered government project sacrificed the trees along a nearby stream for the alleged cause of flood control. Her mother saw that her daughter had what was then widely aspired to as a proper upbringing.

The young Ann saw art rather than nature writing in her future. In fact, she hated camp, preferring scholarly pursuits. In line with this, she earned her B.A. in art history from Wellesley College in 1946 and after that attended graduate school at Radcliffe. There followed various teaching positions, among them at the University of Kansas and at Smith College. In 1952 she married Herman Zwinger, an officer in the U.S. Air Force. For years Ann Zwinger lived a satisfying life as a military wife, moving to various bases across the country while raising her three daughters.

What developed into an enormous midlife career change came after Herman's retirement. Putting down roots in Colorado Springs, Colorado, the Zwingers enjoyed spending summers in their mountain cabin. A visiting literary agent offhandedly suggested that the housewife write a book about Colorado's ecology. The housewife took flame. The result was that rarest of literary events, despite the rosy mythology about instant publishing careers. In 1970 Ann Zwinger's *Beyond the Aspen Grove* became a publishing success, and she has been writing nature books ever since. The statement, however, requires some refining. Though her first volume was about life in the Rocky Mountains, Zwinger became fascinated by the great deserts lying to the south of Colorado Springs, and they became the focus of most of her writing thereafter. Illustrated with her delicate pencil drawings, together her books make up a gracious shelf of information about the region. Joseph Wood Krutch would have been pleased.

Run, River, Run, for example, takes readers on a float trip down the Green, a desert river cutting through portions of Wyoming, Colorado, and Utah. In *A Desert Country near the Sea,* Zwinger goes to the southern region of Mexico's Baja California. True to her dedication to old-fashioned natural history, on such excursions much of the writer's wonder and excitement of exploring the new lands seeps into her prose, yet for the most part Zwinger remains an amiable, if professionally distant, guide. Having both researched the regions thoroughly then next experienced them, Zwinger is the best of docents, taking readers along on her travels and introducing them to the history, geology, flora, and fauna of the areas, and backing up her texts with solid notes. Her scope is both broad and narrow, affably steeping the reader in the landscape. In *Run, River, Run,* she recounts the careers of nineteenth-century fur trappers in the surrounding canyons and, giving them flesh, adds a charming history of the Green River knife, their trusted survival tool. And she doesn't entirely ignore the personal. What it's like to sleep on a damp sand bar deep in the bowels of the Green's canyon while the liquid, aquamarine needle point of the first star glimmers over the dark cliffs high above also comes through. Despite such touches, overall the scholar stands very much behind the prose, lending a solid depth of information to Zwinger's pages.

It would be difficult for writers of any experience to botch a book like *Run, River, Run.* The situation is all to their advantage. The progress of the trip itself, with its changing sights and various stops in this historic place and that, the variety of plants in their highly specialized ecological niches surprising the floaters, provides a ready organizational plan for the book. Adding to the sights going by, the Green is a wild river, with intermittent, roaring, and often dangerous rapids ahead. This keeps the anticipation going with anxieties over approaching challenges, the splashing, engulfing immediacy of kicking white water, and the serene sense of a job well done when the danger is past. Triplet Falls is a case in point, its booming turmoil warning the travelers long before they see this roiling, boiling expanse. Then, inexorably they're pulled speeding into the white mass:

Bob gets a firm grip on the oars and bellows over the pound of the river, "Hang on!" The raft bounds into slick and opalescent troughs, into water spun and syruped into thick loops—magnificent water, charged with energy, revealing little of what enrages it.

Each wave is a watery lion's paw, playfully smacking a gray mouse of a raft with strength to spare. It is pure river on the river's terms. (165)

With such thrills, the fans of nature can't help put down *Run, River, Run* without feeling not only that they've learned about a unique place but more that they've experienced it.

Quite a different challenge was *Wind in the Rock*, Zwinger's next desert book. Here, she explores a barren expanse in southeastern Utah, "Hundreds of miles of rock scarcely blurred by vegetation, rib and vertebra without flesh." Flying with her pilot husband into the area, Zwinger notes its unpromising literary quality: "Beneath the wing, there was not a farm, not a ranch, not a plowed field, and scarcely a trail—total and remote desolation as far as I could see" (4). Her husband winces at the prospect below. Added to the difficulties, there are few people down there to provide human relief to the writing when nature gets dull. On top of that, this is not one single trip with a single theme—running a wild river—to lend a book coherency. Rather, Zwinger has explored the area, sometimes with others, sometimes alone, over a period of several years. It's enough to make a nature writer quail.

Yet for the professional with a pen and fire in the belly, the bigger they are, the harder they fall. Because Zwinger has the knack of sizing up the situation and adjusting her approach, this may be her most skillful and convincing work. After all, nothing is boring in nature to one fascinated by it; facing similar blocks in his path, John Wesley Powell turned a rocky sea of desolation into a wonder, Van Dyke the boredom of sand dunes into one of his most poetic passages. Such excitement alone on the author's part can hone sharp visions.

Sailing into the thick of the difficulties before her, Zwinger writes five longish chapters, one for each of the five canyons she explored and each as if her visit had been one, extended trip. Still, the difficulties innate in the material remain. These five great slashes of rock and sand in the earth are quite similar. How can she justify their separate treatment? Undaunted, she does this in several ways. She concentrates on different aspects of the canyons: the earnest but anguished attempt of the Mormons to colonize Lower Grand Gulch; the story of the ancient, long-disappeared Indians with their kivas and relics in caves waiting to be explored in Upper Grand Gulch. It is here that Zwinger's depth from research pays off. But it is research brought to life, applied to the land she faces. She gives the story of Kokopelli, a flute-playing, humpbacked philanderer, his image often found etched on the canyon walls—and tells his story so well that we almost hear his notes as this rascally figure of Anasazi lore seduces yet one more virgin in his travels.

She meets few people, but she makes the most of them. One area is so ecologically fragile, so jam-packed with Indian ruins—enough in itself to prick up readers' ears—that the Bureau of Land Management insists that even rare visitors have an official guide. Zwinger's is Pete Steele, an old salt of the area who's been a uranium miner, a cowboy, and rodeo clown. They'll be riding horses into the canyon, and they, too, along with the mules of the pack train, become characters. Pete has named one of these Esther, for "a difficult woman with peculiarities" (55). All of this not only is good, lively material, it details the region's peculiar flavor.

However, Zwinger does more than meet people; she begins to interact with them. Zwinger, the naturalist, happiest when she's poring over musty tomes in library basements, begins loosening up, becoming herself a character other than the docent with hair pulled straight back and tied with a rubber band. Now she emerges with more various and personal qualities. She can be the 105-pound housewife dropped off at a bleak trailhead and, staggering under a heavy pack down into the bowels of the earth alone, wondering if she'll make it back out. In contrast, with people around, she can be the slightly caustic schoolmarm. Poking around Slickhorn Canyon on a hot day, her small group pauses for lunch. When she pulls cheese from her pack, it's "the consistency of putty, and the salami tastes like grout." She turns up her nose at the food. Yet "All this," she quips on the foibles of human nature,

boosts my popularity to a new high: I am a source of extras for those who are still hungry, who dig the last pulverized bits out of the corners of their plastic bags, look around wistfully for any tidbits dropped on the rock, and make clutching sounds of unsatisfied hunger. When they get my leftovers there's even an extra bonus: they didn't have to carry them. (153)

It's a neat bit of comic relief. Yet such features are not intrusive; they break the pace but are not frequent, prolonged, or disruptive enough to distract from Zwinger's main focus, the region's natural history.

In fact, for long informative passages, Zwinger only appears to be a bloodless clinician. She keeps her celebratory emotions on short rein, but when she allows them to break through, they are all the more powerful for their timing and calculation, enhancing the emotive movement of her prose. The former art instructor can deliver the geology of the canyons with the precision of a pointing fescue, but, realizing that we are more than geologists, she also steps back and beholds the great cliffs around her with a profound and moving eye:

To me there is an enchantment in these dry canyons that once roared with water and still sometimes do, that absorbed the voices of those who came before, something of massive dignity about sandstone beds that tell of a past long before human breathing, that bear the patterns of ancient winds and water in their crossbeddings. (7)

That is, she can be emotional and accurate all at once.

Nonetheless, the injection of an author's persona can go too far in nature writing. At some indeterminate point, the writing becomes more about the writer than about the supposed subject. Zwinger's work does not approach this shift, though certainly her general trend is to bring personality ever more to the fore. Perhaps too much to the fore. In *The Mysterious Lands*—the title itself echoes with urgings from the publisher's marketing people—readers are ever conscious that they are following a Zwinger who is wandering the Southwest's deserts with a changing entourage of husband, daughter, cousin, and various scientists. This jars the focus on the natural history being discussed. Much had changed in the few short years since Joseph Wood Krutch had the luxury of keeping his private life in the background while offering *The Voice of the Desert* through an intelligent lens. Zwinger gripes that her editors keep hounding her to push more of the personal element into her writing for a modern audience which, in their opinion, needs sugar to help the medicine go down. Dragging her feet while going along with the ploy, Zwinger fears that she is sugarcoating her work "so that somebody will read it" (Rea 25). Whatever one's tastes in the matter, years hence *Wind in the Rock* likely will be considered her most delicate and successful balance of all such features mentioned above.

Given her substance, based on living deeply with the land and its history, a comparison of Ann Zwinger with proponents of desert dreamlands yields sharp differences. Taking the easy way out, they do-si-do themselves into mystic scapes, sometimes fascinating for themselves but lacking corollaries in the real desert, making the desert into a confection. On one of his wonder trips, Barry Lopez exults: "Already I have seen the priest with his Bible bound in wolves' fur and the blackbirds asleep in his hair" (*Desert Notes* 28). Curious images, indeed. Yet Hamlet's vision of a camel in the clouds while he was rocketing himself on the propellant of his ego into a glorious pretense of madness also is surrealistically fetching. But, then, Hamlet was a prince, and for that people paid attention to him; otherwise he likely would have been dismissed as a babbler or worse.

For several reasons, the desert works of Charles Bowden provide a better example of desert writing writhing into a plant sprayed with 2,4-D. First of all, unlike Lopez, who came to his senses and with maturity gained certain substance, as with *Of Wolves and Men,* Bowden shows the opposite drift. He began with a solid desert book, then drifted off beyond mere fantasy into an astounding, if embarrassing, realm of exhibitionism where the egomaniac reigns—thus showing the full force of Sheilaism in our society when given license to bloom. That is, just how far the desert, supposedly beloved by a writer, can be distorted to his ego-driven purposes, the desert paling until the writer becomes the object of his own adoration. Though as readers we have a certain fascination in beholding the process of pathology careening wildly about, still, we feel a little uncomfortable at the spectacle of a person's disintegration become the object of his own celebration. Tacitus, however, no doubt would have understood.

Bowden is a curious blend of a mainstream person adoring his own Bohemianism—a circumstance he himself glories in emphasizing. From Chicago, the Bowden family moved to Tucson, Arizona, around 1957, when Charles was twelve. After graduating from the local University of Arizona with a major in history, Bowden attended graduate school in Wisconsin. Following that, he bounced around for some years. In 1981 he took a job as a reporter for the *Tucson Citizen,* then quit in 1984. Bankrolled by a Tucson supporter, Bowden next founded *City Magazine,* which soon folded. Since then, he has been a freelance writer, "a pastime," he testifies, "which is practically a free ticket to the asylum."[9] Turning out good copy, Paul Brinkley-Rogers characterizes a colorful Bowden: "He celebrates machismo, daring, bravado," while two-fisted Bowden himself maintains that "I speak for the mongrel, the mestizo, the half-breed, the bastard, the alley cat, the cur . . ." (6). In other words, a Robin Hood with bad table manners but a big heart. But more on such things later.

In many ways, Bowden's *Blue Desert* displays a fine, even a remarkable, skill with prose. Though not in the Krutch or Zwinger tradition of natural history, Bowden shows that there are other valid ways to capture the desert. He travels around southern Arizona, writing a series of focused essays about what he finds. In a truly creepy piece, he hikes into a cave far back in the mountains with a scientist studying bats. Standing ankle deep in guano bubbling with writhing beetle larvae, he contemplates the mass of life hanging above and the tragedy of their die-off from DDT. He visits a ranch where the Nature Conservancy is struggling to save the Yaqui topminnow, a small fish native to desert pools, from extinction. He wanders the streets of an isolated town torn by a copper strike, and he hikes a desert stretch where illegal Mexican laborers cross into the United States, their hopes on work in the rich country to the north but sometimes paying the greater price of dying from thirst in that waterless country before they reach their jobs.

With such a method, *Blue Desert* explores not so much the individual wonders of nature but shows the complex, often warring dynamics of man and the land on the contemporary desert.

The emphasis should be on that word "shows." The success of *Blue Desert* comes not so much from the information the book delivers as from the atmosphere created by Bowden's personal anecdotes. An opening note to the book announces that many of the pieces came from the author's work on the local afternoon paper. All to the good. Bowden's journalistic training has served him well in this successful showing rather than telling. Standing in the great darkness of the bat cave, the writer ponders the thousands of creatures clustered immobile on the ceiling high above, waiting for the moment when day dies and they will roar out of the cave in their sudden rush toward nighttime hunting:

They can live in colonies of millions, huge masses of bats squeaking, chattering, and crawling across each other. When big colonies once exited from their caves, the sound, according to early observers, thundered like the roar of white water and the dark cloud could be seen for miles. They fly into the night at about thirty-five miles per hour, then accelerate to around sixty. At dawn, they make power dives back into the cave, sometimes brushing eighty miles per hour.

A few short paragraphs later, Bowden shifts to a different, more intimate tone. When the bats die or infants fall from their perches, the seething mass of larvae in which Bowden stands immediately begins consuming them. Their bones, scattered across the guano in the flashlight beam, present a strange scene, one of a curious, detached beauty: "White bones lace across the dark guano like thin wires. The remnants outline a wing that fell from the ceiling. Small skulls peek through the feces, the tiny craniums empty of brains" (14). Joseph Conrad would have applauded.

Such scenes frequently contain their own comment, often ironic, about the interface of nature and humanity. On a U.S. Air Force gunnery range in western Arizona, pronghorn antelope thrive, not because the military loves large-eyed creatures but because restricted access keeps out poachers, cattle, and other threats to these swift and delicate runners. Plus, the Air Force hopes to spiff up its public image by winning an award for its noble conservation efforts. Following the attempt, Bowden joins several government scientists studying the area's wildlife. So off they go at the crack of dawn, twentieth-century technology borne aloft in a whole bevy of roaring, diving, hunting helicopters. Zooming over the desert, they hope to find a band, net a few members, and affix radio collars for the biological project they hope will lead to the prize.

Finally, when they capture an antelope in a net propelled by a gun, the machines all descend, and the excited men run toward their frightened, trembling prey. Bowden notes that for years people have wondered if antelope make any vocal sounds. Now he has the answer. Caught in an orange maze, the bewildered creature is moaning. As Bowden stands there in the midst of the hubbub, he sees that "a kind of collision between cultures has taken place. Huge machines that fly at eighty miles per hour and drink more than seventy gallons an hour have snared an organism that has raced at fifty miles per hour for millions of years" (25).

Elsewhere, Bowden arrives at the small mining town of Ajo, battering itself in the turmoil of a copper strike. The two sides so hate each other that they have their own bars and would gladly tear each other's throats out. Bowden sits listening for hours as a drunken mine manager vents his bile. Yet in the midst of the strife, all is not concerned with the affairs of battling factions. As the man goes on raving, "Sugar, the bar dog, stares in from the doorway, tail wagging, and her beagle eyes dream of a hand-out" (103).

In his portraits, Bowden gets many things right about the changing desert. He recognizes that the desert tortoise, a slow-moving and vulnerable ancient creature, is what's called an indicator species. When its numbers begin to fall, as many scientists now warn is happening — run over by dune buggies, mindlessly shot and stoned, their habitat replaced by suburbia — the decline signals that the whole ecosystem is in trouble (31). This specific points to a larger truth. In the last century or so, the entire region has suffered the effects of an invasion. People by the millions, hordes of people, have come pouring in to live on the desert. While they preserve a few lava mountains nearby as exotic backdrops, with their freeway systems, lawns, and shopping malls, the new people are remaking the desert according to their wishes (112). This much Bowden has right, though it is but what Joseph Wood Krutch said decades before, repeated with an added, fiery emphasis.

Much of Bowden's writing is immediately convincing and emotionally compelling, as newspaper writing should be, but pulling back from it and considering what he says, rather than how he says it, leads one to believe that Bowden often is stacking the deck to create the immediate emotional impact that sells newspapers. That is, he skews his material for effect until he becomes a broker in half truths and simplistic views. "For a century," the journalist reporting from the desert tells us, "the Anglo world has crushed and buried the Mexican" (58). To a degree, this is true, a statement that is effective in raising readers' hackles over past injustices. What Bowden doesn't say is that upon arriving on the desert centuries ago, the Mexicans, for their part, bludgeoned the Indians they found living there. And before them, the Indians had their go at beating up on weaker tribes. That has been, for better or worse, a historical process going on around the world. And Bowden's view certainly doesn't account for the millions of Mexicans on the other side of the border who would dearly love to escape the poverty and corruption of their native land and enjoy the prosperity in what Bowden paints as a land of repression.

The colorful, though solidly negative, emotionalism, however convincingly presented, becomes Bowden's stock in trade at the expense of understanding the desert's shifting complexities. Rather than praise a society, howsoever wrongheaded in the past, that is beginning to come to its senses and strives to preserve the beleaguered Yaqui topminnow, Bowden makes much of the aging caretaker at the preserve, a redneck anachronism idealizing a past of gunslingers. Now, no doubt, it is more fun to hiss at a villain than it is to honor a saint, though in urging us along in such a direction the writer distorts the situation.

In the process, he does something worse than getting his facts bent into strange shapes. "In the West," he tells us, "nothing done by Americans is for keeps, everything—farms, cities, towns, mines, everything—constitutes a brief raid on the dry land . . ." (105)—a melodramatic and silly statement. Added to that, the world is wrong and Bowden is right. Well, not exactly right anymore. The world is so horrid that Bowden himself, virtuous as he once was, has cracked, having developed a "bad appetite within me for gore, for ruin and bankruptcy" (11). This is Tacitus glorying that he's having a breakdown.

And this is where Bowden's writing, quite promising in patches of *Blue Desert*, goes badly off the tracks and into the swamps of self-absorption, for the writer decides to detail his woes, as if he thinks his readers are eagerly waiting to hear about them. Later on in the book, he starts recounting his drinking problems (161), this preliminary to telling us about his former wife: "She has seen a counselor and this, she tells me, has helped" (166). Adding to her troubles, she develops breast cancer, and Bowden tells us about this, too (166–167). These certainly are misfortunes, but what have they to do with the desert, with a book, in fact, titled *Blue Desert*?

One could hope, vainly in this case, that the writer of an early and potentially fine book would flee from past flaws. Bowden's next book, *Frog Mountain Blues*, supposedly about the Santa Catalina Mountains north of Tucson, instead rushed to embrace the weaknesses. The world, of course, is full of bad books, and the world can simply ignore them, but the sad part is that there is a need for a book-length natural history about this pine-topped range, a precious treasure rising out of the desert and looming over the city. We get some dribbles and drabbles about the mountains themselves, though the setting becomes an excuse for more breast-beating and a reason for the author to talk still more about himself and his not-so-happy childhood in Chicago, apparently far more important to the author than the nature before him.

If anything, the mire of Bowden's work has grown deeper and more quavery. Beginning with a chapter titled "Open the Bottle," *Mezcal* is a drug-drenched, sex-soaked account of Bowden's wanderings across the desert and elsewhere. "I am," the author boasts, "losing my ability to keep things in what is considered their proper place" (99). He presents his ruined state as a superhuman accomplishment, though it comes across as the facile dreams of a teenager placing himself in what he imagines to be romantic heroics. After a prolonged sexual workout in a marijuana-fogged, music-blasted Mexican hotel room, Bowden and his love take a little fresh air. That is, they hit the nearest bars. Beginning with beer, working their way through brandy, and finally getting serious with mescal, they become ever more stupid:

> There is a stone staircase, very wide and grand, sweeping up one side of the Plaza and our table is close by this imperial gateway and Susan sits facing the steps. A dozen men or more stand on the stairway, their brown faces rippling with hope, and stare hard in our direction. Susan tilts back in her chair, her skirt hiked halfway up her thighs. I toss down a shot of mezcal and think I have never tasted anything so warm and good before. "Waiter, más mezcal!"
>
> Susan whispers into my ear, "I am not wearing any panties." (24)

No wonder that Mexicans have low opinions of tourists from the north. In any case, as witty as Susan can be, nothing can ease the pain, whatever it is, that Bowden waves ever more vigorously as the flag of his existence. Gone, then, is all but a thin pretense that this is writing about nature. This is simply babbling from the couch of the analysand, reverting to adolescent fantasies. Sheilaism has come home to roost; the children of the 1960s have triumphed, having now entered the personal desert of themselves. And somehow they expect us to be interested in reading about its exploration.

Should any of this portrait seem too harsh, we might turn to the author himself. He, after all, should be the best guardian of the image he prefers to project. And he presents himself to reporter Paul Brinkley-Rogers in terms even more jejune than those depicted above. Now well into his fifth decade and getting soft around the edges, Bowden says he remains a man "whose appetite for life's gritty pleasures—wine, dope, guns, cheap motels, 24-hour love affairs, violence, danger, speeding tickets, strange characters, profanity and writing—cannot be quenched" (1). In contrast to the inane bluster, some critics might argue that the choice need not be between either the distant Zwinger or the gushing Bowden. In *Refuge* the self-possessed Terry Tempest Williams writes about her desert home in Utah and shows that personal history and natural history can be successfully balanced. If so, it is a balance that can easily topple into the macabre, and even in the much-praised Williams one often puzzles about any necessary relationships between her two, major elements. As Bowden bears witness, when the biographical indulgence isn't carefully reined, we can get the old, laughable cliché of the writer with a whiskey bottle in one hand, a pen in the other, the raving genius about to begin his next masterpiece—that is, the writer as romantic caricature. To such embarrassing ends has much desert writing been turned.

13

PETER REYNER

BANHAM

Wheeled Voyeur

from Overseas

"Where are the camels?"[1] That's what Peter Reyner Banham, a sophisticated architectural historian from England, wanted to know when he
took his first step into the American desert.

We might put hands to mouth to cover our mirth at the question. It
sounds too much like the stock bewilderment of the touring European,
on the qui vive when west of the Mississippi for wild Indians and cowboys shooting up frontier towns. Certainly, *we* know that there are no
dromedaries stepping across the dunes of the West, in their stately, snob-
bish way delicately lifting their legs as they plod over the sands. And
neither are there hook-nosed Arabs prowling about in burnooses. Nor
palm-fringed oases, mysterious places where strange trysts occur while
atonal music wavers through the night. Either Banham is incredibly naive
or he's making a wry joke on himself.

The fact is that Banham, who held a Ph.D. from the University of
London, was neither an artless simpleton nor was he pulling our legs
when he swung open the door of his rental car and made that first footfall
into the Mojave's shimmering heat. He was simply, as he himself admits,
bringing along his childhood mythology about deserts, applying an outlook learned in the green and misty United Kingdom about the Near
East to a superficially similar but radically different landscape. In his case,
it was either the Pip, Pip, Pip of the colonial officer with drawn Webley
leading his men against a rascally band of Bedouins as he spreads British civilization or the legendary figure of English wanderer Charles M.
Doughty probing an Arabia of the last century where, indeed, shy, sloe-
eyed women melted off around corners in their robes and veils and

strange music quavered half the night out of the inscrutable depths of the palms.[2]

Yet totally new experiences can be frightening. Whether learning a new language, facing the task of assembling a new kitchen gadget, or confronting the puzzle of the desert, we learn incrementally, applying what we already know to what's before us. In his case, Banham gives double thanks for the desert concepts forming the baggage of every English schoolboy. Firstly, they spared him the disorientation that can come from facing the unknown by providing reference points, ways to approach a new land. Secondly, because his expectations were so out of line with reality, quickly proving false—it soon became obvious that there were no big-nosed camels out there leering above the creosote bushes and no legionnaires in havelocks scanning the forbidding expanses from the ramparts of forts—it allowed him a quick realization. Since his expectations were "totally inapplicable" in America, Banham shed them like an old, useless skin (*Scenes in America Deserta* 166). In this way, Banham had the advantage of the foreigner. A semipermanent visitor from England, he could objectify the desert as an exotic entity in a way that American tourists, and certainly desert residents dealing with the everyday realities of arid lands, are not likely to do.

We should be so lucky. We grow up with our own set of appealing clichés about deserts. Long before we set foot in a desert, we know what it's going to be like. We know from books, but especially from movies, television specials, and *Arizona Highways*, with their powerful visual impacts sticking in the brain and often overriding everything else, that deserts are going to be colorful places of fascinating diversity, probably even of mystery. Furthermore, deserts are part of our makeup in ways that they are not to Banham and his compatriots. Tales about the arid sweeps are part and parcel of the vivid story of westward movement; furthermore, they are a dramatic part of our country, part of our own natural heritage. Hence, we tend to take them personally. If they are not lands of gold making the prospector hilariously rich, well, then, at least they're lands of freedom nonpareil in a republic that is supposed to be overgushing with that quality but seems to be ever more niggardly in delivering it—but not the desert, where the dune buggy addict or fanatical hiker can spin off endlessly into nature to his heart's content. Yet more than simply freedom, an exotic, near religious place where we can, as romantics have been schooled about nature until they're dizzy with the education—and here nature at its most exotic—find our true, deepest, spiritual selves, à la Lummis, Van Dyke, Nabhan, and the others in that long line of figures in our opalescent desert tradition.

As to illusions, we find it far easier than Banham to preserve them. They are not so far out of whack with reality as to be obviously false when we face the palpable thing. On first view, the mountain range may not be emblazoned with the colors splashed from the painter's upset palette as the tourist magazines led us to believe. Still, those colors are pretty subtle if you study them long enough, and, better, once in a while when we're specially blessed the sun crashes down, and the peaks roar before us with the glow of superheated iron, what we expected at last shown possible, and that's what we bear away as reality.

But what about the unfortunate Banham, stripped of such prejudices, standing there psychologically naked?

Well, not exactly naked. To stand so, totally disarmed and without a set of values, valid or not, for comprehending the surrounding chaos, would lead to insanity. Beyond tales of Doughty and bright legends spun from the British Empire's thrusts into desert colonialism, Banham had his stabilizing, even somewhat conventional, background.

Born in Norwich, England, in 1922, the son of an engineer, Banham himself worked in Bristol as an engineering apprentice in the wartime airplane industry. He married in 1946 and obtained his Ph.D. from the Courtald Institute of Art at the University of London in 1958. After that, he served in various editorial capacities at the *Architectural Review* and lectured at the University of London's School of Architecture. In 1976 he left for the United States to become chairman of the department of design studies at the University of New York at Buffalo. Then he moved on to the University of California at Santa Cruz, where he taught art history. Along the way, he lectured here and there, won various prizes in his field, and wrote books. When he died in 1988 at the age of sixty-six, he left behind him a more than fortunate career as an architectural critic. However, the mere recitation of his accomplishments belies the content of his thought and its unique perspective on deserts. Or, rather, one might say, the shambles he made of how Americans traditionally think of their arid heritage.[3]

In this, one might repeat how white-knuckled Americans are in clinging to traditional, dualistic views of nature. On the one extreme, they think it the raw material fallen from the hand of a beneficent God to be chopped down, dammed, shoveled into furnaces—that is, nature converted and exploited as man chooses. On the other, man is the enemy, nature ruthlessly abused by modern civilization, and every effort should be made to preserve what sad remnants are left of the once-pristine natural heritage. Most of us, of course, vacillate somewhere in the middle, perhaps typically escaping on weekends to sleep out in the cactus flats studded with lava peaks, then returning to the air-conditioned offices and the daily work that allow us the means of our modern ease. Such are our perfectly human, self-serving, and comfortable rationalizations.

Yet exploiter or preservationist, we cling to a certain idealized Weltanschauung, and it's surprising how such viewpoints sometimes find common ground. Take Los Angeles, for instance. Few people in either camp would stand up in public, or less so blurt out at a dinner party, to praise this sprawl of civilization, all but universally scorned as an overpopulated, smog-plagued, freeway-entangled sore, the example par excellence of how bad an urban mistake can get.

However, a good purchase can be had on Banham's thinking by considering his views of the city. He loves its freeways, its crazy mixture of architecture, its restaurants shaped like hats and milk cans. He revels in the urban behemoth, as *Time Magazine* put it in reviewing Banham's *Los Angeles*, for the city's "glorious spontaneity" ("Defending Los Angeles"). In the words of the book's author:

> In one unnervingly true sense, Los Angeles is the Middle West raised to flash-point, the authoritarian dogmas of the Bible Belt and the perennial revolt against them colliding at critical mass under the palm trees. Out of it comes a cultural situation where only the extreme is normal, and the Middle Way is just the unused reservation down the centre of the Freeway. (25)

Well, O.K., we can grant Banham his view, if that's what he likes. After all, art critics have to have *something* new and glittering to say; otherwise, they won't be read. If Banham "was among the first architectural historians to give the same degree of attention to the architecture of the everyday landscape that scholars give to monuments and cathedrals" (Goldberger), we can accept that, if not with certain snideness in our hearts, as the ways academics make splashes in their fields and win prizes for "original" thinking.

Then, on second thought, one suffers a hint of discomfort. What if such a man were turned loose on the desert? What would we get then?

To our horror, in *Scenes in America Deserta*, we get a man who thinks that power lines can enhance a desert view (78), who celebrates the scars of open-pit coal mines for their "grand Miltonic scale" (55), and, worse, makes fun of desert lovers as "maniacs of the ecological generation" (158). No! Still worse, not one to mop his brow as he plods like a commoner over the empty rockiness, as if in some self-enforced rite of romantic purgation, instead Banham celebrates himself, whizzing past such earnest types in his red, rented Mustang, as a "wheeled *voyeur*" (17).

Such appalling blasphemy becomes even sharper when set against the words of heroic desert writer Edward Abbey. Advocate of shedding the technology that he feels represses us, ranger Abbey rails at tourists whose first question upon entering a national park is "Where's the Coke machine?" Along with Thoreau, Lummis, Van Dyke, Krutch, Zwinger— along with just about every nature writer worth his salt in America— Abbey wants to liberate our citizenry of consumerized drones by bringing people closer to nature:

You sir, squinting at the map with your radiator boiling over and your fuel pump vapor-locked, crawl out of that shiny hunk of GM junk and take a walk. . . . Give the kids a break too, let them out of the car, let them go scrambling over the rocks hunting for rattlesnakes and scorpions and anthills. . . . Yes sir, yes madam, I entreat you, get out of those motorized wheelchairs, get off your foam rubber backsides, stand up straight like men! like women! like human beings! and walk—walk—WALK upon our sweet and blessed land! (Desert Solitaire 233)

And there's Banham, whisking along in his red Mustang, all but smoking a big, fat cigar.

Is this some enfant terrible, one of those people who loves to get attention at parties by blurting out shocking absurdities?[4] It would be easy to dismiss him as such. But a closer look shows him a revealing thinker, a disciple of Van Dyke who has gone far beyond his master— and, whatever one thinks of power lines, one of the few in the last several decades to have much new to say about viewing deserts. To understand Banham is to see our deserts with new eyes.

Despite the enviable brightness, the visual radicalism lying behind Banham's writing is not always immediately apparent. For instance, it's always risky for the desert explorer, venturing in a Mustang, no less, to chance the ruts of an unknown, diminishing road, especially late in the day. Yet, casting his fate to the winds, the aesthetician, hungry for visual food, grips the jolting wheel and drives on into the lonely heart of the Mojave. In return, he's rewarded with weird crepuscular effects as massive clouds filter the setting sun and bathe the stark Soda Mountains ahead in a strange "poison orange" (21). Then:

The road . . . climbed a little and turned a few degrees southward, and it was easy enough to park and watch the sunset darken into a ripe fluorescence—the color of iron cooling after coming out of the furnace, evoking a matching glow from any moderately reflective surface like rock fragments on the desert floor, outlining the creosote bushes in dull halos of tenuous red and filling their bulk with solid blue shadow. (Scenes 22)

Echoing the sunset imagery in Van Dyke's *The Desert* (91) and having perfected the ability to display the flickery subtleties of colors, Banham has written a far more than adequate descriptive passage. Many a desert writer would feel immensely blessed to have such words flow from his pen.

Yet there's far more to the Englishman's writing than an admirable talent spinning out a delectable combination of words. Note the depth of this passage, its sociological, historical, if not hallucinogenic, qualities, all rolled into one visual explosion. Again at evening, but this time as Banham approaches Las Vegas, America's Sin City, unusual meteorological conditions produce this:

I had not reckoned with the optical effects of that deceiving desert air, still heated by the ground below and full of the haze of the afternoon. The towers of lights and the changing skysigns were there all right, but wavering dizzily and fractured into flickering filaments and ripples of pink and electric blue and gold, floating above a reflecting pool of mirage in the purple air. If you sought an image of the dissolution of a corrupted civilization you could hardly have done better; yet the effect was more gentle and poetic than that, more like a dream city dissolving in its own ecstasy. (208)

Fetching as it is, the passage would have Van Dyke rotisserating in his grave, for the words disguise a host of underlying aesthetic conflicts. Van Dyke, along with many a modern desert lover, sees man as the enemy,[5] and he makes a large point of eschewing the "human element" in his nature writing (*Autobiography* 168–169). Yet here we have disciple Banham not only glorying in America's most tawdry tourist center, he's floating into his vision on modern air suspension, often insisting that the automobile is the instrument liberating him from physical drudgery so that he can revel in a continuing panorama of optical delights (52). To make Van Dyke and his fellows doubly grind their teeth, Banham purports that the automobile is more than a convenience; under certain conditions it is a *necessary* tool for achieving the sparkle of aesthetic pleasure. Musing on the wonders of Death Valley, he says: "I suspect that the whole effect needs also the forward speed of the automobile to bring the alternating slopes into view at the right pace—at walking speed they would be too far apart in time for the congruence of the successive sweeps, the pattern of alternating slopes to be perceived" (149). At that, Van Dyke must be rending his garments in disgust.

Underlying all this, however, is more than a gentlemanly difference of opinion, opposing ideas on the proper way of enjoying deserts. At its heart lies a fundamental watershed marking two ways of appreciating both art and nature.

While acknowledging the power of romanticism, Spanish philosopher José Ortega y Gasset does not have a high opinion of the movement. Agree or disagree, his explanation, encapsulated in a discussion of *Tristan and Isolde* puts each of us on the spot to decide one path or another. Ortega y Gasset gives Wagner the nod for "darkly stirring music," but, not leaving it at that, the critic asks why people enjoy the opera that so powerfully "makes us weep and tremble and melt away voluptuously." It is because the audience can so readily identify with the actions of the characters in the plot. For a few hours, people can indulge, if vicariously, in the joys and sorrows of the forbidden fruits from an illicit sexual encounter, much as members of the audience perhaps have done themselves, or would like to do, in their own private lives. That is, Wagner works our personal feelings until each of us has a catharsis, writ larger than we can enjoy in our petty lives (26).

According to Ortega y Gasset, that is precisely the problem with romanticism. It is popular because the emotions it generates come easily, but it also limits us to a narrow emotional band found in ourselves, delineated by our personal experiences (5). In short, it is self-indulgent, à la a Charles Bowden or a Sheila Larson. It is a kind of drunken man's pleasure, fueled by the happenstance of indulging in alcohol (27). It quickly evokes good feelings, and, it's oh so easy to reach for the bottle one more time, but it is not satisfying. In this sense, romanticism is restrictive rather than expansive; it involves the pleasures of the familiar, of wading in the comfortable territory of our own clichés, rather than taking us beyond our personal selves.

Yet in a Cartesian sense, what else is there? Surely we know the world only through our own experiences. Despite this truism, there is a choice possible, and the resulting emphasis can make a day-and-night difference. We can dwell on our private circumstances, becoming a Charles Bowden seeing the Southwest in terms of himself, as a stage for exploring his unhappy life. Or we can put the personal circumstances of our lives, our wounded childhoods, financial struggles, and failed love affairs—the dross of human existence not particularly important to the rest of humanity to begin with—in their proper perspective, behind us. Then we can approach a work of art or the desert with our higher faculties at their keenest. Then our search, in the manner of Joseph Wood Krutch, relieved of the weight of daily gripes and moans, will bear a "luminous character" (28). As Ortega y Gasset further distinguishes the two processes, "Life is one thing, art is another" (31). In this way, we have shucked self-indulgence and, girding our loins with the best of ourselves, approach true creativity.

The best example of this ideal embodied in a desert writer would seem to be John C. Van Dyke. He certainly comes across as the wanderer who has abandoned his private life in pursuit of the desert as a wondrous object before him. To him, this vast land is a work of art, worthy of nothing less than his most refined sensibilities brought to bear through his most intense concentration. In his preface to *The Desert*, the art critic pictures himself as a man totally devoted to appreciating the joys of his first love and the greatest work of art of all, the arid lands: "The desert has gone a-begging for a word of praise these many years. It never had a sacred poet; it has in me only a lover" (xi). Furthermore, as he says in his *Autobiography*, scorning the very "human element" (168) that Ortega y Gasset scorns, using the very same words (29), wild "nature itself . . . should be the all-absorbing topic" (168–169). On top of that, as just about everyone comments who studies Van Dyke, there are no people in the book, not a single person. In this sense, *The Desert* seems to be a "pure" work of art. Such circumstances have led Richard Shelton to put the case well. Van Dyke saw the desert as a series of "vast galleries whose works he examined with the intensity of a lover and the precision of a scientist" (xii).

By way of contrast, Banham, also an art critic, can come across as most "impure." Not only does he roar around the desert in his red Mustang, leaving such honest plodders as Van Dyke in his dust, and devote, as we've seen, one of his most poetic passages to the soaring, neon-bathed, nighttime architecture of America's gambling capital. Adding insult to injury, he hobnobs with the people he meets and celebrates as delightful handiwork the various ruins men have left behind on the desert. Then, to our horror, he cavalierly unfolds a folding bicycle and, a twentieth-century clown, rides it, skittering off across the pure flatness of a dry lakebed.[6] Certainly, in contrast to elevated Van Dyke, this Philistine should be relegated to the lowest level of déclassé pretenders.

The irony is that Banham, despite his antics, turns out to be closer aesthetically to the wind-driven snow than Van Dyke, for such judgments as those above are not informed by close reading. Typical of Van Dyke, as we've seen in an earlier chapter, he's a grand deceiver; his work is not always what he leads us to believe. Embedded in the "pure" aestheticism of *The Desert* is a contrary theme. On this point, it is not accurate to say that there are no people in his desert classic. One person looms over the entire book, permeating it with his pained presence—and what a fellow he is! It is none other than Van Dyke himself. From the beginning, he sets up the book as a grand tour. Using the first person, he addresses his readers, inviting them to escape humdrum existence, mount up, and ride along with him "beyond the wire fence of civilization" (x). That is, coloring the whole book thereafter is the image of the stalwart and experienced frontiersman showing us the sights. False as we've seen this picture to be, faked to burnish up the book's heroic authority, readers are easily taken in by it.

Our guide's presence is there in more important ways. Van Dyke doesn't seem to be a very happy man. In fact, he's quite obviously a misanthrope. Pausing here and there, he delivers sermonettes on what's wrong with the world—primarily, it turns out, man himself, whose "boot mark in the dust smells of blood and iron" (vii–viii). Well, we can grant him that. Depicting man as the great destroyer heightens the beauty and value of the pristine nature before us. Yet Van Dyke, often a complex writer, won't let it rest at that. Despite the immediate lures of nature, it happens that it has a rather testy, and fatal, side. Every living thing in its domain either "pursues or is pursued." Beyond nature's skin-deep beauty, we see a vicious, endless circus of ripping, tearing, and devouring: "The bounding deer must get away; the swift-following wolf must not let him" (155). And not only for the animal world. Bedazzled by nature's loveliness, the surface beauty wrought by struggle for perfection (171), man admires, but he, too, is sucked into its churning maws (230–231). On top of that, a fellow is lucky if nature first doesn't drive him mad in the process, just for the fun of it (107). So we get, not pure aestheticism at all, but the tortured and doomed romantic hero whose temporary ecstasies and long-term agonies color the whole. True, Van Dyke spares us the specifics of his Sturm und Drang, thus saving himself from the diminishment of the mundane; what we have for the book's underlying persona is Bowden without the particulars.

It happens that the two books of Van Dyke and Banham, separated by roughly eighty years, concentrate on the Mojave Desert of Southern California, yet their treatment of the region is quite different. Banham is broader, taking in the whole of the landscape. He also is far more relaxed. He has few axes to grind; he is not the doomed romantic driven into the Mojave by an unnamed turmoil in his soul. Rather, he's out to enjoy what he sees, and often there is a riffle of pleasant laughter surrounding his progress. He is, he chides himself to the point of boasting, "the archetypical British tourist" (3). It is true that out there in the Mojave he "uncovered an aspect of myself that I did not know" (18). But he's not going to tell us about it. Having read and appreciated the artistic passages

Peter Reyner Banham

of the grim and humorless Van Dyke (153–154), Banham is not going to "fall into a Wertherish reverie of introspection" (18). He is the art historian, an educated European out to enjoy America's landscape, out to see what there is to see out there in this vast nook, this strange surprise of the Mojave. If that means chatting with the Nipton Troll, a man "quite mad" and "more or less clean" who lives in a road culvert and is writing a report about the desert for a Lord Fleet Thompson of London, so be it (59). The desert engenders such curiosities, and all of them interest Banham. Or if it means jouncing over bad roads, only to see, suddenly there before him, the jewel of an oasis, the little settlement of Kelso, "bounded by well-trimmed hedges" and a tidy railroad station in the Spanish-Colonial style, all the better. Banham wants to learn about all that he sees, not just nature or officially designated art. Kelso sparks the historian in him, and he muses on the infinite variety of adjustments man has made to live in this landscape (24).

That puts John C. Van Dyke and Peter Reyner Banham at loggerheads. Van Dyke purports to be the holier-than-thou aesthetician, untainted by the lowbrow human associations in which Banham exults. Yet in the topsy-turvy territory where literature, art, and nature meet, as we've seen, Van Dyke is awash in his own personal doom, while Banham, at times a reveler in the desert antics of his fellowmen, comes out far ahead in the race to be pure. Banham adds a delightful complication to the issue. Although he takes a cheery potshot or two at Van Dyke, razzing him for the demeanor of one who never smiles and treads about in thick-soled shoes (158), who doesn't understand the flora and fauna he discusses (157), and, following his histrionic urges, whirls out affected passages in the ornate Art Nouveau style, the amazing thing is that Banham enthusiastically confesses that he and Van Dyke are aesthetic brothers, seeing the desert in much the same way (154).

Yet to sort out what is going on here is to appreciate Reyner Banham's refinement of Van Dyke's way of seeing the desert.

If anything, Van Dyke is solidly consistent. Despite the wildness occurring within them, his chapters are well organized, each dealing in turn with animals, flora, mirages, and such. *The Desert* starts at point *A* and marches its way steadily to point *Z* with admirable aplomb, along the way playing intriguing variations of chords blending the author's angst with his wonder at the marvels before him in an inextricable whole of writer and content. This is not true of Banham, and his quite different method hardly is a fault but, rather, it places him a step or two ahead of Van Dyke in convincing complexity. Banham is not so brusque as to tell us what he's doing; he simply shows us, planting the evidence and letting us figure it out.

A key to this lies in the otherworldly evocation of Las Vegas quoted several pages back. Here, the towers and lights of Sin City seen from a distance at evening waver into a flickering mirage before the awed traveler. At the end of the paragraph, Banham suggests, "If you sought an image of the dissolution of a corrupted civilization," this would be it, "a dream city dissolving in its own [sinful] ecstasy" (208). We can only imagine what kind of a moralistic roar Van Dyke would have worked himself into had he confronted such a blot of call girls and slot machines rising in conglomerated affront on his beloved desert.[7]

Note, however, that Banham very carefully uses the conditional "if." That is, if you'd care to put a moral spin on the scene, you might see it as a city glorying as it dissolves in its own ecstasy of corruption. Not that *Banham* sees it that way. He only allows for the possibility. The city might be perceived as a lesson in the wonders of human follies, as a vista of pure artistic excitements, or as both at once. Banham, then, is writing two books that consist of two perspectives interleaved in one volume. A man curious about the phenomenon of people and their ways in the desert, he takes in this aspect, too, as part of the scene. Novelist and critic David Quammen faults Banham for this because the venturing Englishman sometimes slights the Yarrow's lizards and jumping cholla for meditations on the works of man (9). Be that emphasis as it may, Banham makes clear that it's the desert context of whatever he's viewing that makes it lovely. What lends Scotty's Castle in Death Valley remarkable qualities is not the architecture itself—its "Hispanic whimsy" really would be quite commonplace in, say, Florida—but "where it stands." The context of an "almost abstract wilderness" gives the castle its radiance (35). Hence, though Banham may pause to dwell at length on a work of man, it's really the desert he's talking about in terms of aesthetics, as the value-imparting essential.

Thus, Banham goes beyond Van Dyke on at least two scores. Van Dyke's condemnation of the human element, after all, is a little silly, as if one must pull back from his joy and turn away repentant if he discovers himself admiring anything to do with human hands. Abandoning such provincialism, Banham widens Van Dyke's perspective and treats the visual whole of the desert, and he bears out in practice what Van Dyke only talked about in theory while really having his own concerns, disguised, at heart. Whatever the circumstances behind the creation of the things before him, Banham's ultimate pleasure has little or nothing to do with himself personally but everything to do with the "unalloyed pleasure" of the visual experience. That is, the harvest of accidental joy when "cresting a hill, or rounding a bluff and seeing some shape or color, rock or river, that temporarily commands one's total attention" (218). Aesthetically, one hardly can get "purer" than that.

Banham expends many pages mulling over the aesthetics of sight and the pleasure from deserts in particular. Doggedly asking himself, "What is it in these scenes that produces these seemingly uncontrollable responses?" (218), he goes over the old but telling distinctions, as applicable to literature as to art, between the Picturesque and the Sublime (221). He courses through Gaston Bachelard's widely read *The Poetics of Space* (62) and fondly remembers when he first ran across Van Dyke's book, in a linen closet in Pasadena. The prose "still sparkles in memory" whenever Banham is in the Southwest (153). These are intricate, yet cheery explorations, pleasures in themselves to follow because, unlike many a philosopher, Banham doesn't let the theory fly off into the ether but keeps pulling it back to test it against our experience of the physical world.

Ultimately, like Einstein wrestling to discover a unified field theory explaining the Universe, all such approaches fall short of achieving a watertight case for desert aesthetics. Eminent Bachelard, "who writes so engagingly and with flashes of deep penetration about the interior spaces of the house, even on the interiors of 'drawers, boxes, and closets,'" becomes "skimpy and self-defensive" when he approaches Banham's topic. Frenchman Bachelard, Banham reminds us, never saw a desert, and thus is not much help (62–63). In contrast, Van Dyke's descriptive reactions ring true. Basically, he is an abstractionist, enjoying forms and colors for their own sake, though Van Dyke is not a theorist and can't say *why* he finds them stimulating (223). Is this, then, all mystery or at least is it inexplicable, the entire complex of who we are both individually and as members of a culture gawking as our optic nerves twitch with joy?[8] Certainly the unknowability of deserts, the lure of the "well-hidden secret" (48), keeps romantics' hearts fluttering and heightens their anticipation, as Banham readily admits. On this, hardly a religious man, Banham nonetheless goes on to quote Balzac's epigrammatic proclamation, "The desert is where God is and man is not" (16).[9]

Banham, however, is merely playing with us in his lighthearted, professorial way. A writer who can be trickier, though more honest, than Van Dyke, he is setting us up for the more solid suggestions of his later pages. Here he takes yet another step or two beyond his mentor.

"What is it in these scenes that produces these seemingly uncontrollable responses?" It is a question Banham asks with special intensity regarding Cave Mountain, a monstrous prospect rising boldly before the motorist, as if I-15 will take him at eighty miles per hour slamming through the mass and into the very bowels of the mountain:

. . . by midafternoon a combination of dust and air and the sun getting round behind the mountain (and behind the dust) produces enough luminosity in the atmosphere to provide a layered visual separation of successive outcrops along the spur. Such visual separation by veils of luminous air between ranges of mountains is, of course, one of the most commonplace visual enchantments and delights of desert landscapes. . . . (151)

In the strictest sense, the scene is not Sublime. Sublimity, implying awe, also implies danger in that realm where physical circumstances color our perceptions of beauty. For that reason, Manly gazed on the prospect of barren mountain rising ahead over barren mountain, and because of the danger involved in crossing the ranges, felt a divine shiver from nature. One might get a hint of a similar reaction by standing on the edge of the Grand Canyon, gazing into the abyss below, and experiencing the queasiness of vertigo which influences the Canyon's visual impact. Yet the motorist, though perhaps in a state of wonder, feels no such threat from the great mass of Cave Mountain.

With its storms, swirling wind and water, the desert can be violent, if briefly, but Banham argues that what underlies most people's memory of the desert is its grand repose. Hence, the desert makes us contemplative. The mind relaxes, reaching out to embrace the scenes before us. And in that way, in the way that the act of meditation can become, viewing deserts tends to be addictive (219). Yet there's more going on here, and it lies in that area where optical physics affects our emotional reactions. Van Dyke often talks of the desert's colored air, and now Banham suggests that our "mysterious" response to what we see, as in the example of Cave Mountain, has to do with the separation of colors from their objects, "of color from substance," stretching the mind toward a delicious entertainment of abstractions (223) that results in our "spooky" reaction to deserts.[10]

Although Banham's theory certainly does not tell all, Ortega y Gasset would be pleased. In a remarkable breakthrough, Banham has gone farther than any other desert writer—Dutton, Powell, Austin, Krutch, name anyone you will—both in removing the plaguing hounds of self-absorption from desert appreciation and in providing at least a framework for further theoretical exploration.

Finally, however, like Einstein, Banham, too, throws up his hands at explaining the marvel—which, by definition, can't be explained. Those who worry that Banham, going away from the personal self, may be too bloodless, too clinical, are wrong. Unlike the romantic self-seekers such as Bowden, Banham has "not 'found myself.'" Rather, he has become released from personal, often self-destructive, dross for something far better. "I have lost myself" in the beauty of the desert exults Banham on his last page, and if anything "I understand myself less than I did before." He continues to the conclusion of the book: "What I have truly found, however, is something that I value, in some ways, more than myself" (228). And that is exactly what many a religious leader claims is necessary for the highest sense of human fulfillment.

EPILOGUE

The Mountain,
a Beetle, and the
Thief in the Night

When a jocular Godfrey Sykes pitched onto his head and waved his legs against the Mexican sky to celebrate the conquest of a desert peak by imitating its insect namesake, he was unwittingly sending a message freighted with meaning.

Today, the genre of desert writing seems to be in a bind. The realists represented by Powell, Hornaday, and Krutch have had their day, and it has been a bright one. Drawing heavily on science, leaning on reason, they have described the workings of the desert, its geology, exotic plants, and animals, while coloring their books with a fervid wonder at what lay before them. It's with a thrill that we join Joseph Wood Krutch to behold God's Hand rising in the sky over the desert vastness and tag along with the crafty Browne in a parlay with Yuma Indians.

That is, such writers have explored the desert, and we have seen it with new eyes along with them. What, then, is a young author, writing in their vein, to do? In noble fashion, the major and most exciting work has been done. What is left is filling in the outlines of a diminished desert. Yet we hardly can imagine a treatise on the life cycle of the Pinacate beetle, fascinating as it is, gripping the public as did Hornaday's book about his journey through the marvelous, then little-known, corner of Mexico that is the insect's home. The work focused on the beetle—or on the saguaro or the denning of coyotes—will appeal mostly to students in those particular fields, and their number is understandably limited. How many herpetologists are there in the country, or even specialists in *Canis latrans?* And whom would they speak to about their enthusiasm over the recent work on their subject?

So with an eye on keeping a readership, and, indeed, on exercising their own general interests, writers have swung the other way. Traveling through the deserts, now fenced and marked by the boundaries of national parks and game preserves, desert venturers can no longer climb a cliff as did Powell and declare as they overlook the sea of a stony wilderness that "barren desolation is stretched before me; and yet there is a beauty in the scene." Beauty there still is out in the desert, thank goodness for those who have worked over the decades to preserve it, but its celebration is deflated, the sharp edge of thrills once honed by daily dangers blunted by the host of footprints (and tire tracks) behind every writer and every reader now beholding the arid sweeps.

"Make it new," said Ezra Pound to poets, but the good advice of his *Cantos* haunts today's desert writers.

Reacting to the above, and in a trend already evident in the later works of Ann Zwinger, no longer able to say much new about what's before them, writers have resorted to documenting their personal experiences, the problems of sleeping out in a desert sand storm and the minor joys of finding an unexpected flower blooming in a crevice. Younger writers, such as Bruce Berger and Page Stegner, certainly reflect this. Their writing often is delicately woven in literary terms, for which they deserve every credit. But the inescapable fact, no matter what their finesse, is that they insistently contribute one volume after another to the category of "What I Did When I Traveled in the Desert"—a desert already familiar to us. Worse are less honorable writers who avoid the problem by reducing the desert to a confessional stage. Such is hardly the fare—contrasting with a Dutton or a Krutch—that lifts the reading public by the ears.

For that, the realists are rapidly losing ground.

Taking their place in increasing numbers are the fabulists. They, of course, also have a tradition, some of it, as with Van Dyke, heady and moving. Whether we're talking of a tree inexplicably bursting into flame as if sparked by a Divine Hand to save a freezing Cabeza de Vaca or Cozzens' fantastically vertiginous landscapes, the exotic desert always has lent material for craving, overactive imaginations, both of writers and readers. Today, the real desert before us often falls short of the Technicolor hyperactivity demanded by generations with tastes schooled by the constantly changing stimuli of television. And falls short, too, given the heavy burden moderns bored with their regularized lives have imposed on nature, of this most otherworldly of nature's landscapes asked to fill our spiritual ennui. As if, since we say we love nature, we also insist that it's nature's job both to entertain and heal us.

Sometimes the more ordered a society becomes, the more embedded in civilized routines, the more it yearns for compensating mystical experiences. And so we get writers, whether cynically snuffling up their sleeves at the public's sheep-like naiveté or convincing themselves that they believe such phenomena because their psychic need is so desperate, turned novices rolling around on the floors of desert shacks looking for their spiritual spots and another, Ezekiel-like, beholding, not the starry Hand of God rising, marvelous enough in itself, but surreal whirlings of lights in the sky spun from the author's wish-fulfillment.

Such writing, if handled well, can be artistic at times and even convincing. Yet it is not really nature writing but rather a rejection of nature and an insult to it, as is a plasticized Disneyland an insult to soul-shaking folklore. And so we get a hotel in desert Las Vegas featuring its own air-conditioned desert offering tourists a momentarily stimulating, although hardly profound, experience of the desert.

That brings us to another reason why many writers are biting the ends of their pencils, facing an even more dire threat to their profession. If upended, tottering Godfrey Sykes was flashing a sign, it was but a hint compared to another performance, Walt Disney's *The Living Desert*, appearing only forty-six years later. No matter that much of the film was fudged to impress viewers and so sell tickets. As has been seen, books can be faked, too. What counts is the onset of a massive cultural change as the electronic media has pushed the written word aside. Generations ago, nature guide Enos Mills boasted that children arriving at his lodge in idyllic Estes Park soon gave up the "movie talk" filling their heads for the deeper pleasures of waiting expectantly by a beaver pond (161). He must have had a special touch. Increasingly, children and adults alike want to learn about deserts not through direct experience or through books, both requiring engagement, a certain personal investment, but through a media partial to sleight of hand, that is, skewed information with a cotton-candy fluff. A writer may ponder a timeless desert scene of little apparent activity, where nothing much is happening, and get a thoughtful essay out of it. Few people, however, are willing to watch twenty minutes or an hour of such stasis, such non-happening.

It is this fairly recent development that has little beads of blood breaking out on the foreheads of serious desert writers. All the more so because the force of television and film has influenced publishing, resulting in the supercolored, histrionic coffee-table books about deserts that ape their competition. And tourism has followed suit, for we are Romans, not Greeks. Those "outback" excursions through Navajoland where the dusky shepherd, appropriately jeweled, blanketed, and mounted on a palomino, appears on cue from out of nowhere, and the cameras snap their excited little clicks. So, countering Austin, Krutch, Abbey, and others who plead for the land, people's appreciation of what they claim to "love" is based less and less on direct experience and more and more on make-believe. No wonder the shallow fabulists are having such a happy time of it. Their success is dipped from the same slick come-ons that sell wash-day miracle soaps.

Although "success" hardly is the appropriate word. Year after year, desert books come pouring off the presses—and, whether by realists or fabulists, quickly move from the store shelves into the remainder bin. Perhaps it is a symptom of our culture that we now have in desert writing, as in so many other aspects of our national life, so few large, authoritative, and widely acknowledged worthies. Gone are the days—this is a descriptive statement, although partially a lamentation—when Joseph Wood Krutch's *The Voice of the Desert* went through reprinting after reprinting, read *and discussed* by tens of thousands of intelligent readers, in fact by a large portion of people who were educated, mentally alive, and well-read. Now, desert writers, whatever their degree of literary talent, have their following, but, much like the audience for poetry, it is small and often associated with a coterie in academe.

That's not to say that the jig is up for desert writing. Surely, despite the enormous talents of the past, not everything has been said about our deserts, and just as surely the written word has not been eclipsed by the electronic media. Instead, the two represent diverging functions. There will always be an audience seeking the deeply moving over tinsel, and that most likely will be from engagement with prose rather than with an endless procession of flickering images.

It is to say, however, that, as is always true of the arts, what has been done in the past, no matter how ingenious or banal, will not suffice as a model for the future. In the late 1960s, Edward Abbey came crashing into desert writing seemingly from nowhere, half philosopher, half bandido, to rejuvenate the genre. What is needed now is not another Edward Abbey from the same craggy mold but a new, convincing, and challenging voice. Time after time, as with the abrupt, buoyant epiphany of Peter Reyner Banham, it has happened in desert literature when least expected, and it will happen again. As always, it will come as a thief in the night and suddenly be there, assuming its presence. The only thing not known is from what direction it will come and in what apparent shape it will appear. Not knowing either only whets our taste for the coming surprise.

NOTES

INTRODUCTION

1. According to the layman's rule of thumb, a desert is a place receiving ten inches or less of moisture a year. Scientists' various definitions add complex dimensions. The several formulas for determining a desert take into consideration not only the total amount of precipitation, but such features as soil, wind, and temperature conditions. Similar criteria are used to distinguish one desert from another, as the Chihuahuan, Sonoran, and Great Basin of the American Southwest—and beyond that, to designate subdivisions within larger deserts. The niceties can become highly refined. For a clear presentation of such natural history, see Peggy Larson's *The Deserts of the Southwest*. In the present book, "desert" is a generic term, used interchangeably in the singular and plural.

2. The conflicting attitude applies generally over the years to our industrializing yet romantic nation. First we crushed nature; then we idealized it. Roderick Nash studies the long, ongoing process in *Wilderness and the American Mind*.

1. CABEZA DE VACA

1. My *Alvar Núñez Cabeza de Vaca* outlines his life, analyzes his work, and comments on recent scholarship.

2. As might be guessed, Cabeza de Vaca's idealism, his advocacy of fair dealings with Spaniards and Indians alike, did not sit well with conquerors reveling in slavery and rapine. The colonists under his administration revolted and sent their governor back to Spain in chains (Cabeza de Vaca, *The Account* 13–14).

2. WILLIAM L. MANLY

1. There is some evidence, little developed and inconclusive, of another hand at work in the book (Lawrence Clark Powell, "William Lewis Manly's *Death Valley in*

'49" 31, 33, 52). Whatever the case, Edwards assures us that Manly is "historically sound" (*The Valley Whose Name Is Death* 89).

3. J. ROSS BROWNE AND SAMUEL W. COZZENS

1. The precise dates of Cozzens' stay in the Arizona Territory are not known. Historian Hubert H. Bancroft says that Cozzens "visited the country in 1858–60" (519). Legal records reveal that Cozzens received a judgeship in the Territory in 1860 (*Appointment and Commission of Samuel W. Cozzens*).

2. On this point, Bancroft says that although Cozzens' book is "not grossly inaccurate," it is "of a somewhat sensational type" (519). Bancroft is being far too kind.

4. CHARLES F. LUMMIS

1. A color reproduction of *On the Coast of California* appears in Holmer's article (8).

2. Fleming summarizes Lummis' life and work.

3. For James' life and work, see Wild, *George Wharton James.*

5. MARY AUSTIN

1. For instance, her *Earth Horizon* condemns the shameless gossip about Lummis' love affairs, then on the same page gleefully passes on a tidbit or two (292).

2. This outline follows Austin's autobiography, *Earth Horizon.*

3. An interesting contrast is Austin's second book of essays about the desert, *The Land of Journey's Ending*, appearing twenty-one years after her first. An outstanding book, nevertheless by comparison, it suffers from what Larry Evers calls the author's "magisterial tone" (xviii), a result of Austin's ravaging ego fed by her national fame. *The Land of Journey's Ending* was an attempt to recapture her earlier, innocent self, but by then it was too late for her.

4. 1 Kings 21:1–29.

6. JOHN C. VAN DYKE AND THE DESERT AESTHETICIANS

1. Lawrence Clark Powell, *Southwest Classics* (327). Powell further hails Van Dyke as the first in "the illustrious lineage of desert writers" (315).

2. John Muir, letter to Howard Palmer, 12 December 1912.

3. For recent scholars who continue to beat their heads, often blissfully, against the walls of the landscape's beauty, see Bachelard's *The Poetics of Space* and Yi-Fu Tuan's *Topophilia.*

4. The following details of Van Dyke's life and thinking about art are expanded in his autobiography.

5. That's just part of a complex story. Readers taken by intrigues will be de-

lighted at Van Dyke, a man who throve on plots. Lurking beneath his trips to the Southwest for his health were escapes from a scandal resulting from an illegitimate daughter sired with the wife of a fellow faculty member at Rutgers and a bizarre escapade involving a bag of money carried deep into Mexico for Andrew Carnegie (Teague and Wild 20–22; Wild, "The Homestead Strike and the Mexican Connection").

6. But from the palette of which painter? My "How a London Madman Painted Our Deserts" explains that while viewing the arid lands Van Dyke often saw them through the eyes of a favorite English painter, Joseph M. W. Turner. The bright, whirling colors in Van Dyke's book echo the wild manner in Turner's canvases from his later, impressionistic period. See, for instance, Turner's *The Fighting "Témémaire"* (1838) or the still wilder abstraction of blurred oranges and whites in his *Sun Setting over a Lake* (c. 1845).

7. For more on the comparison of Van Dyke and Austin, see two separate articles, Buck and Wild, and Wild, "Sentimentalism in the American Southwest."

8. Having his chuckle, Van Dyke worked pretty hard at the deception. Such books as *The Open Spaces* and his *Autobiography* are laced with combat with thieves and wolves and with Van Dyke's cliff-hanging athletic feats in the Western wilds. Van Dyke was in fact a sickly man for much of his life, sometimes unable to mount the lecture platform, let alone a horse.

9. To be fair about it, in those days nature seemed vast by comparison to human inroads. One could, then, appreciate nature, as did Carnegie, even while destroying it.

10. We do not have the letter, but Van Dyke's squid-like reply to it exists (Teague and Wild 59–61).

11. Doubling the irony here, it's a curious comment on human psychology to consider how eagerly readers have swallowed Van Dyke's self-projected image as a desert hero. Despite the widespread reading of his book, over the decades not one scientist, literary critic, hiker, naturalist, or desert devotee of whatever intensity and persuasion has challenged Van Dyke in print on such matters. The one possible exception is the single and rather mild observation by Peter Reyner Banham that Van Dyke "does not always understand the life forms he describes" (*Scenes in America Deserta* 157). Perhaps tellingly in our need for heroes, Banham was not an American but an Englishman. More on Banham and Van Dyke will be seen in the final chapter.

7 · WILLIAM T. HORNADAY

1. Some years later, MacDougal would lead a rather different expedition, frolicking out into the desert with a Mary Austin hoping to recharge her spiritual batteries from more direct contact with the earth—and, some say, with MacDougal.

2. The group also included a Jesse T. Jenkins and a George Saunders, about whom little is known. Fontana expands on the members of the expedition (xxii–xxxi).

3. My *Pioneer Conservationists of Eastern America* summarizes Hornaday's life and work (94–105).

4. Some of Hornaday's information quite understandably has not worn well over time. For example, he seems to accept the wisdom of the day concerning thirteen species of coyote (313), whereas today scientists accept only one, the difference

in size and color now accounted for by geography and individual differences. However, Hornaday lived in a time of taxonomic proliferation, and in this he is reflecting the thoughts of his fellow scientists. In the main, Hornaday's information, unlike Van Dyke's, is as accurate as he could have made it.

5. In their separate works, Reiger and Trefethen make persuasive cases that hunter/naturalists have been the nation's foremost preservationists.

8. JOHN WESLEY POWELL AND WILLIAM E. SMYTHE

1. Howard Mumford Jones (8). His *O Strange New World* details such excitements.

2. The best overview of Powell is Stegner's *Beyond the Hundredth Meridian.*

3. It is obligatory to say at this point in recounting the Powell story that only six cheering men shot out of the depths of the canyon to amaze a Mormon settler named Asa fishing on the bank. Early in the expedition, one man deserted, and only two days before Powell's exit from his gloomy tomb of rock, three others, fearing the roar of the final cataracts, hoofed it out of the canyon in hopes of reaching the nearest Mormon village. Unknown to Powell at the time of his emergence from the Grand Canyon, they lie bloated in the sun, riddled with Shivwit arrows.

The seething haystacks and rocks also took their toll on the boats. Powell regretfully left his flagship, the *Emma Dean,* named for his wife, behind after it was shivered beyond repair by an especially bad bout with some rapids.

4. For literary effect, Powell adjusted some details of the adventure; for instance, combining several explorations of the canyon region and weaving them into one continuous story. In the main, however, his account is reliable.

5. Good summaries of Smythe's career are Lawrence B. Lee's Introduction and his "William Ellsworth Smythe and the Irrigation Movement."

6. The beginnings of Anglo mania for large-scale irrigation in California went back to the 1850s, predating Smythe some forty years. Scoffers, however, considered many of the early schemes grandiose and impractical, as, indeed, a good number of them were (W. Storrs Lee 132–137).

7. Caption to Powell photo preceding 261.

8. Smythe details the picture in two chapters, "The Blessing of Aridity" (30–40) and "The Miracle of Irrigation" (41–48).

9. J. SMEATON CHASE

1. For the bare bones of Chase's life, see Hart and "Chase, J[oseph] Smeaton."

2. Lawrence Clark Powell's *California Classics* quotes a poignant example from what sounds like a draft of Chase's will (206).

3. Chase does not give the year, although several references to the ongoing war in Europe offer a rough time frame (217, 296, 355). On this journey he was riding a tough, docile, and lovable Indian pony he named Kaweah, after the horse of earlier Sierra adventurer Clarence King (85).

4. Chase's book reproduces an Eytel painting, the ghostly *Moonlight Sonata* (opposite 38) and praises the artist's conscientious work for giving "... a truer rendering

of the desert than do sensational canvases . . ." (29). For an ample selection, as well as a biographical sketch, of work by this kindly but brave desert explorer, see Hudson. Apparently, monkish Eytel came as close as anyone to being a genuine desert saint. In companion articles, Jaeger and Elwood offer heartwarming vignettes of humble Eytel. James devotes early pages of *Wonders* to praising both the talents and character of Eytel, his illustrator and frequent companion in the author's desert travels (1:xxxvii–xliv). Originals of Eytel's paintings are in the holdings of Palm Spring's splendid Desert Museum.

The mention of Eytel brings up a separate but related issue. Physically isolated though they were at times, desert devotees in those days often had intricate connections with other aficionados spread across the desert. In this fraternity, relations sometimes were brotherly, at other times not; and, either way, they could get complicated. As mentioned, in 1918, J. Smeaton Chase supplied most of the photographs for the illustrated edition of John C. Van Dyke's *The Desert*, a sharp deal for Scribner's. Before that, Carl Eytel did the lovely drawings for George Wharton James' *Wonders of the Colorado Desert.* However, James had gripes. He claimed, in public, no less, that Van Dyke had stolen from him the photo Van Dyke used for the frontispiece of *The Desert* (James 1:xxviii–xxix). Whether the accusation was true or not, James, a Southwestern hustler and editor of the Radiant Life Press, was not always pure in his dealings. He got his hands on some early correspondence of John Muir, and in a letter dated 16 July 1908 to Muir, James hinted at a payoff if Muir would like the correspondence back.

As it happened, Muir's daughter Helen, seeking a cure for her respiratory problems, was staying in the Mojave Desert north of Palm Springs, at the ranch of Theodore Strong Van Dyke, a brother of John C. Van Dyke. Given his wanderings and affability, Chase likely knew Theodore, a California writer in his own right who welcomed artistic and scientific types to stay in the small houses dotting his ranch. Hence, the possible contact resulting in Chase's sale of photos for use in John C.'s famous desert book. In any case, despite the desert appreciation going on at the ranch, life there was not always happy (Wild, "John Muir and the Van Dyke Ranch," parts 1 and 2). The connections go on and on. The affairs among these people, who advocated the simple life, rarely were simple.

10. JOSEPH WOOD KRUTCH

1. For Krutch's life and analysis of his work, see Pavich and the longer study by Margolis.

2. *Statistical Abstract of the United States, 1970* (21).

3. *Statistical Abstract of the United States, 1990* (36).

4. Margolis explores the rather ironic relationship between Krutch and wealthy amateur naturalist Bechtel (207–211).

11. EDWARD ABBEY

1. For whimsical effect, Abbey liked to say that he was born in the village of Home, Pennsylvania, a stretching of the truth scholars have gladly repeated. Al-

though such a place exists, James M. Cahalan recently pointed out that in fact Abbey was born in the hospital at Indiana, Pennsylvania, a town about ten miles south of Home (96–97).

2. The most thorough study to date of Abbey's life and work is James Bishop's *Epitaph for a Desert Anarchist*. See also two literary studies with some biographical information, Ann Ronald's *The New West of Edward Abbey* and Garth McCann's shorter *Edward Abbey*.

3. We should criticize this book with some forgiveness. At the time of its writing, Abbey was grieving the loss of his third wife, Judy Pepper, from leukemia. Nonetheless, the book's faults are but exaggerations of those found in most of his other novels.

4. See, for example, *Resist Much, Obey Little*, the Festschrift edited by James Hepworth and Gregory McNamee.

5. In his short list of suggested readings, Abbey recommends Van Dyke (239). Far more telling is a comparison of the prefaces of the two books, each stating the impossibility of fully capturing the essence of the lover, each using the word "impression," and each bittersweet in taking the stance of the lone rebel pained at the loss of natural beauty. To both Abbey and Van Dyke, the world was damned, and their celebrations were but existential gestures, the best they could do to find joy as a temporary salve to gloom in an ultimately meaningless world.

6. In this sense, one might argue that, with his appeal to middle-class upstarts, Abbey was not nearly so radical as he's sometimes made out to be. See Wild, "Edward Abbey: The Middle-Class Maverick."

7. For an everyday picture of working with Abbey, see Wild, "Into the Heart's Wild Places."

12. ANN ZWINGER AND CHARLES BOWDEN

1. Carlos Castañeda, *The Teachings of Don Juan* (14–19).

2. Barry Holstun Lopez, *Desert Notes* (40).

3. Lopez, *Desert Notes* (41).

4. Gary Paul Nabhan, *Desert Legends* (2–3).

5. Nabhan, *Desert Legends* (77). Nabhan's escape hatch in such scenes, presented as if they actually happened, is the "re-storying" in the subtitle. Van Dyke similarly gave himself considerable wobble room by using the word "impression" in his preface to *The Desert* (xi).

6. Castañeda is the exception. Bursting on the scene during the freewheeling drug enthusiasms of the 1960s, his initially popular study of Yaqui Indian shamanism has since suffered from serious doubts about its authenticity. See de Mille.

7. John M. Ellis develops the idea in "The Western Tradition of Political Correctness."

8. The summary of Ann Zwinger's life follows Wild's *Ann Zwinger* (5–10).

9. Biographical sources for Bowden should be approached with caution. The quote, along with some of the other information, is from material provided by Bowden's publisher, the University of Arizona Press. Much of the story of Bowden's life comes through in bits and pieces in his own books. However, one needs to be on guard when reading the statements Bowden makes about himself. For instance,

the first sentence of *Blue Desert* reads: "I have lived in the Sonoran Desert since I was a boy . . ." (1). Yet it is clear from the information Bowden supplied to the publisher mentioned above that as an adult Bowden spent considerable time living in Wisconsin and Illinois.

13. PETER REYNER BANHAM

1. Banham, *Scenes in America Deserta* (161).

2. Acknowledging the impact of such dreamstuff, Banham's *Scenes in America Deserta* echoes the title of Doughty's 1888 volume, *Travels in Arabia Deserta*.

3. Good sources for Banham's life are Goldberger and "Banham, (Peter) Reyner," the rundown on him in *Contemporary Authors*.

4. Recalling Banham's ability to annoy fellow academics, Michael McNay comments on the "gaudy plumage" of the professor's "*lèse majesté*" and answers in the affirmative.

5. The very first page of *The Desert* rails: "What monstrous folly, think you, ever led Nature to create her one great enemy—man!" (vii).

6. See the jaunty photograph in *Scenes* (opposite 120).

7. He didn't, of course. In Spanish, Las Vegas means the meadows, and though there is no record of Van Dyke visiting the place, if he had he would have seen some pleasant expanses of green grass, cottonwoods, and running water, a small oasis in the midst of unrelieved sandy flats and bare, distant mountains where teamsters converged from miles around to rest in the cool shade while their weary stock drank their fill. The livelier activities for which Las Vegas is now known are fairly recent. They began to appear, like the slow eruption of an iridescent mushroom out of the desert, in the 1930s, when the huge workforce needed to construct nearby Hoover Dam called for lusty entertainments. For a brief but admirable history of Las Vegas, see David Darlington (241–248).

8. See, for example, John Gage's study of how the meanings assigned to various colors have changed in cultures down through the centuries.

9. Banham gives the wrong source for the quotation. He says that he is quoting Frank Lloyd Wright, who in turn, Banham maintains, is quoting Victor Hugo. However, the words are not from Hugo but from the last page of Balzac's short story "Une Passion dans le Désert." The original reads, "[Le désert] c'est Dieu sans les hommes" (1084). For the English translation of Balzac's weirdly telling story about deserts, upsetting in a way we feel when approaching a deep truth we hadn't expected about ourselves, see "A Passion in the Desert."

10. Perhaps, we might suggest, as Banham does not, that such strangeness combines with the vastness and sensory deprivation of deserts to send a person reeling back into hallucinogenic areas of his own brain, for some a horrifying, for others a pleasurable, experience. In any case, the implications of what Banham does approach can get gnarly. Why bother with deserts? Why not instead sit gawking mindlessly at endless color stimulations seen on video tapes? And then, too, the swirling colors of oil slicks and the boiling clouds from nuclear explosions certainly have their visual excitements. Such are the risks when phenomena are divorced from their impacts.

BIBLIOGRAPHY

Abbey, Edward. *Abbey's Road.* New York: E. P. Dutton, 1979.

———. *Beyond the Wall: Essays from the Outside.* New York: Holt, Rinehart and Winston, 1984.

———. *Black Sun: A Novel.* New York: Simon and Schuster, 1971.

———. *The Brave Cowboy: An Old Tale in a New Time.* New York: Dodd, Mead, 1956.

———. *Desert Solitaire: A Season in the Wilderness.* New York: McGraw-Hill, 1968.

———. *The Fool's Progress: A Novel.* New York: Henry Holt, 1988.

———. *Jonathan Troy: A Novel.* New York: Dodd, Mead, 1954.

———. *The Journey Home: Some Words in Defense of the American West.* New York: E. P. Dutton, 1977.

———. *The Monkey Wrench Gang.* Philadelphia: J. B. Lippincott, 1975.

———. "Some Implications of Anarchy." *Thunderbird* 6 (March 1951): 3–9.

Appointment and Commission of Samuel W. Cozzens, 1860. First Judicial District, Pima County, of the provisional government of the Territory of Arizona. Signed at Tucson on 5 April 1860, by L. S. Owens, Governor. Special Collections, University of Arizona Library, Tucson.

Austin, Mary. *The American Rhythm.* New York: Harcourt, Brace, 1923.

———. *The Arrow Maker: A Drama in Three Acts.* 1911. Rev. ed. Boston: Houghton Mifflin, 1915.

———. *Earth Horizon.* Boston: Houghton Mifflin, 1932.

———. "Inyo." *Overland Monthly* 34 (July 1899): 49.

———. *The Land of Journey's Ending.* 1924. Intro. Larry Evers. Tucson: University of Arizona Press, 1983.

———. *The Land of Little Rain.* Boston: Houghton Mifflin, 1903.

———. "The Pot of Gold." *Munsey's Magazine* 25.4 (July 1901): 491–495.

———. "Regionalism in American Fiction." *English Journal* 21.1 (January 1932): 97–107.

Bachelard, Gaston. *The Poetics of Space.* 1958. Translated by Maria Jolas. Boston: Beacon Press, 1969.

Balzac, Honoré de. "A Passion in the Desert." 1832. *The Human Comedy.* Translated by J. Alfred Burgan and Peter P. Breen. Vol. 34. Philadelphia: George Barrie and Son, 1896. 49 vols. 3–24.

————. "Une Passion dans le Désert." 1832. *La Comédie Humaine.* Edited by Marcel Bouteron. Vol. 7. Paris: Editions Gallimard, 1955. 12 vols. 1071–1084.

Bancroft, Hubert H. *History of Arizona and New Mexico, 1530–1888.* San Francisco: The History Company, 1889. Vol. 17 of *The Works of Hubert Howe Bancroft.* 39 vols.

Banham, Peter Reyner. *Los Angeles: The Architecture of Four Ecologies.* London: Penguin Press, 1971.

————. *Scenes in America Deserta.* Salt Lake City: Gibbs M. Smith, 1982.

"Banham, (Peter) Reyner." *Contemporary Authors.* 1st ed. Edited by Ann Evory. Vols. 29–32. Detroit: Gale Research, 1978. 100 vols. 41.

Belden, L. Burr. "Manly of Death Valley." *Westways* 56.11 (November 1964): 27–28.

Bellah, Robert N., et al. *Habits of the Heart: Individualism and Commitment in American Life.* Berkeley: University of California Press, 1985.

Bingham, Edwin R. *Charles F. Lummis: Editor of the Southwest.* San Marino: Huntington Library, 1955.

Bishop, James, Jr. *Epitaph for a Desert Anarchist: The Life and Legacy of Edward Abbey.* New York: Atheneum, 1994.

Bourdon, Roger Joseph. "George Wharton James: Interpreter of the Southwest." Dissertation. University of California, Los Angeles, 1965.

Bowden, Charles. *Blue Desert.* Tucson: University of Arizona Press, 1986.

————. *Frog Mountain Blues.* Tucson: University of Arizona Press, 1987.

————. *Mezcal.* Tucson: University of Arizona Press, 1988.

Bright, Marjorie Belle. *Nellie's Boardinghouse: A Dual Biography of Nellie Coffman and Palm Springs.* Palm Springs: ETC Publications, 1981.

Brinkley-Rogers, Paul. "Blood Feud: Renegade Tucson Writer Attacks American Myths." *Arizona Republic* [Phoenix] 18 September 1995: C1, 6.

Browne, J. Ross. *Adventures in the Apache Country: A Tour through Arizona and Sonora, 1864.* 1869. Edited by Donald M. Powell. Tucson: University of Arizona Press, 1974.

————. *Etchings of a Whaling Cruise, with Notes of a Sojourn on the Island of Zanzibar.* 1846. Edited by John Seelye. Cambridge: Harvard University Press, 1968.

Buck, Wendy, and Peter Wild. "Viewing America's Deserts, Part 5. Two Desert Radicals: Mary Austin and Her 'Mentor.'" *Puerto del Sol* 31.2 (Summer 1996): 258–276.

Cabeza de Vaca, Alvar Núñez. *The Account: Alvar Núñez Cabeza de Vaca's Relación.* 1542. Translated by Martin A. Favata and José B. Fernández. Houston: Arte Público, 1993.

————. *The Narrative of Alvar Núñez Cabeza de Vaca.* Translated by Buckingham Smith. Washington, D.C.: George W. Riggs, 1851.

Cahalan, James M. "'My People': Edward Abbey's Appalachian Roots in Indiana County, Pennsylvania." *Pittsburgh History* 79.3 (Fall 1996): 92–107.

Carmony, Neil B., and David E. Brown. Introduction. *The Wilderness of the Southwest: Charles Sheldon's Quest for Desert Bighorn Sheep and Adventures with the Havasupai and Seri Indians.* By Charles Sheldon. 1979. Edited by Neil B. Carmony and David E. Brown. Salt Lake City: University of Utah Press, 1993.

Cassidy, Ina Sizer. "I-Mary and Me: The Chronicle of a Friendship." *New Mexico Quarterly* 9.4 (November 1939): 203–211.

Castañeda, Carlos. *The Teachings of Don Juan: A Yaqui Way of Knowledge.* Berkeley: University of California Press, 1968.

Cather, Willa. *Death Comes for the Archbishop.* New York: Knopf, 1927.

Chase, J. Smeaton. *California Coast Trails: A Horseback Ride from Mexico to Oregon.* Boston: Houghton Mifflin, 1913.

————. *California Desert Trails.* Boston: Houghton Mifflin, 1919.

————. *Our Araby: Palm Springs and the Garden of the Sun.* Pasadena: Privately printed, 1920.

————. *Yosemite Trails: Camp and Pack-Train in the Yosemite Region of the Sierra Nevada.* Boston: Houghton Mifflin, 1911.

"Chase, J[oseph] Smeaton." *National Cyclopaedia of American Biography.* New York: James T. White, 1958. 42:317.

Cheaves, Sam Frank. *Child of the Sun: A Historical Novel Based on the Journey of Cabeza de Vaca across America.* Santa Fe: Sun, 1986.

Cozzens, Samuel Woodworth. *The Marvelous Country: Three Years in Arizona and New Mexico.* 1876. Minneapolis: Ross and Haines, 1967.

"Cozzens, Samuel Woodworth." *Appleton's Cyclopaedia of American Biography.* Edited by James Grant Wilson and John Fiske. New York: D. Appleton, 1887. 1:763.

Darlington, David. *The Mojave: A Portrait of the Definitive American Desert.* New York: Henry Holt, 1996.

"Defending Los Angeles." *Time Magazine* 98 (August 1971): 41.

de Mille, Richard. *The Don Juan Papers: Further Castañeda Controversies.* 1980. Belmont, Calif.: Wadsworth Publishing Company, 1990.

Doughty, Charles M. *Travels in Arabia Deserta.* 1888. New York: Random House, 1947.

Dutton, Clarence E. *The Tertiary History of the Grand Cañon District.* 1882. Santa Barbara: Peregrine Smith, 1977.

Edwards, E. I. "Death Valley's Neglected Hero." *The Westerners Brand Book 12.* Los Angeles: Los Angeles Westerners, 1966. 59–73.

————. *The Valley Whose Name Is Death.* Pasadena: San Pasqual Press, 1940.

Ellis, John M. "The Western Tradition of Political Correctness." *Academic Questions* 5.2 (Spring 1992): 24–31.

Elwood, Lloyd. "Of Such as These Is the Spirit of the Desert." *Desert Magazine* 11.11 (September 1948): 18.

Evers, Larry. Introduction. *The Land of Journey's Ending.* By Mary Austin. Tucson: University of Arizona Press, 1983. ix–xxv.

Fink, Augusta. *I-Mary: A Biography of Mary Austin.* Tucson: University of Arizona Press, 1983.

Fiske, Turbesé Lummis, and Keith Lummis. *Charles F. Lummis: The Man and His West.* Norman: University of Oklahoma Press, 1975.

Fleming, Robert E. *Charles F. Lummis.* Western Writers Series no. 50. Boise: Boise State University, 1981.

Fontana, Bernard L. Introduction. *Camp-Fires on Desert and Lava.* By William T. Hornaday. 1908. Tucson: University of Arizona Press, 1983.

Foote, Timothy. "1846 — The Way We Were — and the Way We Went." *Smithsonian* 27.1 (April 1996): 38–46, 48, 50–51.

Gage, John. *Color and Culture: Practice and Meaning from Antiquity to Abstraction.* Boston: Little, Brown, 1993.

Goldberger, Paul. "Reyner Banham, Architectural Critic, Dies at 66." *New York Times* 22 March 1988: B5.

Gordon, Dudley. *Charles F. Lummis: Crusader in Corduroy.* Los Angeles: Cultural Assets Press, 1972.

Greeley, Horace. *An Overland Journey from New York to San Francisco in the Summer of 1859.* 1860. Edited by Charles T. Duncan. New York: Alfred A. Knopf, 1964.

Hart, James D. *A Companion to California.* Berkeley: University of California Press, 1987. 90–91.

Hepworth, James, and Gregory McNamee, eds. *Resist Much, Obey Little: Some Notes on Edward Abbey.* Salt Lake City: Dream Garden, 1985.

Hoffer, Eric. *The Ordeal of Change.* 1963. New York: Harper and Row, 1967.

Holmer, Richard. "Currier & Ives Do California." *Californians* 12.6 (1995): 8–11, 51.

Hornaday, William T. *Camp-Fires on Desert and Lava.* 1908. Tucson: University of Arizona Press, 1983.

——. *Free Rum on the Congo, and What It Is Doing There.* Chicago: Woman's Temperance Publication Association, 1887.

——. *Thirty Years War for Wild Life: Gains and Losses in the Thankless Task.* New York: Scribner's, 1931.

Hudson, Roy F. *Forgotten Desert Artist: The Journals and Field Sketches of Carl Eytel, an Early-Day Painter of the Southwest.* Palm Springs: Desert Museum, 1979.

Ingham, Zita, and Peter Wild. "The Preface as Illumination: The Curious (If Not Tricky) Case of John C. Van Dyke's *The Desert.*" *Rhetoric Review* 9 (1991): 328–339.

Jaeger, Edmund C. "Art in a Desert Cabin." *Desert Magazine* 11.11 (September 1948): 15–19.

James, George Wharton. Letter to John Muir, 16 July 1908. John Muir Papers. University of the Pacific, Stockton, Calif.

——. *The Story of Captain: The Horse with the Human Brain.* Pasadena: Radiant Life Press, 1917.

——. *The Wonders of the Colorado Desert.* 2 vols. Boston: Little, 1906.

Jefferson, Thomas. *Notes on the State of Virginia.* 1783. Edited by Merrill D. Peterson. *Writings.* New York: Library of America, 1984. 123–325.

Jones, Howard Mumford. *O Strange New World; American Culture: The Formative Years.* New York: Viking, 1964.

"Joseph Wood Krutch." *New York Times* 26 May 1970: 40.

Krutch, Joseph Wood. *The Desert Year.* 1952. Tucson: University of Arizona Press, 1985.

——. *The Forgotten Peninsula: A Naturalist in Baja California.* New York: William Sloane, 1961.

——. *The Measure of Man: On Freedom, Human Values, Survival, and the Modern Temper.* Indianapolis: Bobbs Merrill, 1954.

——. *The Modern Temper: A Study and a Confession.* 1929. New York: Harcourt, Brace, 1956.

——. *More Lives than One.* New York: William Sloane, 1962.

——. "Preface." *The Modern Temper: A Study and a Confession.* By Joseph Wood Krutch. 1929. New York: Harcourt, Brace, 1956. xi–xiii.

——. *The Twelve Seasons: A Perpetual Calendar for the Country.* New York: William Sloane, 1949.

———. *The Voice of the Desert: A Naturalist's Interpretation.* New York: William Sloane, 1955.

Langlois, Karen S. "A Fresh Voice from the West: Mary Austin, California, and American Literary Magazines, 1892–1910." *California History* 69.1 (Spring 1990): 22–35, 80–81.

Larson, Peggy. *The Deserts of the Southwest.* San Francisco: Sierra Club Books, 1977.

Lee, Lawrence B. Introduction. *The Conquest of Arid America.* 1900. Rev. ed. 1905. Seattle: University of Washington Press, 1969. xxix–xliii.

———. "William Ellsworth Smythe and the Irrigation Movement: A Reconsideration." *Pacific Historical Review* 41.1 (August 1972): 289–311.

Lee, W. Storrs. *The Great California Deserts.* New York: G. P. Putnam's Sons, 1963.

Lewis, Meriwether, and William Clark. *History of the Expedition under the Commands of Captains Lewis and Clark.* Philadelphia: Bradford and Inskeep, 1814.

Limerick, Patricia. *Desert Passages: Encounters with the American Deserts.* Albuquerque: University of New Mexico Press, 1985.

Long, Haniel. *Interlinear to Cabeza de Vaca.* Santa Fe: Writers' Editions, 1936. Rpt. *The Marvelous Adventures of Cabeza de Vaca.* London: Souvenir, 1972.

Loomis, Noel M., and Abraham P. Nasatir. *Pedro Vial and the Roads to Santa Fe.* Norman: University of Oklahoma Press, 1967.

Lopez, Barry Holstun. *Desert Notes: Reflections in the Eye of a Raven.* Kansas City: Sheed, Andrews and McMeel, 1976.

———. *Of Wolves and Men.* New York: Scribner's, 1978.

Lummis, Charles F. *The Land of Poco Tiempo.* 1893. New York: Scribner's, 1928.

———. *Some Strange Corners of Our Country: The Wonderland of the Southwest.* 1892. Tucson: University of Arizona Press, 1989.

———. *A Tramp across the Continent.* New York: Scribner's, 1892.

Lutz, Tom. *American Nervousness, 1903: An Anecdotal History.* Ithaca: Cornell University Press, 1991.

Manly, William Lewis. *Death Valley in 49.* 1894. New York: Wallace Hebberd, 1929.

Margolis, John D. *Joseph Wood Krutch: A Writer's Life.* Knoxville: University of Tennessee Press, 1980.

Marsh, George Perkins. *Man and Nature.* 1864. Edited by David Lowenthal. Cambridge: Harvard University Press, 1974.

Maximilian, Prince of Wied-Neuwied. *Travels in the Interior of North America.* 1839. Translated by H. Evans Lloyd. London: Ackermann, 1843.

McCann, Garth. *Edward Abbey.* Western Writers Series no. 29. Boise: Boise State University, 1977.

McNay, Michael. "Profession: Enfant Terrible." *Guardian* [Manchester, England] 26 October 1968: 7.

Mills, Enos A. *The Adventures of a Nature Guide.* Garden City, N.Y.: Doubleday, 1920.

Muir, John. Letter to Howard Palmer. 12 December 1912. John Muir Papers. University of the Pacific, Stockton, Calif.

Murie, Margaret. "Inner Ingredients Inspire Others." *High Country News* [Lander, Wyo.] 23 September 1977: 3.

Nabhan, Gary Paul. *Desert Legends: Re-Storying the Sonoran Borderlands.* New York: Henry Holt, 1994.

Nash, Roderick. "Conservation as Anxiety." *The American Environment: Readings in the History of Conservation.* Edited by Roderick Nash. Reading, Penn.: Addison-Wesley, 1968. 85–93.

———. *Wilderness and the American Mind.* 3d ed. New Haven: Yale University Press, 1982.

Nentvig, Juan, S. J. *Rudo Ensayo: A Description of Sonora and Arizona in 1764.* Translated by Alberto Francisco Pradeau and Robert R. Rasmussen. Tucson: University of Arizona Press, 1980.

Ortega y Gasset, José. *The Dehumanization of Art and Notes on the Novel.* 1925. Translated by Helene Weyl. Princeton: Princeton University Press, 1948.

Pavich, Paul N. *Joseph Wood Krutch.* Western Writers Series no. 89. Boise: Boise State University, 1989.

Pilkington, William T. *My Blood's Country: Studies in Southwestern Literature.* Fort Worth: Texas Christian University Press, 1973.

Powell, Donald M. Introduction. *Adventures in the Apache Country: A Tour through Arizona and Sonora, 1864.* By J. Ross Browne. 1869. Edited by Donald M. Powell. Tucson: University of Arizona Press, 1974. ix–xv.

Powell, John Wesley. *Exploration of the Colorado River of the West.* Washington, D.C.: U.S. Government Printing Office, 1875.

———. *Report on the Lands of the Arid Region of the United States.* Washington, D.C.: U.S. Government Printing Office, 1878.

Powell, Lawrence Clark. *California Classics: The Creative Literature of the Golden State.* 1971. Santa Barbara: Capra Press, 1989.

———. *Southwest Classics: The Creative Literature of the Arid Lands.* 1974. Tucson: University of Arizona Press, 1982.

———. "William Lewis Manly's *Death Valley in 49.*" *Westways* 62.11 (November 1969): 30–33, 52.

Quaife, Milo Milton. Introduction. *Death Valley in 49.* By William Lewis Manly. 1894. Edited by Milo Milton Quaife. Chicago: Lakeside Press, 1927.

Quammen, David. "The Rattlers Are Missing." *New York Times Book Review* 20 February 1982: 9, 27.

Rea, Paul W. "An Interview with Ann Zwinger." *Western American Literature* 24 (1989): 21–36.

Reid, Mayne. *The Scalp Hunters: Or, Adventures among the Trappers.* New York: Robert W. De Witt, 1856.

Reiger, John. *American Sportsmen and the Origins of Conservation.* 1975. Rev. ed. Norman: University of Oklahoma Press, 1986.

Reisner, Marc. *Cadillac Desert: The American West and Its Disappearing Water.* New York: Viking, 1986.

Ronald, Ann. *The New West of Edward Abbey.* Albuquerque: University of New Mexico Press, 1982.

Roosevelt, Theodore. "The Strenuous Life." *The Strenuous Life: Essays and Addresses.* New York: Century, 1902. 1–21.

Roper, Laura Wood. *FLO: A Biography of Frederick Law Olmsted.* Baltimore: Johns Hopkins University Press, 1973.

Ruxton, George Frederick. *Life in the Far West.* 1849. Edited by Leroy R. Haven. Norman: University of Oklahoma Press, 1951.

Sheldon, Charles. *The Wilderness of the Southwest: Charles Sheldon's Quest for Desert Bighorn*

Sheep and Adventures with the Havasupai and Seri Indians. 1979. Edited by Neil B. Carmony and David E. Brown. Salt Lake City: University of Utah Press, 1993.

Shelton, Richard. Introduction. *The Desert.* By John C. Van Dyke. 1901. Salt Lake City: Peregrine Smith, 1980. xi–xxix.

Slovic, Scott. *Seeking Awareness in American Nature Writing: Henry Thoreau, Annie Dillard, Edward Abbey, Wendell Berry, Barry Lopez.* Salt Lake City: University of Utah Press, 1992.

Smythe, William E. *City Homes on Country Lanes.* New York: Macmillan, 1921.

————. *The Conquest of Arid America.* 1900. Rev. ed. 1905. Intro. Lawrence B. Lee. Seattle: University of Washington Press, 1969.

————. *History of San Diego, 1542–1908.* San Diego: History Company, 1908.

Statistical Abstract of the United States, 1990. 110th ed. Washington, D.C.: U.S. Department of Commerce, Bureau of the Census.

Statistical Abstract of the United States, 1970. 91st ed. Washington, D.C.: U.S. Department of Commerce, Bureau of the Census.

Stegner, Wallace. *Beyond the Hundredth Meridian: John Wesley Powell and the Second Opening of the West.* Boston: Houghton Mifflin, 1954.

————. Introduction. *The Exploration of the Colorado River.* By John Wesley Powell. 1875. Abridged ed. Chicago: University of Chicago Press, 1957. xi–xxi.

Teague, David, and Peter Wild, eds. *The Secret Life of John C. Van Dyke: Selected Letters.* Reno: University of Nevada Press, 1997.

Thoreau, Henry David. "Walking." 1862. *The Writings of Henry David Thoreau.* 10 vols. Boston: Houghton Mifflin, 1893. 9:251–303.

Trefethen, James B. *Crusade for Wildlife: Highlights in Conservation Progress.* Harrisburg, Penn.: Stackpole, 1961.

Tuan, Yi-Fu. *Topophilia: A Study of Environmental Perception, Attitudes, and Values.* Englewood Cliffs, N.J.: Prentice-Hall, 1974.

Van Doren, Carl. "Mary Hunter Austin, 1868–1934." *New York Herald Tribune Books* 26 August 1934: 6.

Van Dyke, John C. *The Autobiography of John C. Van Dyke: A Personal Narrative of American Life, 1861–1931.* Edited by Peter Wild. Salt Lake City: University of Utah Press, 1993.

————. *The Desert: Further Studies in Natural Appearances.* 1901. Intro. Peter Wild. Baltimore: Johns Hopkins University Press, 1999.

————. *The Desert: Further Studies in Natural Appearances.* 1901. Photographs by J. Smeaton Chase. New York: Scribner's, 1918.

————. *In Egypt: Studies and Sketches along the Nile.* New York: Scribner's 1931.

————. *The Meadows: Familiar Studies of the Commonplace.* New York: Scribner's, 1926.

————. *The Money God: Chapters of Heresy and Dissent concerning Business Methods and Mercenary Ideals in American Life.* New York: Scribner's, 1908.

————. *The Open Spaces: Incidents of Nights and Days under the Blue Sky.* New York: Scribner's, 1922.

————. *Principles of Art.* New York: Fords, Howard, and Hulbert, 1887.

————. *Rembrandt and His School: A Critical Study of the Master and His Pupils, with a New Assignment of Their Pictures.* New York: Scribner's, 1923.

————. *What Is Art? Studies in the Technique and Criticism of Painting.* New York: Scribner's, 1910.

Van Dyke, Theodore Strong. *Millionaires of a Day: An Inside History of the Great Southern California "Boom."* New York: Fords, Howard and Hulbert, 1890.

————. *Southern California: Its Valleys, Hills, and Streams; Its Animals, Birds,* etc. New York: Fords, Howard, and Hulbert, 1886.

Walker, Clifford. *Back Door to California: The Story of the Mojave River Trail.* Barstow: Mojave River Valley Museum Association, 1986.

Walker, Franklin. *A Literary History of Southern California.* Berkeley: University of California Press, 1950.

Wheat, Carl I. *Trailing the Forty-Niners through Death Valley.* San Francisco: Privately printed, 1939.

Wild, Peter. *Alvar Núñez Cabeza de Vaca.* Western Writers Series no. 101. Boise: Boise State University, 1991.

————. *Ann Zwinger.* Western Writers Series no. 111. Boise: Boise State University, 1993.

————. "Edward Abbey: The Middle-Class Maverick." *New Mexico Humanities Review* 6 (Summer 1983): 15–23.

————. *George Wharton James.* Western Writers Series no. 93. Boise: Boise State University, 1990.

————. "The Homestead Strike and the Mexican Connection: The Strange Story of 'Honest' John McLuckie." *Pittsburgh History* 80.2 (Summer 1997): 60–69, 74.

————. "How a London Madman Painted Our Deserts." *North Dakota Quarterly* 63.2 (Spring 1996): 5–17.

————. "Into the Heart's Wild Places: Edward Abbey, 1927–1989." *Sierra* 74 (May–June 1989): 100–101.

————. "John Muir and the Van Dyke Ranch: Intimacy and Desire in His Final Years, Part 1." *John Muir Newsletter* 5.3 (Summer 1995): 1, 4–5.

————. "John Muir and the Van Dyke Ranch: Intimacy and Desire in His Final Years, Part 2." *John Muir Newsletter* 5.4 (Fall 1995): 1, 3–5, 6.

————. *Pioneer Conservationists of Eastern America.* Missoula, Mont.: Mountain Press, 1985.

————. *Pioneer Conservationists of Western America.* Missoula, Mont.: Mountain Press, 1979.

————. "Sentimentalism in the American Southwest: John C. Van Dyke, Mary Austin, and Edward Abbey." *Reading the West: New Essays on the Literature of the American West.* Edited by Michael Kowalewski. New York: Cambridge University Press, 1996. 127–143.

Wild, Peter, and Neil Carmony. "The Trip Not Taken; John C. Van Dyke, Heroic Doer or Armchair Seer?" *Journal of Arizona History* 34.1 (1993): 65–80.

Williams, Terry Tempest. *Refuge: An Unnatural History of Family and Place.* New York: Pantheon, 1991.

Worster, Donald. *Rivers of Empire: Water, Aridity, and the Growth of the American West.* New York: Pantheon, 1985.

Wynn, Dudley. "Austin, Mary." *Dictionary of American Biography.* Edited by Robert Livingston Schuyler and Edward T. James. New York: Scribner's, 1944. 10: Sup. 1, 34–35.

Zwinger, Ann. "The Art of Wandering." *Orion Nature Quarterly* 5.1 (1986): 4–13.

————. *Beyond the Aspen Grove.* 1970. Tucson: University of Arizona Press, 1988.

————. *A Desert Country near the Sea: A Natural History of the Cape Region of Baja California.* 1983. Tucson: University of Arizona Press, 1987.

————. *The Mysterious Lands: A Naturalist Explores the Four Great Deserts of the Southwest.* 1989. Tucson: University of Arizona Press, 1996.

————. *Run, River, Run: A Naturalist's Journey down One of the Great Rivers of the American West.* 1975. Tucson: University of Arizona Press, 1987.

————. *Wind in the Rock: The Canyonlands of Southeastern Utah.* 1978. Tucson: University of Arizona Press, 1988.

————. "A World of Infinite Variety." *Antaeus* 57 (1986): 34–44.

INDEX